COLD WAR DIPLOMACY

American Foreign Policy,
1945-1975

NORMAN A. GRAEBNER
University of Virginia

D. VAN NOSTRAND COMPANY, INC.
New York • *Cincinnati* • *Toronto* • *London* • *Melbourne*

To Cathy

D. Van Nostrand Company Regional Offices:
New York   Cincinnati

D. Van Nostrand Company International Offices:
London   Toronto   Melbourne

Published by D. Van Nostrand Company
450 West 33rd Street, New York, N.Y. 10001

10 9 8 7 6 5 4 3 2

Foreword

If the Cold War continued through 1975 it was a different struggle from that which existed fifteen years earlier when the first edition of this volume appeared. Yet it was not totally apparent why and how the Cold War had changed; indeed, countless Americans persisted in their belief that the Soviet-American confrontation remained as threatening and dangerous in 1975 as it had appeared to be at mid-century. They charged that all official and academic arguments in behalf of détente merely accepted a subordinate position for the United States and ignored the dangers which such resignation entailed. Still the repeated denials that any significant change had occurred in the Soviet-American relationship after 1960 demonstrated the extent to which time had, for others, transformed that relationship.

Initially the Cold War resulted from a myriad of major and minor disagreements which flowed from the determination of the victorious allies of 1945 to restore war-torn Europe to a condition which conformed to their perceptions of an ideal world. For the United States and Britain that best of all worlds conformed overwhelmingly to that fashioned at Versailles; for the Soviets the postwar era required, if it would satisfy historic Russian purposes at all, the elimination of the Versailles Treaty's essential provisions, especially its Eastern European settlements and its reaffirmation of Western predominance in Europe. This massive divergence in purpose, rendered inflexible by a profound conflict over the ultimate intentions implied by competing ideological imperatives, gradually disintegrated into a Cold War.

That world which called upon the United States for leadership after 1945 was neither simple nor reassuring, and nowhere in the American tradition was there much patience with the complexities of the international environment. Refusing to accept the infinite variations of national interest in world politics, the United States attempted to reduce the globe to more easily understandable and manageable proportions by remaking it in the American image with ample projections of power and influence. The nation's immediate postwar endeavor was the encouragement of world commerce through the greater stabilization of currency and the expansion of trade and investment through such international agencies as the International Monetary Fund, the World Bank, and the General Agreement on Trade and Tariffs. These international instruments received reinforcement from the Truman Doctrine, the Marshall Plan, the Technical Assistance Program, and a variety of regional and bilateral economic arrangements. Despite the American responsibility for financing and managing much of this postwar reconstruction, the effort in no measure exceeded the capabilities of the United States. The limited objectives of international stabilization and economic expansion marked the perimeters of basic American interests and thus, in large measure, the limits of successful national action.

Whatever the danger of Soviet expansionism in postwar Europe, those who advocated a strong anti-Soviet posture could point to a worldwide Soviet-based campaign of ideological belligerency against the West and its institutions. Within the Soviet bloc itself, there was no absence of tyranny and terror: the relentless persecution of dissenters, the dispatching of thousands to concentration camps, the notorious "show trials" designed to silence artists and writers who revealed a glimmer of independence. France and Italy had large and growing Communist parties with assumed ties to the Kremlin. Indeed, for those who engaged in the exercise of warning the nation against Soviet behavior there was no apparent limit to condemning evidence. The existence of internal tyranny, defended with ideological rationalizations, was neither proof of external Soviet expansionism nor necessarily a workable guide to Western policy. Yet for such devotees of toughness as Dean Acheson and John Foster Dulles, analytical subtleties were synonymous with softness. The eventual United States involvement in Vietnam and its resultant horrors were implicit in their program, for the decision to aid South Vietnam was consistent with earlier anti-Soviet policy.

Anticommunism proved from the beginning to be a deceptive standard for United States relations with the U.S.S.R., for it weakened the traditional restraints of American conservatism and propelled the nation into objectives it could not achieve. The ease whereby the United States gained its immediate postwar objectives created the illusion that its new global posture reflected a permanent arrangement of power in the world. What contributed to the illusion of permanent power was the wartime destruction of all the imperial structures which had established the boundaries of traditional United States influence. The war had not only destroyed the power of Germany and Japan but also produced the final disintegration of the British and French empires. As a result, Walter Lippmann observed, "we flowed forward beyond our natural limits and the cold war is the result of our meeting the Russians with no buffers between us. The miscalculation . . . falsified all our other calculations—what our power was, what we could afford to do, what influence we had to exert in the world." In time American commitments would require a realistic re-evaluation.

What divided Americans in their attitudes and purposes toward Russia after mid-century was not their profound disagreements over Soviet behavior or the nature of the Soviet regime. What separated them was their varying perceptions of what United States foreign policy could and needed to achieve. Whereas the day-to-day policies of the United States sought to halt the spread of communism in all its forms, the nation's official long-range purpose demanded no less than the diminution of Communist power and ideology until they ceased to be threats to Western security. What mitigated the intensity of the Cold War was less the change within the Soviet sphere than what occurred within the United States itself. The internal manifestations of Soviet power remained unchanged: the totalitarian nature of the Soviet regime, the acceleration of its defense effort, and the continuation of its anti-Western ideological crusade even while its diplomatic style became more moderate. But changes in United States policy transcended style to include substance as well, for American far more than Soviet intent defied the realities of postwar Europe and Asia. Whereas the U.S.S.R. had anchored its long-term diplomacy to the legitimization of political and territorial arrangements which its power had created earlier, the United States pursued long-term goals where neither American power nor even clear American interests were present.

How long could policies attached to goals which had no clear relationship to power, interest, or even intent remain serious? Washington never developed one program designed to free Eastern Europe or China of Communist control. Having coexisted successfully with an allegedly expansionist Russia for a full generation, countless Americans by 1970 were ready to accept the conclusion that their leaders had overestimated the Soviet danger. Concomitantly they revealed a greater tolerance toward conditions which they could not and would not change. Eventually, they understood, the United States would of necessity terminate its futile search for the lost world of Versailles and accept the world which existed. Détente, whatever its ramifications for peace and security, reflected essentially a tardy American recognition that the Europe wrought by Hitler's defeat had become a permanent feature of international life.

Charlottesville, Virginia   NORMAN A. GRAEBNER

Contents

PART ONE

American Foreign Policy, 1945-1975

One

Introduction: The Isolationist Tradition

The thirty years from 1945 to 1975 comprised for the American people an original experience. Never before in a time of comparative peace were they so fully involved in world affairs. As the guardians of Western civilization, Americans had little choice, for that civilization had entered upon troubled times. Tragically the suicidal tendencies within Western Europe, characterized largely by that region's inability to integrate the German Empire into its political structure, had the effect of propelling two great powers to the forefront of world politics. That the United States and Russia in 1945 would face one another across a weak and demoralized Europe was predicted by the mere act of crushing the might of Germany. But in itself, this apparent military necessity presaged no unique or permanent American involvement in affairs beyond its own shores. Indeed, most Americans assumed that with the establishment of peace the two great Allies, through their cooperation and mutual support of the decisions of the United Nations, would guarantee at last the creation of a new world order based on law and justice. Repeatedly during the war the Soviets accepted in formal agreement the principle of self-determination for all Europeans as embodied in the Atlantic Charter of August 1941. Beyond victory lay a world not unlike that of the early interwar years, with Europe sufficiently stable to permit an American retreat from it.

What perpetuated the nation's traditional illusion of isolation, even at a time of total involvement, was the fact that the war always remained far from its own shores. Since German power, once disposed of by an Allied victory, would entail no continuing infringement on Western security, the United States really had no foreseeable political or military interest in postwar Europe other than that of imposing some restrictions on the defeated nations. Nothing about the war itself challenged the American isolationist tradition.

Only the most astute observers during World War II could see that the United States, in its pursuit of total victory, was helping to create a new balance of power that would prove to be as unacceptable as that created by Hitler. For the more complete the defeat of Germany, the more thorough would be the Soviet dominance of Eastern Europe and the destruction of the traditional balance of power. Any return to normalcy required Russia's withdrawal to both its prewar boundaries and, in general, its prewar status in world affairs—to be achieved automatically through the Soviet acceptance of the principle of self-determination of peoples. Fundamentally, the Atlantic Charter promised a postwar world without permanent victors or permanent losers. For the American people, having suffered no invasion, this was both a feasible and a moral arrangement.

But Russian vulnerability to penetration from the west, demonstrated again in the recent experience of war, prompted the Kremlin to seek some tangible evidence of victory. Unfortunately, the Soviets could not impose their will on regions subject to their armies without both defying their wartime commitments to self-determination, and raising doubts regarding their ultimate intentions. It was not certain that the U.S.S.R., having broken one set of promises, would not continue its westward course as subsequent opportunities presented themselves. When American leadership in 1947 became convinced that the Soviet Union represented an expansive rather than a stabilizing force in European politics, it wrote its fears into the nation's economic and military containment policies. But even these momentous decisions comprised no sharp break with the nation's traditional distaste for power politics. As in previous twentieth-century involvements in European affairs, the United States quickly identified its military and diplomatic entanglements with a new crusade for freedom.

This deepening commitment to the safety of Western Europe and the increasing emphasis on military preparedness created the notion that the United States had at last entered upon a career not unlike those of the great powers of the past. This was not true. If the United States, because of its wealth and power, had a continuing impact on events throughout the world, its policies had far more in common with the

Wilsonism and isolationism of the interwar years than with the *realpolitik* of a Richelieu, Canning, or Bismarck. For what distinguished the statesmanship of such men was not the wielding of massive power or the inclination to interfere but the accurate and painstaking definition of their nations' interests in terms of available power and the interests of others. Not since the nineteenth century had the United States analyzed its needs in such concrete terms. Between the wars the inclination of American leadership to embrace the cause of humanity permitted it to come to grips with nothing.

This tendency to pursue abstractions rather than concrete interests continued to dominate American diplomacy in the postwar era. The central fact in the country's response to the Soviet challenge was the absence of any clearly-defined body of objectives that had some relationship to American capability or even genuine intention. If future historians, examining these troubled years, could credit the United States with a truly beneficial role in world affairs, it would be not because this nation held within its grasp an unprecedented capacity to destroy or because it was adept at verbalizing utopias for itself, neither of which required much imagination, but because it recognized its fundamental interests amid the varied challenges of the age and defended them with determination.

What gave consistency to the American outlook on the world after 1900 was the essential fact that the United States entered the present century as a satiated power. For such a nation there is always an identity between its interest in stability and its appeal to abstract principles, for the application of democratic and legal processes to international affairs assures not only the continuance of peace and order but also the perpetuation of the established hierarchy of power. Were the United States an aggressive, imperialistic country, as it was during much of the nineteenth century, its diplomatic language would contain fewer references to principle. In large measure the postwar appeal to the concepts of the Atlantic Charter, like the prewar appeal to the sanctity of treaties, appeared to much of the globe as an inexpensive, if futile, effort of the United States to deflate its enemies. During the 1930s the perennial refusal of the country to concede its principles and demand nothing less than their fulfillment forced American leadership to respond to the threats of German and Japanese aggression with little but words of disapprobation. After World War II this deeply-ingrained habit of over-demanding reduced much of the nation's action toward the Kremlin to a similar pattern of behavior, for nothing else remained.

It is tragic that this neglect of the fundamental obligation of government to maintain some relationship between ends and means in national action accustomed the American people to expect too much of foreign policy. Herein lay the traditional American dilemma. Whatever the energy or determination of its antagonists, the nation was always assured that it could anticipate the eventual collapse of its enemies and the creation of the illusive world of justice and freedom. Certainly all United States diplomatic relations with the U.S.S.R. and mainland China after 1950 were anchored to that assumption. What is dangerous in any promise of victory at little or no cost is the resultant failure of leadership to prepare the people either for peace or for war. This was perilously true in the troubled days before Pearl Harbor; it was equally true in the 1950s and 1960s. Not until 1970 and thereafter was the government of the United States prepared to accept the existence of postwar Russia and China largely on their own terms.

This country's permanent involvement in world affairs made unprecedented demands upon its resources and its energies. Far less obvious, but far more disturbing, was the nation's perennial inability to divest itself of its isolationist habits. It continued throughout the 1950s to expect too much of its enemies and too little of itself under the unshakable assumption that its superior virtue somehow eliminated the need to pay the normal price of creating a well-conceived hierarchy of interests and preparing itself and others to make concessions on matters of secondary importance in the interest of stability and peace. The refusal of the United States to define its requirements in negotiable terms permitted it no escape from the diplomatic challenges of the 1930s except that of war. Yet it learned so little from that experience that after 1945 it neglected again, in its appeal to principle, to define those areas of turmoil and conflict where its interests and its capabilities converged. In the long run a nation cannot escape its challenges. The substitution of words of disapprobation and other devices of drift for serious negotiation are at best a play for time beyond which the concrete issues in conflict must always be resolved either by diplomacy or by war.

Two

Divided Europe:
Foundations of the Cold War

For the American people in 1945, victory over the Axis was synonymous with utopia. The nation's giant crusade against "the makers of war, the breeders of hate," as President Franklin D. Roosevelt had termed the German leaders, had managed to assign all the world's evil to the enemy of the moment. Through crushing military force the peace-loving nations would now disarm the criminals and adopt measures to prevent them from disturbing the peace again. Under Secretary of State Joseph C. Grew, in January, anchored his optimism for the future to the "upsurge of determination among the peoples of the world as has never before been seen in history—the determination that war, like slavery and disease, must go." Beyond the destruction of Germany and Japan, then, lay not a continuance of the struggle for power among nations, but a new era of international cooperation based on the principles of the Atlantic Charter.

This mood of assurance that the year would reap a harvest, not of victory alone, but of lasting peace, continued to mount throughout the spring of 1945. The apparent agreements of the Big Three at Yalta in February was evidence enough that the wartime unity of the great powers would continue into the postwar world. The American and Soviet acceptance of the United Nations Organization was merely the final guarantee that the search for world order would not fail. The reaffirmation of the principles agreed to at Dumbarton Oaks in the fall of 1944 demonstrated, in the words of *Time*, "that World War II was

7

not being fought in vain." Senator Alben W. Barkley of Kentucky characterized the Yalta Conference "as one of the most important steps ever taken to promote peace and happiness in the world." The President confirmed the deep sense of achievement when he reported to a joint session of Congress on March 1 that "never before have the major Allies been more closely united—not only in their war aims but in their peace aims." The Crimean Conference, he added hopefully, "spells the end of the system of unilateral action and exclusive alliances and spheres of influence and balance of power and all the other expedients that have been tried for centuries—and have failed. We propose to substitute for all these a universal organization in which all peace-loving nations will finally have a chance to join."

Whatever doubts the national leadership harbored concerning Russia's postwar intentions—and they were considerable—were not conveyed to the American people. The U.S.S.R. had subscribed to the principle of self-determination of peoples as embodied in the Atlantic Charter. This action enrolled that country in the legion of the good and appeared to assure its cooperation in the creation of the new postwar order. The new President, Harry S. Truman, gave public expression to his confidence in May on the occasion of VE Day: "United, the peace-loving nations have demonstrated in the West that their arms are stronger by far than the might of dictators or the tyranny of military cliques that once called us soft and weak." What the President failed to observed at that moment of triumph was that Russia was not necessarily peace-loving in the American sense, and that without its support the democracies would not have won at all. This was not a victory of democracy alone, but democracy supported by the world's greatest dictatorship, the Soviet Union.

THE NEW BALANCE OF POWER

What mattered to thoughtful Americans in early 1945 was the impact of Germany's impending collapse on the European balance of power. That the traditional balance of Europe could not survive a total victory of either Germany or Russia over the other had been clear to students of European affairs since the turn of the century. Following the Nazi invasion of Russia in June, 1941, the proponents of Versailles could sustain the established treaty structure only by disposing of both Russian and German power—something which the Russian Revolution had permitted them to achieve in 1919 to preserve a modicum of balance in postwar Europe. They would not do so again for the reason that the Soviet Union in victory would emerge from the war as Europe's leading military power. In a letter to Secretary of State Cordell Hull of May 1944, Admiral William D. Leahy recognized the changes being wrought in world politics by the Russian victories on the Eastern front. "In appraising possibilities of this nature," he wrote, "the outstanding fact to be noted is the recent phenomenal development of the heretofore latent Russian military and economic strength— a development which seems certain to prove epochal in its bearing on future politico-military international relationships, and which has yet to reach the full scope attainable with Russian resources." Already the forces of the U.S.S.R. had moved from the defensive to the offensive, and were beginning their sweep into Rumania, Hungary, Poland, and the Baltic states. In the months that followed it became clear that Russia, not Britain, would succeed Germany as the major force in European affairs.

In retrospect it was obvious that two world wars had hurried along the fundamental process of bringing the United States and the U.S.S.R. to the forefront of world politics. These wars had dragged a reluctant United States to the center of the world stage as the dominant power of the Western world. During World War I, the Russians, following the devious route of revolution, broke out of those internal restraints imposed by Czarist tradition and began their preparation for industrial and technological expansion. World War I itself eased the way for Russia's new assault on the historic forces that had confined that nation's influence and prestige. The Versailles Conference of 1919 dismembered Turkey and Austria, two of the five empires which had contained Russian expansion in recent times. World War II destroyed what was left of the old balance of power in Eastern and Central Europe. By 1945 Germany was in ruins; England and France were weakened almost beyond recall as major forces in world politics. At last the West, through the process of self-destruction—a process for which Germany must carry the chief responsibility—had removed from Eastern European affairs all five of the great nations which only a long generation earlier appeared capable of limiting Russian ambition with relative ease.

THE WARTIME CONFLICT OVER EASTERN EUROPE

American leadership was scarcely prepared for the vast changes occurring in Europe. What mitigated the reaction to Russia's burgeoning strength was the knowledge that the basic decisions which had created the new order of power were made in Berlin, not in London, Moscow, or Washington. The Russian gains of 1944 and 1945 resulted less from Soviet aggressiveness than from Germany's collapse. But what disturbed Washington in this massive transfer of power was the question of Soviet purpose. Long before 1945 the well-established facts of international life scarcely warranted any Western expectation of a new world order based on the Wilsonian principles of self-determination. Throughout the war it was clear that Allied interests coincided only on the issue of defeating the common enemy. The United States and Great Britain entered the war seeking nothing but peace and stability in world affairs. They had written their moral and limited purpose into the Atlantic Charter as early as August 1941. In this document, they promised Eastern Europeans as well as their own citizens a postwar settlement based on the principle of self-determination of peoples. For the Kremlin this repudiation of the tangible and lasting emoluments of victory was never an acceptable basis of action. Whether Russia eventually signed the Atlantic Charter or not, she would not settle for a world based on the principle of self-determination. Any assumption that she would expected too much denial of that country's historic problems and ambitions.

At no time during the war did Stalin hide his intention of creating a new European order which would serve the interests of the Soviet Union. For centuries the rulers of Russia had viewed the disallowance of Poland and other areas of Eastern Europe to any antagonist as a matter of life and death. The ease with which the anti-Soviet governments of Slavic Europe fell into Nazi hands prompted Stalin in December 1941, to demand of Anthony Eden that Britain recognize the "Curzon Line" as the new Soviet-Polish frontier as well as the transfer to Russia of certain Rumanian military facilities. To Secretary of State Cordell Hull it was unthinkable that Russia should gain any territorial concessions as the result of the war. He reminded Eden that the postwar policies of the United States

have been delineated in the Atlantic Charter which today represents the attitude not only of the United States but also of Great Britain and of the Soviet Union.

In view of this fact in our considered opinion it would be unfortunate were any of the three governments, now on common ground in the Atlantic Charter, to express any willingness to enter into commitments regarding specific terms of the postwar settlement. Discussions between the several governments looking toward fullest possible agreement on basic policies and toward later arrangements at the proper time and with full public knowledge will of course be expected to continue. Upon the conclusion of hostilities those nations contributing to the defeat of the Hitler forces will join in an effort to restore peace and order. The participation at that time of the Soviet Government will be no less than that of Great Britain and our own. In order not to jeopardize the aims we shall all share in common looking to an enduring peace, it is evident that no commitments as to individual countries should be entered into at this time. It would be unfortunate if we should approach the peace conference thus hampered. Above all there must be no secret accords.

Churchill agreed, writing to Eden in January 1942, that "there can be no question of settling frontiers until the peace conference."

Throughout the war years Roosevelt and Churchill were held to the principle of postponement by the combined pressures of the Eastern European governments in exile, military advisors motivated by the single-minded purpose of defeating the Axis powers, the requirement of national unity in the successful conduct of the war effort, and Roosevelt's own self-assurance that he could remove the deviations of purpose among the Allies in due time with personal diplomacy. Secretary Hull, moreover, was reluctant to face the great political questions of the war before it was necessary. (*See Document No. 1 on p. 171.*) But what bothered some observant Americans was the danger that Soviet ambition might expand with the success of the Red Army if no agreements were reached while the Russians still required American cooperation. Walter Lippmann analyzed the high cost of procrastination in January 1945. "A very large part of our present difficulties," he wrote, "may be traced to the policy of reiterating high principles and of postponing the settlement of concrete issues. . . . For the effect of urging postponement in the name of high principles has been to . . . nullify our own influence in favor of moderation and compromise. Thus the more we preached high principles and postponed settlements the greater became the gap between our principles and what was happening."

Soviet determination to maintain the newly created hegemony in Eastern Europe flowed as much from the experience of war as from historic ambition. That Russia, unlike the United States and Britain, was invaded by German armies made certain the disruption of Allied interests vis-à-vis Germany with the destruction of Nazi power. Western security interests required nothing of a defeated Germany other than a general settlement which, with minor guarantees against the resurgence of German nationalism, would conform to the principle of self-determination. For the United States and England there was no dichotomy between wartime principles and national purpose. Russian interests, on the contrary, required territorial and political guarantees against the recurrence of direct invasion from the west. In the Soviet occupation and control of Eastern and Central Europe lay the only apparent rewards of victory. To win acceptance of such an altered structure of European politics, the Kremlin had no choice but to extend to the West proposals for the division of Europe into spheres of influence.

In the American refusal to recognize a Soviet sphere in Eastern Europe lay a disturbing irony. During the war few Americans detected the contradiction between the encouragement of the Russians to destroy Nazi power across Eastern Europe and the constant assurance which Roosevelt and Hull conveyed to the American people that the peace settlement would conform to the principles of the Atlantic Charter. Yet Stalin made no secret of his determination to foster governments in Eastern Europe friendly to the U.S.S.R. Never again, he warned Ambassador W. Averell Harriman, would he tolerate a belt of anti-Soviet governments along Russia's western frontiers. Roosevelt and Churchill responded to their dilemma both by promising the peoples freed from German domination that they would be permitted self-determination and by assuring Stalin that the West was cognizant of his interest in pro-Soviet governments along the Russian periphery. Churchill explained Western intentions in February 1945: "The Poles will have their future in their own hands, with the single limitation that they must honestly follow, in harmony with their allies, a policy friendly to Russia. This is surely reasonable."

Unfortunately, by 1945 the Western powers could no longer guarantee even limited self-determination to the people of Eastern Europe. The West could not defeat the Axis without turning over control of Slavic Europe to Russian armies. By early 1945 Soviet forces, in pushing their way into Germany and Austria, had swept across Poland, Czechoslovakia, Rumania, Bulgaria, and Hungary. In addition, the Soviets had established their influence in Communist-ruled Yugoslavia and Albania. Obviously, there was no power in Europe that could force Russia's withdrawal to its borders of 1939. That country's new accretion of strength would drive it toward policies designed both to force an acceptance of the new status quo in Eastern and Central Europe and to guarantee its security against a resurgent Germany.

THE YALTA CONFERENCE

The Yalta Conference of February 1945 became a traumatic experience because it exposed in one massive revelation, for those who chose to read its lessons, what the United States government had suppressed with remarkable success through three years of war. How could a democratic leadership reiterate the principles of the Atlantic Charter and admit publicly that these principles meant nothing to an ally whose defection would mean the failure of policy? It seemed better to dispose of the German problem unencumbered by doubts and permit the Soviet challenge to pass unnoticed under the assumption that it could be disposed of later or avoided completely. Even before Roosevelt left for the Crimea late in January, the State Department made it clear that the time had passed when the United States could control events in Eastern Europe. In a sense Western Europe had given up that control when it failed to protect Czechoslovakia and Poland from German and Soviet encroachment in 1939. Nothing remained with the end of fighting to counter the Soviet military position except the Russian signature on the Atlantic Charter. Unless the West chose to threaten the Soviets with military force, there was little left in the Western arsenal except paper agreements and the willingness to resort to moral pressure.

Having lost control of Slavic Europe to Russian armies, the Western Allies attempted to salvage what they could of the Atlantic Charter in the form of a Declaration on Liberated Europe. Under it the Big Three pledged themselves to assist the former Nazi satellites "to solve by democratic means their pressing political and economic problems" and to acknowledge "the right of all people to choose the form of government under which they will live." This so-called Yalta Charter was Roosevelt's final and futile effort to prevent the creation of a Soviet sphere of influence in Eastern Europe.

Even before the Yalta Conference, Soviet policy toward Poland had put the wartime alliance to the test. Early in January 1945, a Moscow broadcast announced that the U.S.S.R. was recognizing the Lublin Committee as the provisional government of Poland. Clearly this group, by Western political standards, was not representative of the Polish people. Britain and the United States continued to recognize the exiled Polish government in London. The *Manchester Guardian* predicted that the Lublin group would win because the Soviets had control of Poland. Roosevelt complained to Stalin on February 6, "It seems to me that it puts all of us in a bad light throughout the world to have you recognizing one government while we and the British are recognizing another in London." At Yalta a few days later the Soviets promised to include Poles from abroad in the Lublin government. How this agreement could be implemented was not evident.

This clear Soviet defiance of the Atlantic Charter in the first postwar effort at political reconstruction in Eastern Europe produced a wide variety of reactions in the Western world. The London Poles denounced the Yalta communiqué as a violation of the principle of self-determination. Charles Rozmarek, president of the Polish-American Congress, declared: "It is with sorrow, dismay and protest that we greet the decision of the Big Three to give all land east of the so-called Curzon line to Russia in direct contradiction to all sacred pledges of the Atlantic Charter. This tragic revelation is a staggering blow to the cause of freedom." The Chicago *Tribune* observed simply that American morality and diplomacy had hit a new low at Yalta. Meanwhile, the State Department assured the American people that the principles of the Yalta Declaration would be effective in practice; alone they would terminate any danger of spheres of influence in Europe. "The British and Soviet Governments, with the United States," declared James C. Dunn, State Department spokesman, over NBC, "are pledged to consult with each other constantly in every part of liberated Europe." Perhaps Senator Arthur H. Vandenberg's noted speech of January 10, 1945, epitomized the American dilemma. He demanded the right for Americans to criticize Soviet action, but he refused to face the central challenge—that beyond peace the United States would be forced to concede either its principles or its alliance with Russia.

In London Churchill defended the Yalta agreements before the House of Commons late in February as the best that could be obtained. "Only one link in the chain of destiny," he said, "can be handled at a time." On the following day Captain Thorneycroft reminded the House of Commons that the difficulty between East and West was not Poland at all, but rather the growing conflict between American idealism, embodied in the Atlantic Charter, and Russian realism, embodied in the historic advice and ambitions of the Czars. The process of adjusting these differences, he predicted, would be a long and painful one. (*See Document No. 2 on p. 176.*)

Stalin, in lieu of any settlement, proceeded to turn liberated Europe into a Soviet sphere of influence. Late in February he dispatched Soviet diplomat Andrei Vishinski to Bucharest to force King Michael to appoint the Soviet puppet, Petra Groza, as head of the new Communist-dominated government of Rumania. Early in March, Foreign Minister Vyacheslav Molotov demanded that the old Lublin regime form the core of the provisional government of Poland promised at Yalta. The pattern of Soviet policy was clear. Using his political and ideological identification with local Communist leaders, Stalin gradually established a series of friendly Communist governments in the areas occupied by Soviet troops.

EASTERN EUROPE AND POSTWAR RECONSTRUCTION

Clearly the United States would not and could not control the destiny of Eastern Europe. Still Washington chose to make that region's future the central issue of postwar reconstruction. Why the United States displayed this interest in a region of little historical importance to it must find its explanation in the conditions that prevailed in 1945 and thereafter. In part the pressures on American leadership were domestic—the refusal of the powerful Slavic minorities in the United States, especially the Polish American Congress, to countenance any agreement that would recognize Soviet control of any Slavic region. This minority received open, vigorous support from much of the nation's conservative, Republican, and Catholic press. The realization that the threat to self-determination emanated from the same Communist power which, in victory, had uprooted the old European balance of power, convinced at least a minority of Americans that Soviet behavior endangered Western security and for that reason could not be tolerated. This fear of additional Soviet encroachment became more pervasive with the passage of time.

Roosevelt and Hull, with their promises of a postwar era built on the principles of the Atlantic Charter, created visions of an ideal world which much of the American population shared in 1945. The nation's wartime leadership had promised too much and expected too much to recognize the Soviet sphere of influence. Roosevelt, during his last weeks as President, saw that the big-power unity for which he had struggled so hard throughout the war years was eluding him and the country. Outwardly he remained optimistic to the end. Shortly before his death he wired to Churchill: "I would minimize the general Soviet problem as much as possible because these problems, in one form or another, seem to arise every day and most of them straighten out. . . ." Privately, the President was less sure. In a series of dispatches to Stalin he reminded the Soviet leader that in his defiance of wartime agreements he was destroying the unity that the Western world had been led to expect. "You must believe me when I tell you," he wrote early in February, "that our people at home look with a critical eye on what they consider a disagreement between us at this vital state of the war.'' In an eventual mood of desperation, Roosevelt wrote to Stalin on April 5, one week before his death: ''It would be one of the greatest tragedies in history if at the very moment of victory now within our grasp such distrust and such lack of faith should prejudice the entire undertaking after the colossal losses of life and material and treasure involved.''

Thereafter the actual record of Soviet repression, reported in detail by American officials, created a strong conviction within the United States government that political structures based on such repression did not merit recognition. Still if the United States was not concerned about the absence of representative government in Russia, it was neither logical nor fruitful to demand representative government in the Slavic states where American political interests and the possibilities for controlling events were no greater than in Russia itself. For the United States to behave as if it could influence the destiny of regions under Soviet control was undignified and misleading.

For some Americans of the immediate postwar era—and even more for the revisionist historians of the 1960s—the Truman administration's concern for Eastern Europe centered as much on the economic open door as on free elections. Both American purposes, if achieved, would limit the new Soviet hegemony and permit free competition in that region. For many key United States officials any effort to restrict unlimited international trade and investment in Europe endangered both peace and prosperity. Still Eastern Europe had never been economically important for the United States. American assets in the Slavic states were never more than 12 percent of all such assets in Europe, and the bulk of that investment was concentrated in Poland, Czechoslovakia, and Hungary. Traditionally United States exports to Eastern Europe totaled approximately 2 percent of the nation's total exports. By mid-century, despite a brief recovery after the war, that trade had become almost nonexistent.

Still United States officials opposed Soviet domination of even the limited trade and investment opportunities that existed in Slavic Europe. Beginning in 1944 Russian officials began to claim industrial property in Rumania and other neighboring countries, some of it American-owned, as reparations. Washington immediately condemned such action as a violation of American rights and interests. During 1945 Russia sought and gained a wide variety of special economic advantages designed to divert the trade of the Slavic countries eastward. In May, Elbridge Durbrow of the State Department's Division of Eastern European Affairs warned that Soviet trade agreements with the Eastern European regimes might "create an almost airtight economic blackout in the entire area east of the Stettin-Trieste line." In August 1945, Ambassador to Poland Arthur Bliss Lane objected to the Soviet-Polish trade agreement of July as "contrary to our foreign economic policy of encouraging free private trade among nations." Polish officials reminded Lane that they could preserve some remnant of national independence only by acceding to Kremlin demands.

Differences between East and West over Eastern Europe moved quickly beyond the point of reconciliation. Ambassador Harriman reported from Moscow in May 1945: "I am afraid that Stalin does not and never will fully understand our interest in a free Poland as a matter of principle. The Russian Premier is a realist in all of his actions, and it is hard for him to appreciate our faith in abstract principle. It is difficult for him to understand why we should want to interfere with Soviet policy in a country like Poland which he considers so important to Russia's security unless we have some ulterior motive." What disturbed Churchill was the Soviet policy of creating a distinct zone in Eastern Europe. He wired Truman on May 12, urging some settlement with the Kremlin even at the cost of principle:

I am profoundly concerned about the European situation. I have always worked for friendship with Russia, but like you, I feel deep anxiety because of their misinterpretation of the Yalta decisions, their attitudes toward Poland, their overwhelming influence in the Balkans . . . and above all their power to maintain very large armies in the field for a long time. . . . Surely it is vital now to come to an understanding with Russia, or see where we are with her, before weakening our armies mortally or retiring to the zones of occupation. . . . Of course we may take the view that Russia will behave impeccably, and no doubt that offers the most convenient solution. To sum up, this issue of a settlement with Russia before our strength has gone seems to me to dwarf all others.

Walter Lippmann voiced the same impatience with the tendency toward drift. He asserted on May 8 that Europe actually was divided into two exclusive spheres of influence, one dominated by the United States and the other by the U.S.S.R., each limited largely to its own sphere. "No nation, however strong," he wrote, "has universal world power which reaches everywhere. The realm in which each state has the determining influence is limited by geography and circumstance. Beyond that realm it is possible to bargain and persuade but not to compel, and no foreign policy is well conducted which does not recognize these invincible realities."

THE ILLUSION OF POWER

That vast body of mutual wartime interests, centering in the quest for victory, which had permitted American leadership to postpone all fundamental decisions relative to Soviet intention, no longer existed. But Roosevelt had simply created no policy for dealing with Stalin's postwar behavior. During the war Allied decisions had assumed a cooperative peacetime Russia, principled by Western standards; in 1945 the Western powers faced a new Russia, vastly augmented in ambition, aggressiveness, and size, determined to pursue its historic interests—which the Atlantic Charter could not serve—in world affairs. The Soviet challenge was limited, but the Kremlin's designs on Eastern Europe were unmistakable. Any American response that came to grips with the problem had either to recognize the Soviet sphere, in an effort to minimize its scope, or to seek the strength to undo it. But from the beginning the United States government sought to avoid the choice. It rejected the consequences of the war under the assumption that it could, with superior military and economic power, through trade restrictions and eventually military alliances, compel the Soviets to conform to its principles of postwar European reconstruction. It was this illusion that propelled the United States into foreign policies which would never have much relationship to either the nation's power or its basic intentions.

Still the illusion of power was strong. The United States emerged from the war the most powerful nation in history, with the world's largest and best equipped navy and air force. What magnified that predominance was the death and devastation which all other major nations had suffered during the war. President Harry S. Truman, who succeeded Roosevelt in mid-April 1945, revealed that consciousness of power when he told his cabinet on April 23, before a meeting with Soviet Foreign Minister V. M. Molotov, that "if the Russians did not wish to join us [at the United Nations Conference in San Francisco] they could go to hell." Vandenberg found enough solace in these words to confide in his diary, "FDR's appeasement of Russia is over." The United States and the U.S.S.R. could live together successfully, the Senator was convinced, "if Russia is made to understand that we can't be pushed around." The new Secretary of State, James F. Byrnes, asserted later that "the only way to negotiate with the Russians is to hit them hard, and then negotiate."

So confident were such leaders of American military superiority that the rapid demobilization of the nation's armed forces from 12

million in 1945 to 1.5 million in 1947 did not create a sense of insecurity. Even at reduced levels that power seemed sufficient to
guarantee the peace. For some the atomic bomb was merely the final
assurance that the United States could manage Europe's reconstruction in accordance with its principles. If the bomb worked, Truman remarked shortly before the Potsdam Conference of July–August 1945,
"I'll certainly have a hammer on those boys [the Russians]." The
bomb was needed, observed Secretary Byrnes, not to defeat Japan, but
to "make Russia manageable in Europe." At Potsdam Truman received news of the successful atomic test at Alamogordo, New
Mexico. The effect on the President was dramatic, for Churchill recalled, "Truman was evidently much fortified by something that had
happened and . . . he stood up to the Russians in a most emphatic and
decisive manner. . . . He told the Russians just where they got off and
generally bossed the whole meeting."

Within days Truman made the fateful decision to use the bomb
against Japanese targets. Whether his purpose was simply to terminate
the Pacific war quickly or to create an implied threat in future negotiations with the Russians remains a subject of controversy. At any rate,
the two interpretations create no direct conflict, for Truman could well
have had both intentions in mind. Thereafter, the bomb was present at
every meeting. Shortly before the London Conference of September
1945, Secretary of War Henry L. Stimson confided in his diary that
Byrnes "was very much against any attempt to cooperate with Russia.
His mind is full of his problems with the coming meeting . . . and he
looks to having the presence of the bomb in his pocket so to speak.
. . ." But Byrnes and his successors were careful not to employ the
bomb as a threat. There could be no atomic diplomacy, for the United
States had no historic political or economic interest in a free Eastern
Europe of sufficient magnitude to establish the credibility of an atomic
threat to achieve it.

Still the Truman administration regarded the bomb of sufficient
military importance that it chose, despite its sharply divided counsels,
to protect the nation's assumed monopoly of knowledge regarding its
creation. For Stimson it appeared essential that the United States share
the secret with the Russians in a display of trust. American-Soviet relations, he warned, "may be irretrievably embittered by the way in
which we approach the solution of the bomb with Russia. For if we fail
to approach them now and merely continue to negotiate with them,
having this weapon rather ostentatiously on our hip, their suspicions
and their distrust of our purposes and motives will increase." During

the spring of 1946, after months of internal debate, Truman adopted the plan formulated by Bernard Baruch, which would have placed atomic control in the hands of the United Nations, but under conditions which would have protected the United States monopoly for a number of years. The Soviets rejected the plan and proceeded to develop their own atomic program.

In Europe the administration had no interest in applying even the conventional power that remained in its possession. Joseph E. Davies, Truman's special envoy to London, warned him that Churchill was too much concerned with British interests on the Continent. With his advisors concurring, the President decided against using the matter of retirement to agreed zones of occupation for the purpose of bargaining. It seemed to make little difference, for in June the President announced a settlement of the Polish issue, adding confidently that the Russians were anxious to get along peacefully with the American people. Harry Hopkins, on a special mission to Moscow, had convinced Stalin that the United States was not trying to force on Poland a government unfriendly to the U.S.S.R. Ambassador Harriman reached a final agreement on June 22, 1945, to establish a new provisional government for Poland.

Americans who had no interest in military power at all found their real hope for a peaceful future in the events at San Francisco, where from April to June 1945, spokesmen for the victorious nations succeeded in framing the United Nations Charter. For many the U.N. simply became the end of foreign policy. Here at last was the forum before which the law-abiding countries could summon criminal aggressors and demand their compliance with international law.

Yet in the context of big-power rivalry it was clear that the new U.N., like the League of Nations before it, would serve largely as an instrument of evasion. Among sovereign states no international organization can ever be more than an agency of individual national policies. The United Nations could not terminate the struggle for power and prestige among the countries of the world. Nor could it achieve genuine concert in international affairs or force its decisions through collective action on any major power. It could only provide a public forum where nations would add new political instruments to the traditional weapons of diplomacy—where they would resort to legalism in manipulating the procedure of the organization and turn all serious debate into appeals for world sentiment. Since such weapons could have no viable effect on the actual distribution of power in the world, the battles of the U.N. would remain barren. No minority would permit its power or security to be jeopardized by the vote of the majority. Voting could never be as important as the agreement to consult. If the U.N. created an excellent piece of machinery to bring nations together for debate, it did not create a new international order. And nothing would destroy it more quickly than the insistence that it perform as if some new order in international society had actually been established.

For some Americans the power that mattered in controlling European reconstruction was economic, not military. This country's productivity during the last year of the war completely outstripped that of the European countries; with the onset of peace it reached approximately half that of the entire world. Such power added to Washington's aura of confidence. As early as March 1944, Ambassador Harriman observed that "economic assistance is one of the more effective weapons at our disposal to influence European political events in the direction we desire." That Russia might become subject to American economic power seemed clear in January 1945, when the Soviet government handed Harriman a request for long-term credits totaling $6 billion. The arrangement proposed terms favorable to Russia, but, the Kremlin argued, its orders for railroad and industrial equipment would be placed in the United States. For Harriman and Assistant Secretary for Economic Affairs William Clayton, United States economic power was so awesome that it could give the United States the needed leverage to control events in Eastern Europe. Clayton favored delay in granting credits because, he insisted, an American loan remained "the only concrete bargaining lever for use in connection with the many other political and economic problems which will arise between our two countries." Thereafter the subject receded; the Big Three avoided it at Yalta in February, and at Potsdam in August.

Meanwhile on May 11, 1945, three days after peace came to Europe, Truman abruptly cut Lend-Lease aid to Russia. Whether the President hoped through this action to exert economic pressures on the Soviets to force agreement on other issues or whether he was merely complying with the congressional order that Lend-Lease terminate with the end of the war remains unclear. Still the two interpretations are not mutually exclusive, for Truman sought to satisfy Congress and was not averse to revealing his growing displeasure at Soviet behavior. Harry Hopkins in Moscow assured Stalin that the United States, as a powerful country, had no desire to put pressure on the Soviet Union, but the administration assumed correctly that its decisions on Lend-Lease would antagonize the Russians. Perhaps that irritation would influence United States-Soviet relations for the better by reminding the

Russians that they would need to bargain for what they received from the United States. Stimson argued that United States power, atomic and economic, would be effective in dealing with the Russians. In a diary notation of May 14, 1945, Stimson wrote: "They can't get along without our help and industries and we have coming into action a weapon which will be unique."

Truman's decision on Lend Lease, which he admitted was unnecessarily harsh, did not change any Russian policy, but it was a demonstration of American dissatisfaction. Thereafter the United States continued to stall on the question of a loan to Russia, determined to use its economic power to force Soviet concessions in Europe. Early in March 1946, the State Department announced that it had lost the Russian loan request. Within weeks the loan became a dead issue. Truman had no desire to confront Congress on the matter; the Kremlin would not compromise any of its political interests in Slavic Europe to obtain American credits.

THE POSTWAR CONFERENCES

Truman, Churchill, and Stalin met at Potsdam in mid-July 1945, accompanied by their foreign ministers and military advisors, endowed with the power to establish the foundations of peace. Yalta had been a conference of commanders-in-chief; Potsdam was a meeting of political leaders confronted with the obligation to block out the territorial, economic, and administrative arrangements for reconquered Europe. The conference achieved quick agreement on the establishment of the Council of Foreign Ministers. On the concrete issues of Germany and Eastern Europe there was no possible compromise. Stalin employed every device and agreement to maintain the maximum degree of Soviet prestige, power, and security. When he failed to win concessions, he favored postponement. The Big Three agreed eventually that Germany should be demilitarized, denazified, and democratized. For reparations, each occupying power was authorized to remove property from its own zone and to seize German assets abroad. The four occupying commanders were designated a control council to decide matters affecting Germany as a whole.

Stalin remained totally adamant on the question of Eastern Europe's future. "A freely elected government in any of these East European countries," he admitted simply, "would be anti-Soviet, and that we cannot allow." The United States, Byrnes assured a suspicious

Molotov, "sincerely desires Russia to have friendly countries on her borders, but we believe they should seek the friendship of the people rather than of any particular government." His government, said Byrnes, did not wish to become involved in the elections of other countries; it merely desired to join other nations in observing elections in Italy, Greece, Hungary, Rumania, and Bulgaria. Vigorous Western protests against Stalin's unilateral violation of the Yalta agreements resulted in some revision of procedural matters, but left all fundamental issues substantially untouched.

At Potsdam world politics began to assume a bipolar structure. The leading nations, already distrustful of the United Nations, were beginning to seek security in their own resources. "As a result," ran John Fischer's judgment in *Harper's* of August 1945,

most of the lesser nations are now being drawn by a sort of Law of Political Gravity into the orbit of one or the other of the two Super-Powers. So far neither Russia nor the United States has yet completed its protective belt of satellites. Some areas are being tugged both ways, like small planets caught between two great stars.

As long as the tugging continued, predicted Fischer, the relations between the two great powers would remain tense. The postwar period of "grinding adjustment" had arrived. To avoid war, added Fischer, the United States and the U.S.S.R. had no choice but to accept the sphere of influence of the other. Since Soviet power was dominant in Eastern Europe, eventually the Western nations would be forced to concede with whatever grace they could muster. The unity that remained after Potsdam was limited to rhetoric that could shield the vast conflicts apparent on every issue.

At the Council of Foreign Ministers meeting at London in September 1945, the trend toward a permanently divided Europe became inescapable. At the conclusion of the conference the London *Observer* warned that there could be no "shirking from the unpleasant fact that, without agreement between Moscow and the West, a line drawn north and south across Europe, perhaps somewhere in the region of Stettin to Trieste, is likely to become more and more of a barrier separating two very different conceptions of life." Soviet intransigence at London had the effect of driving the Western ministers into a solid, opposing bloc. When it became obvious to the Soviets that every issue resulted in the combined opposition of the United States, England, France, and China, they finally broke up the conference by demanding that France and China be excluded from the crucial decisions.

At London Molotov made it clear that Russia's price for cooperation was Western recognition of the new satellite governments of Eastern Europe. Byrnes assured Molotov again that the United States was not interested in seeing anything but governments friendly to the Soviet Union in Eastern Europe. Molotov replied that this could not be true. The Radescu regime in Rumania, which had been hostile to Russia, he said, had received cordial American and British support. Yet, he added, when the Groza government, which was friendly to the Soviet Union, was established, the Western powers had withdrawn their recognition. Byrnes replied that Soviet pressure had forced the Groza regime on the Rumanian people. "Our objective," Byrnes explained, "is a government both friendly to the Soviet Union and representative of all the democratic elements of the country." The Secretary countered Molotov's continuing demand for security against Germany with an offer binding the United States to that nation's demilitarization for twenty-five years. Such a security pact appeared to the Russians less substantial than an arrangement based on their own power. Eventually Byrnes returned to the United States, unable to modify Soviet intransigence on any of the fundamental issues dividing the world.

Without special preparation or Republican advisors, Byrnes traveled to Moscow in December 1945, against the judgment of veteran diplomats and correspondents. "I believed," he wrote in his defense, "that if we met in Moscow, where I could have a chance to talk to Stalin, we might remove the barriers to the peace treaties. The peace of the world was too important for us to be unwilling to take a chance on securing an agreement after full discussions." Byrnes eventually gained Stalin's acceptance of a peace conference, but he was forced to compromise his London stand.

Byrnes, with his advisors, chiefly Ambassador Harriman and career officer Charles E. Bohlen, was convinced at Moscow that the continued nonrecognition of the Soviet hegemony would achieve nothing for the United States. (In October and November the United States had extended recognition to the provisional governments of Austria and Hungary.) At Moscow, without denying American principles, Byrnes accepted the existing regimes of Rumania and Bulgaria. Stalin agreed to a token representation of pro-Western parties and pledged early free elections. If these agreements represented some retreat from the previous American position, they recognized essentially that the United States had few choices remaining.

THE HARDENING AMERICAN RESPONSE

Byrnes' search for a decision at Moscow terminated abruptly the optimistic American attitude toward Russia, born of wartime collaboration. Tragically, the continued Soviet determination to maintain political control of Eastern and Central Europe unleashed in the United States a variety of equally determined pressures against any concession of principle. Truman, in his Navy Day speech of October 27, 1945, declared that this nation would never recognize any government established by force against the freely expressed will of the people. Walter Lippmann retorted that the President's generalizations would do little for negotiations. "We do indeed live in a marvelous age," he added caustically, "having succeeded not only in tapping the sources of atomic energy but the source of moral revelation as well."

Embarrassed by Byrnes' concessions at Moscow, Truman dated his break with his Secretary from that conference. He recorded in his *Memoirs:* "My memorandum (January 5, 1946) to Brynes . . . was the point of departure of our policy. 'I'm tired of babying the Soviets,' I had said to Byrnes, and I meant it." Jonathan Daniels, in his biography of Truman, quoted the President as saying, "Byrnes lost his nerve at Moscow." He accused Byrnes of not keeping him informed and of talking to the radio without his permission. Admiral Leahy, Truman's personal Chief of Staff, took the lead in condemning the Moscow Declaration. James V. Forrestal, Secretary of the Navy, lauded the President's firmness and suggested that the United States increase its capabilities to meet new dangers. From Moscow Harriman encouraged the administration to get tougher with the Russians, and in May 1946, George F. Kennan, Harriman's assistant, was recalled from Moscow to advise the State Department on Russian matters.

But the chief movement for a "get tough" policy centered in Republican leadership. Congressional Republicans had supported Roosevelt's wartime policies and decisions. But by the autumn of 1945 it was quite obvious that the wartime effort had brought the nation far less security and peace than the President had promised or that American expenditures had warranted. Republicans now demanded of Truman what Roosevelt had failed to achieve: a world of justice built on the Atlantic Charter.

Following the collapse of the London Conference, John Foster Dulles, Republican foreign policy spokesman, cautioned a national radio audience that Soviet intransigence was designed to determine if this nation would really hold to its principles. Early in October 1945, the Senate Foreign Relations Committee pressed Byrnes to "get tough" with the Russians. On November 1 the House of Representatives, with only two Republicans in opposition, passed an appropriations bill barring the use of American funds in the Russian satellites. This bill died in the Senate Appropriations Committee, but it revealed a decided shift in Congress, especially among Republicans, toward the new anti-Soviet attitude. Then on December 5, a committee of House and Senate Republicans issued a policy statement chiding the administration's policy in Eastern Europe:

We believe in fulfilling to the greatest possible degree our war pledges to small nations that they shall have the right to choose the form of government under which they will live and that sovereign rights and self-government shall be restored to those who have been forcibly deprived of them. We deplore any desertion of these principles.

Following the Moscow Conference, Republican leaders became increasingly critical of the administration's failure to free the countries of Eastern Europe from Soviet influence. Representative Clare Booth Luce, in February 1946, publicly denounced the Truman leadership for ignoring its commitments to the Atlantic Charter, for the dismemberment of Poland, and for its failure to carry out the principle of self-determination in the Russian satellites. Late that month Vandenberg warned the Senate of the growing rivalry between the United States and the U.S.S.R. He concluded:

If this is so . . . I assert my own belief that we can live together in reasonable harmony if the United States speaks as plainly upon all occasions as Russia does; if the United States just as vigorously sustains its own purposes and its ideals upon all occasions as Russia does; if we abandon the miserable fiction, often encouraged by our own fellow travelers, that we somehow jeopardize the peace if our candor is as firm as Russia's always is; and if we assume a moral leadership which we have too frequently allowed to lapse. The situation calls for patience and good will; it does not call for vacillation. . . . There is a line beyond which compromise cannot go—even if we once crossed that line under the pressures of the exigencies of war. But how can we expect our alien friends to know where that is unless we re-establish the habit of saying only what we mean and meaning every word we say?

This posture of toughness toward Russia permitted the Republican leadership to identify itself with the normally Democratic urban groups of Eastern European and Catholic background. Herein lay the chief significance of the Soviet issue in American politics. Catholic editors and writers of Eastern European origin, supported by such national pressure groups as the Polish-American Congress, took the lead in charging past American and British policies for the loss of Eastern Europe. Editor James M. Gillis of the *Catholic World* observed in May, 1946, that "if the real Poland can never speak again, the shame of the democracies and the futility of the UN are both revealed." The writer placed the blame on those who led the United States into war to save Poland from the Nazis and then threw the country to the Russian wolves. "That's why some of us, contemptuously branded isolationists," ran his conclusion, "are chary of assuming international obligations which we know we cannot fulfill, and which not even the most rabid interventionists honestly intend to fulfill."

These strident demands for the triumph of principle held the nation to its inflexible posture toward the U.S.S.R. But nowhere did they suggest any course of action which had a serious relationship to the limitless goals which they created. Few Americans would have favored decisions more explicit than those prescribed by Vandenberg. When it became obvious that the new Polish government was involved in a series of political murders in Poland, Byrnes instructed the American Embassy in Warsaw to "inform the Polish government that we are relying on that government to take the necessary steps to assure the freedom and security which are essential to the successful holding of free elections." Vandenberg objected immediately, declaring that it was not enough to rely on the Polish government to "vindicate the honor and the pledge of the United States of America." We must rely, he said, "on our own moral authority in a world which, in my opinion, craves our moral leadership." Such firmness did not mean war, he insisted in a passage reminiscent of the internationalism of the interwar years:

It means, first, that we must insistently demand prompt and dependable assurances that the Yalta and Potsdam pledges in behalf of free elections be effectively fulfilled. It means, in other words, that we shall lift the powerful voice of America in behalf of the inviolable sanctity of international agreements to which we are a party. If this does not suffice, it means, then, that we shall scrupulously collect our facts; draw our relentless indictment if the facts so justify; and present it in the forum of the United Nations and demand judgment from the organized conscience of the world.

This illusion that moral force would permit the United States to turn the Soviets out of Eastern Europe enabled national leaders to escape the intellectual dilemma posed by their determination both to sustain their demands on Russia and to dismantle the American military establishment. On matters of national defense the Republicans, despite their verbal expectations of greater success abroad, were considerably behind the national administration in maintaining the nation's military structure. The policy of toughness assured economy-minded isolationists that they could win the struggle for Europe without encumbering the country with additional expenditures. Whatever the needs of the hour, demobilization was in the air, and the majority of both parties accepted the obligation to reduce the size of the armed forces. Already the dichotomy, familiar enough in American experience, between the demands placed on national performance and the almost total neglect of means, had become characteristic of the nation's behavior. For the moment it mattered little, for no level of American preparedness would produce the desired Soviet capitulation to Western demands.

Churchill battled this trend in his famous speech at Fulton, Missouri, in March 1946. Assuring the nation that he spoke for himself alone, the British leader alluded to an *Iron Curtain* descended across the European continent. He did not claim to know the limits of the expansive and proselytizing tendencies of either Russia or the Communist international. But the challenge, he said, required a "fraternal association of English-speaking peoples," and "intimate relationships between our military advisors, leading to a common study of potential dangers, the similarity of weapons and manuals of instruction, the interchange of officers and cadets at technical colleges" and "joint use of all naval and air force bases in the possession of either country all over the world." Russia, he believed, did not desire war, but, he added, "I am convinced that there is nothing they admire so much as strength and there is nothing for which they have less respect than for military weakness." *(See Document No. 3 on p. 181.)*

Truman, although present at Fulton, disclaimed all responsibility for Churchill's speech. White House Press Secretary, Charles G. Ross, reported that the President did not know of its contents, and at the Jackson Day dinner two weeks later the President himself made no reference to it. Thus Truman succeeded in escaping much of the bitter condemnation of Churchill's plea for an Anglo-American alliance. Members of Congress and the American people in general were still reluctant to commit American power permanently to the defense of Europe. Churchill's program appeared to call for a return to power politics and would merely force the Russians to create a countering alliance. To Pearl S. Buck, speaking at Town Hall, Churchill's speech was a catastrophe because it threatened to split the world. The British statesman was hailed and jeered on his procession through New York, and a leftist demonstration outside the dinner hall lasted for two hours. Senator Arthur Capper of Kansas, a noted Republican, took a parting shot at Churchill by charging him with trying to "arouse the people of the United States to commit the country to the task of preserving the farflung British Empire." What Churchill's speech seemed to indicate was that most Americans, whatever their feeling toward Russia, would retreat from any program that required more of the United States than moral disapprobation.

THE PARIS CONFERENCES OF 1946

Byrnes after the Moscow Conference began to respond to the pressures of the right. At a cabinet luncheon late in January he complained that the attacks of Vandenberg and Dulles on his actions were largely partisan. Then in a radio report of February 28, to counter the charges of appeasement, he assumed a position as firm as Vandenberg's (one wit termed this speech the Second Vandenberg Concerto). To reestablish a nonpartisan approach to foreign policy, Byrnes invited both Vandenberg and Tom Connally, the Democratic leader of the Senate, to accompany him to the Foreign Ministers meeting at Paris late in April. Thereafter, the Republican attacks on Executive leadership began to diminish, whereas at Paris Connally criticised Byrnes for trying too hard to please Vandenberg. Upon his return to the Senate in May, Vandenberg reported that the American delegation had maintained absolute unity on every issue. American policy, he said, was based on the "moralities of the Atlantic and San Francisco charters," as well as "the practical necessities for Europe's rehabilitation." That sort of foreign policy, he concluded, he would support under any administration.

To one high French official, Byrnes at Paris "gave the impression of a clever politican determined not to give an inch." His only concern, it seemed, was to put the onus of deadlock on the Soviet government. Every maneuver exposed another irreconcilable conflict. The Secretary terminated one especially futile session with the observation, "Can we at least agree upon adjourning until Monday?" On another occasion Vandenberg reported that the score for the conference was "no runs, no hits, and a lot of errors (but not by us)." By mid-May Connally observed that both Byrnes and Vandenberg believed United States-Soviet relations had fallen into a bottomless pit. The only alternatives remaining for the West were surrender or recess. In his report to the Senate, Vandenberg insisted that delay was preferable to error. "We can compromise within the boundaries of a principle," he admitted. "We can no longer compromise principles themselves."

When the Paris conference reconvened in July, Byrnes demanded a settlement. He warned Molotov that if there was no agreement on an early meeting of the 21-nation peace conference, the Western nations would proceed to negotiate a separate treaty with Italy. If one world was impossible, the West would simply organize the area outside the Soviet orbit. Byrnes' policy of firmness and patience gradually shifted to one of firmness without patience, for behind American pressure was the determination to reduce the nation's troop strength in Europe. It seems incredible that the Secretary should have been forced to bargain with the Russians at all. As Anne O'Hare McCormick wrote in July, "When Americans demand in one breath that their government take a firm stand on principle and in the next that the bulk of our forces be withdrawn from Europe, they should not complain of unsatisfactory compromises. We cannot stand and move away at the same time." Despite this apparent impatience, Byrnes won substantial concessions from the Russians on an Italian treaty, with a free city of Trieste and British control of the former Italian colonies.

THE FUTILITY OF THE MORAL RESPONSE

American "get tough" policy after 1945, which never comprised more than a change of style, satisfied the domestic requirements of a government that had somehow to promise powerful pressure groups and politicians that it would secure the triumph of self-determination. Yet in the new rhetoric lay eventual tragedy, for it convinced too many Americans that there was some special power in words and created the illusion that the choices before the nation in its negotiations with the Soviet Union were much broader than the presence of Red armies in all regions of dispute suggested. The "get tough" attitude gave nothing away, but it assured no settlements on American terms.

Henry A. Wallace, Secretary of Commerce, took the lead in criticizing the nation's stereotyped response to the question of exclusive spheres of influence in Europe. In a memorandum to the President of July 23, 1946, he admitted the administration's success in achieving bipartisan cooperation in its new attitudes toward Russia, but he questioned whether unity built on currying conflict abroad was advisable. "I think there is some reason to fear that in our earnest efforts to achieve bipartisan unity in this country," he warned, "we may have given way too much to isolationism masquerading as tough realism in international affairs."

On September 12, at Madison Square Garden, Wallace called for a policy of peaceful competition with Russia. What mattered, he said, were not peace treaties over Greece and the German satellites, but peace between the United States and Russia. "On our part," he said,

we should recognize that we have no more business in the *political* affairs of Eastern Europe than Russia has in the *political* affairs of Latin America, Western Europe, and the United States . . . whether we like it or not, the Russians will try to socialize their sphere of influence just as we try to democratize our sphere of influence. This applies also to Germany and Japan. The Russians have no more business in stirring up native Communists to political activity in Western Europe, Latin America, and the United States than we have in interfering with the politics of Eastern Europe and Russia.

Wallace did not regard Russia an immediate danger to Western Europe; for that reason he denied the need of an active policy of force. But he voiced clearly his belief that merely getting tough would not secure the fulfillment of the aspirations of Yalta. Western toughness would always be matched by that of the Kremlin. In the conflict over Eastern Europe, he knew, the Soviets held the overwhelming advantage. Their defense was not based on claims and aspirations, but on physical occupation and military power. Walter Lippmann wondered again why the nation preached high ideals for Eastern Europe when it had established its own sphere of influence in the Pacific north of the equator.

For the Russians Byrnes' continuing reliance on moral force rather than bargaining to have his way seemed quite incomprehensible. In *Speaking Frankly,* Byrnes acknowledged that the Russians had analyzed his methods precisely. After one heated session at Paris, Charles E. Bohlen, advisor to the American delegation, remained behind to converse with a member of the Soviet delegation. "The Soviet representative," reported Bohlen, "said it was impossible for him to understand the Americans. They had a reputation for being good traders and yet Secretary Byrnes for two days had been making speeches about principles—talking, he said, like a professor." With all sincerity, the Soviet delegate added, "Why doesn't he stop his talking about principles, and get down to business and start trading?"

Such reliance on moral force created some illusion of ultimate success. Yet as a substitute for concrete policy it comprised largely an escape from responsibility. In December 1946, Lippmann analyzed succinctly why American action would continue to reap little but futility:

Mr. Byrnes, Mr. Vanderberg, Mr. Connally, and Mr. Truman had been schooled in the Senate, and Mr. Bevin in the Trades Union Congress and in Parliament. Unable to induce or compel M. Molotov by what they regarded as diplomacy, they sought to outvote him, and to arouse public opinion against him. The theory of this procedure was that by bringing issues to a public vote an aroused public opinion would do to the Russians what it has done now and then to Tammany Hall and Mayor Hague, to Mr. Joe Martin and Senator Taft.

But to apply the methods of domestic politics to international politics is like using the rules of checkers in a game of chess. Within a democratic state, conflicts are decided by an actual or a potential count of votes—as the saying goes, by ballots rather than bullets. But in a world of sovereign states conflicts are decided by power, actual or potential, for the ultimate arbiter is not an election but war.

Two disturbing postwar trends, each destroying the illusion of one world, converged during the summer and autumn of 1946. The first was the unbroken increase in tension between East and West. What had begun as a verbal struggle over the future of the Russian satellites had, in the absence of any diplomatic agreements, degenerated into a conflict of immense hostility. Byrnes recognized this alarming quality in the debate raging across Europe. "The thing which disturbs me," he observed late in October, 1946, "is not the lettered provisions of the treaties under discussion but the continued if not increasing tension between us and the Soviet Union." The second trend of 1946 was the further structuring of a bipolar world—an evolution characterized both by the gradual assumption of Western leadership by the United States and the simultaneous conclusion among the lesser countries of the West that the position of neutrality between the giants was no longer tenable. As the astute London *Observer* commented on October 27, 1946: "Our relations with America and Russia are not the same. Those with America, though our views and interests are far from identical, are easy and friendly, and we cannot view America as a potential menace to our existence. The same cannot, unfortunately, be said of Russia. . . ."

For Byrnes the conflict between the United States and the U.S.S.R. was still sufficiently limited to rule out the rearming of Germany or Japan. Nor had he any desire to break off negotiations with the Soviets. If the postwar experience had been hard on the nerves of diplomats, he wrote, war would be harder on the lives of millions. Diplomacy offered no panaceas. To build a lasting peace required far more diligence and imagination than suggested by the optimism which still anticipated unilateral Russian concessions and the pessimism which anticipated the ultimate triumph of justice only at the end of another war. But the one essential national decision—that of defining American interests in the context of both a divided world and a new balance of power—still awaited a more propitious time.

The Structure of
Containment

What characterized American foreign policy in the late 1940s was its gradual retreat from an offensive to a defensive posture. Until 1946, Soviet ambitions appeared limited to regions already under the dominance of the Red Army. The notion that Russia's forward position was only the initial step in a general assault on the free world was scarcely in evidence. It was Western policy, with its avowed purpose of deflating the Soviet hegemony, that maintained a spirit of aggressiveness. Soviet power was finite; its existence was disturbing only to the extent that it underwrote the new Communist regimes of Eastern Europe. The assumption that Stalinist behavior posed a moral rather than a physical challenge created the illusion that a sufficient response lay somewhere in the realm of verbal disapprobation. This permitted American leadership to sustain its expectation of eventual Soviet capitulation at the same time that it continued to reduce the size of the nation's military establishment. Soviet intransigence throughout 1945 and 1946 was more productive of frustration than of fear.

Throughout 1946 Russia's hegemony in Eastern Europe still represented a status quo policy, disagreeable but no direct threat to Western security. But the Soviet influence in northern Iran, a region still in flux, appeared early in 1946 as a special threat to Iranian independence, Middle Eastern peace, and the strategic interests of the Western World. Russia had encouraged the Communist-dominated

Tudeh Party of Azerbaijan in northern Iran to challenge the Teheran government. In August 1945, the Tudeh Party openly rebelled and demanded independence for Azerbaijan. Stalin reminded Byrnes in Moscow during December that Soviet troops stationed in that region were there legally to protect the Baku oil fields and Russia's southern frontier. At the U.N. in January 1946, Teheran accused the Russians of meddling in Iranian affairs. Shortly thereafter the United States and Britain withdrew their forces from Iran. The Russians warned that they would keep their troops in Iran until the new Iranian government, formed late in January under Ahmed Qavam, offered an acceptable settlement. During March the Russians, failing to keep the Iranian question off the U.N. agenda, walked out of the Security Council.

Finally in April the Soviets gained an accord with Iran whereby they agreed to evacuate the country within six weeks in exchange for a Soviet-Iranian oil pact. American officials applauded the Soviet withdrawal but moved privately to prevent the ratification of the oil agreement. Eventually in October 1947, the Iranian parliament rejected the oil agreement overwhelmingly. Thus the Russians, who had regarded the oil agreement as fair, a quid pro quo for withdrawal, lost the oil concession as well. Truman boasted later that he had sent an ultimatum to the Russians, demanding that they evacuate Iran. No ultimatum, if prepared, was ever sent, but the assumption that words had been effective in freeing Iran reaffirmed the popularity of the "get tough with Russia" slogan. United States officials, refusing to recognize the quid pro quo in the initial Soviet-Iranian agreement, assumed that the Soviets had retreated under pressure. Byrnes insisted that the Kremlin complied with the decision of the Security Council because it was "not yet ready or willing to be isolated from the rest of the world." John Foster Dulles concluded that the Soviet withdrawal "occurred under an influence far more persuasive than military force; namely, the force of world opinion."

Eventually the limited conflict over Iran and Eastern Europe forced the West to think in the traditional terms of power politics. To adapt its policies to the new conditions of international life, Western leadership had to evaluate both the strength of the West to protect its interests in a new era of struggle and to define the long-range motivations, intentions, and capabilities of the U.S.S.R. The isolationist tendencies in American attitudes toward world affairs—the inclination to drift under the assumption that the nation was really quite invincible and that most problems eventually resolved themselves without American involvement—predicted a slow and painful adjustment in both the material and conceptual framework of national policy. That the Kremlin presented a challenge to American complacency was clear, but beyond acknowledging a divided world Washington officials seemed incapable of agreeing on either the character or the magnitude of the Russian threat.

THE QUESTION OF SOVIET INTENTIONS

President Harry S Truman and his advisors attempted to parry Soviet demands abroad and reassure the American people at home. The first eighteen months of postwar maneuvering produced a series of Allied treaties with such former Nazi satellites as Italy, Hungary, Bulgaria, and Rumania, but these agreements scarcely infringed on Soviet dominance behind the Iron Curtain. In his address before the U.N. General Assembly in October 1946, the President minimized the apparent East-West conflict. "The war has left many parts of the world in turmoil," he admitted. "Differences have arisen among the Allies. It will not help us to pretend that this is not the case. But it is not necessary to exaggerate the differences. . . . Above all, we must not permit differences in economic and social systems to stand in the way of peace either now or in the future." But in his State of the Union message three months later, Truman issued a warning to the Congress. "We live in a world in which strength on the part of the peace-loving nations is still the greatest deterrent to aggression . . . ," he said, "When a system of collective security under the United Nations has been established we shall be willing to lead in collective disarmament, but, until such a system becomes a reality, we must not again allow our weakness to invite attack." Clearly, Soviet behavior had prompted the administration to examine the whole question of Western security vis-à-vis the U.S.S.R. Behind this obvious shift toward a stronger policy at the beginning of 1947 was the crystallization of the administration's concept of Soviet intentions.

Russian experts in the West had begun their search of the Soviet past for clues which might expose that nation's long-range objectives. George F. Kennan wrote from Moscow in February 1946: "The Kremlin's neurotic view of world affairs is the traditional and instinctive Russian sense of insecurity. . . . Russian rulers . . . have learned to seek security only in patient but deadly struggle for the total destruction of rival power, never in compacts and compromises with it." Kennan warned the administration that the Kremlin would exert unrelenting pressure on the international system in an effort to undermine its opposition. It would accept no permanent *modus vivendi* with the United States until it had achieved the disruption of Western society. "This political force," ran Kennan's conclusion, "has complete power of disposition over the energies of one of the world's greatest peoples and the resources of the world's richest national territory." No longer, he believed, could the West escape a long-term struggle for power and prestige with the Soviet Union, but he carefully avoided any suggestion of policy that would terminate the struggle on Western terms.

Soviet intransigence soon convinced Western leaders that not even Western Europe was immune to either Communist infiltration or direct Soviet attack. The precipitate demobilization of British and American troops had created a military vacuum on the continent. By 1947 the United States Congress had reduced the peacetime strength of the nation's armed forces to 1,550,000 men and had instructed the Pentagon to contract even this number to slightly over a million before the end of the year. The U.S.S.R. had six million under arms in 1946 and had already retooled its aircraft industry. Still its monopoly in atomic weapons, added to its many industrial and technological advantages, gave the United States a military capability superior to that of the U.S.S.R.

More obvious than the relative decline of Western military power after 1945 was the dislocation of the Western European economies. The vast reduction of European productivity, plus the shortage of capital to rebuild it, created such an enormous dollar gap in trade with the United States that the European continent by 1947 was on the verge of bankruptcy. Inflation merely widened the dollar gap. Britain no longer had the financial resources to pay for the heavy importation of vital food and raw materials. In February 1947, the British government issued a White Paper on economic conditions which the London *Times* described as "the most disturbing statement ever made by the British government." Drought destroyed much of France's wheat crop in 1946; a severe winter left little wheat for the 1947 harvest. Elsewhere Western Europe had come within a hairsbreadth of total economic collapse. Europe was, Churchill recalled later, "a rubble heap, a charnel house, a breeding ground of pestilence and hate." Everywhere agricultural production was low, factories were closed, and millions drifted about, unemployed. *The New York Times* reported in February 1947, that severe food shortages confronted victor and vanquished nations alike. Thriving on such chaos, the Communist parties of Western

Europe were in the political ascendancy. For Western Europe the first line of defense against the dual forces of starvation and communism was the undiminished productivity of the United States.

THE TRUMAN DOCTRINE

Several factors converged by early 1947 to place American policy vis-à-vis the U.S.S.R. on the defensive. First came the conviction that the Kremlin, if concerned in its diplomacy with the stability of a divided Europe, actually represented a long-term danger to the entire structure of Western civilization. The conviction among Americans that the Soviet Union represented a global, ideological danger came haltingly and unevenly. But during 1946 that conviction gripped the emotions of an increasingly large number of American writers, public officials, and political leaders. William C. Bullitt, in his book *The Great Globe Itself,* expressed the burgeoning fears of countless Americans: "As conquest of the earth for Communism is the objective of the Soviet Government, no nation lies outside the scope of its ambitions. . . . The Soviet Union is unique among great powers. It is not only a state but also the headquarters of an international faith." At issue was no longer Soviet defiance of wartime principles; now it was the threat of further Russian expansion. The recognition of Europe's economic and military collapse merely confirmed the new mood of national insecurity.

Greece and Turkey, both strategically important to the defense of Western Europe, were the principal points of danger. Greece was in a state of complete economic exhaustion. Greek Communists, moreover, had mounted a guerrilla attack on the British-sponsored conservative government. So fragile was the Athens regime that its very existence depended on occupying British forces. Then in February 1947, the British Embassy in Washington informed the Truman administration that Britain could no longer afford to carry the economic and military burden of keeping Greece out of Communist hands. General George C. Marshall, Secretary of State since January 1947, recognized the significance of the British withdrawal. Unless the United States assumed the former British commitments, he warned, the pro-Soviet elements in Greece would take over the country.

Truman agreed with Marshall on the requirement of economic relief for Greece and Turkey. Marshall, with the approval of the President, assigned the task of formulating a new American policy to Under Secretary of State Dean G. Acheson. Late in February, to assure Congressional support, the President held a briefing session during which Marshall and Acheson explained to Congressional leaders the possible consequences of a Communist takeover in Greece. Vandenberg advised the President that if he wanted an aid program for Greece and Turkey he had no choice but to appear before Congress in person and there convey to the nation the perceptions of danger shared by members of the administration. To many Washington officials, the struggle for Greece was the opening round of a vast ideological struggle between Soviet communism and Western democracy. So Vandenberg regarded it. Forrestal asserted at a cabinet meeting early in March that if the United States would win the competition, it would "have to recognize it as a fundamental struggle between our kind of society and the Russians' and that the Russians would not respond to anything but power."

Truman's message to Congress, on March 12, 1947, defined the conflict between the United States and the U.S.S.R. in broad ideological terms and announced this nation's intention to go to the assistance of free governments everywhere. *(See Document No. 4 on p. 186.)* "At the present moment in world history," he declared, "nearly every nation must choose between alternative ways of life. The choice is not often a free one. . . . I believe that it must be the policy of the United States to support free peoples who are resisting attempted subjugation by armed minorities or by outside pressures." He called for a Congressional appropriation of $400 million for economic and military aid to Greece and Turkey. Beyond these two countries the so-called Truman Doctrine was simply a vague and indeterminate commitment to support freedom.

In general the Truman speech had the desired effect upon the nation; it received praise from much of Congress and the press. But some thoughtful Americans criticized the new doctrine for confusing the issue between the United States and the Soviet Union and for defining the American commitment in vague generalities at a time of trial. Western security demanded the prevention of further Russian expansion. But the President's message identified American interest in Greece and Turkey, not with the maintenance of the European balance of power, but with the defense of freedom even where it scarcely existed. The Truman Doctrine seemed to promise salvation to the world. It perpetuated the nation's habit of refusing to separate what was essential from what was desired. Kennan objected to the President's reference to an ideological struggle between two ways of life and to the open-end commitment to aid free peoples everywhere. To

Walter Lippmann the new policy was so general that it had no visible limits. He reminded the national leadership that a crusade was not a policy. "A policy, as distinguished from a crusade," he wrote, "may be said to have definite aims, which can be stated concretely, and achieved if the estimate of the situation is correct. A crusade, on the other hand, is an adventure which even if its intentions are good, has no limits because there is no concrete program. To substitute specific aims for vague hostilities is the statesman's business in a time of trouble and danger."

Congress straddled the issue of the Truman Doctrine's meaning. James Reston of *The New York Times* wrote on March 23 that Congress was "neither repudiating the broad principle laid down in the Truman Doctrine . . . nor following the implications of that principle to the end." Vandenberg, chairman of the Senate Foreign Relations Committee following the 1946 Republican sweep, steered the President's aid measure through Congress without difficulty. "It is a plan," he assured the Senate, "to forestall aggression which, once rolling, could snowball into global danger of designs. It is a plan for peace. It is a plan to sterilize the seeds of war." By May the measure had passed both houses of Congress and had become the official policy of the United States. To the extent that the Truman Doctrine comprised a feasible effort to keep Greece and Turkey in the Western bloc, it coincided with American security interests in Europe. To the extent that it promised the eventual triumph over communism, it comprised a moral crusade that would both falter before its impossible goals and prevent any negotiated settlement with the Kremlin. Under the conviction that the source of conflict between the two great powers was not Russian imperialism but international communism, the East-West struggle finally transcended Eastern Europe to blanket the entire globe.

THE MARSHALL PLAN

Whatever the ultimate necessity of facing Moscow's ideological challenge, the immediate issue of 1947 was the concrete one of stabilizing Europe. From this objective evolved the American policy of containment, defined with some precision by Kennan in his article, "The Sources of Soviet Conduct," written under the pseudonym of "X" in the July 1947 issue of *Foreign Affairs*. Kennan offered three postulates regarding Soviet beliefs and expectations. The first of these was the Kremlin's acceptance of a fundamental antagonism between capitalism and communism which ruled out any community of interests between the U.S.S.R. and the nations of the West. Second, the Soviets believed that since capitalism in this competition was doomed, there was no need to engage in all-out war. Third, the Soviet assumption of Kremlin infallibility rendered useless any effort to argue with Russian diplomats, for all important decisions were made at the top level.

But Kennan anticipated a time of successful United States-Soviet diplomacy. The Russian economy, he believed, was basically weak and would force the Kremlin to concede eventually to Western economic superiority. Kennan declared that there was a strong possibility "that Soviet power, like the capitalist world of its conception, bears within it the seeds of its own decay, and that the sprouting of these seeds is well advanced." This led the Russian expert to propose a quiet and restrained policy of containment. He summarized his position with some cogency:

In these circumstances it is clear that the main element of any United States policy toward the Soviet Union must be that of a long-term, patient but firm and vigilant containment of Russian expansive tendencies. It is important to note, however, that such a policy has nothing to do with outward histrionics: with threats or blustering or superfluous gestures of outward "toughness."

In April 1947, Marshall created a Policy Planning Staff in the State Department and instructed its director, George Kennan, to prepare an economic recovery program for Europe. Kennan was determined from the beginning to extricate American foreign policy from the ideological context in which the Truman Doctrine had placed it. On May 8 Under Secretary of State Dean Acheson, in a speech before the Delta Council at Cleveland, Mississippi, warned the nation that it must undertake the economic reconstruction of Europe. Acheson, substituting for the President, was clearly announcing the burgeoning program of the administration. His speech, unlike the Truman Doctrine, did not declare ideological war on communism, but Acheson defined the American intention. "Free people," he said, "who are seeking to preserve their independence and democratic institutions and human freedoms against totalitarian pressures, either internal or external, will receive top priority for American reconstuction aid." In his memorandum of May 23 Kennan concluded that any effective reconstruction program would require European initiative. "With the best of will," he wrote, "the American people cannot really help those who are not willing to help themselves." On May 27 Will Clayton, Marshall's chief adviser on economic affairs, reported on a six weeks' survey of

Europe. He argued that the United States had persistently underestimated the wartime damage to Europe's economy. Only an expanded program of American aid could save Western Europe from economic and political disaster. The Policy Planning Staff favored such a program but encouraged the Secretary to direct any national effort toward the concrete problems of poverty and hunger, not toward the eradication of communism.

These two documents became the basis of Marshall's momentous speech at Harvard University on June 5. The Secretary again spoke of the needs of the European countries. "It is logical," he said, "that the United States should do whatever it is able to do to assist in the return of normal economic health in the world, without which there can be no political stability and no assured peace." Leaving behind all ideological implications, Marshall followed the outline developed by the Policy Planning Staff. "Our policy," he declared, "is directed not against country or doctrine, but against hunger, poverty, desperation, and chaos." Marshall offered American aid to all nations that would cooperate in the program. The Marshall Plan, as the Secretary's proposals came to be called, demanded that the initiative be taken by the European nations as they determined their own needs. *(See Document No. 5 on p. 190.)*

Britain and France responded to Marshall's proposal enthusiastically. Late in June Molotov met with the British and French foreign ministers to discuss the possibilities for an overall European economic recovery program. That the Russians appeared serious was demonstrated by the eighty economic advisors who accompanied Molotov to Paris. From the outset, however, Soviet preferences varied greatly from those of the British and French delegates. At the first meeting Molotov suggested that the delegates request the exact amount that would be forthcoming from the United States before they submitted an integrated plan. The British and French ministers, understanding the American political system, disagreed. At the second meeting Molotov accepted collaboration in principle, but only to the extent that each country would make its needs known to Washington directly. The Russians had no interest in a joint program which would compel them to furnish economic data to other countries. Molotov insisted also that the former enemy states, including Germany, should be barred from the program. The third meeting, on June 30, was even more divisive, with Molotov again rejecting the concept of a closely coordinated program for Europe. Already Western observers suspected that Moscow was attempting to sabotage the Marshall Plan.

The fourth session produced no agreement; the fifth session of July 2 was Molotov's last. He accused the United States of attempting to dominate Europe and to penetrate the Soviet sphere by insisting that future economic decisions serve the interest of all-European recovery to the detriment of the Soviet bloc. American officials predicted correctly that Russia would not join a program financed and directed by the United States. But if the Soviet rejection of the Marshall Plan would further divide Europe, the Kremlin would bear the responsibility.

Having boycotted the Marshall Plan, the Soviets negotiated a number of restrictive trade agreements with the countries of Eastern Europe. By 1948 they had transformed their sphere into that monolith whose existence Washington had long assumed. Meanwhile Britain and France, early in July 1947, sent invitations to twenty-two European countries to meet in Paris to discuss Europe's economic requirements. Eight Iron Curtain countries, under heavy Soviet pressure, refused to attend. Eventually the Western nations agreed on their specific needs; the United States Congress responded in 1948 with the first of a series of extensive appropriations. So successful was the new program that by mid-century western Europe was not only on the road to recovery but had already, in many categories, reached or exceeded prewar production figures. Unable to influence Europe's reconstruction in accordance with its principles, the United States employed its vast economic power with telling effect where it mattered. The outflow of American goods and dollars in the form of world trade and investment, added to the Truman Doctrine and the Marshall Plan, created both an international prosperity and a worldwide American influence which few could have anticipated in 1945. The rebuilding of western Europe (and Japan), and the maintenance of a stabilizing military and economic structure, all reflecting the country's financial and technological predominance, remained the essence of the nation's postwar international achievement.

CONTINUED SOVIET PRESSURE ON EUROPE

Two events of 1948 deepened the East-West conflict by demonstrating the willingness of the U.S.S.R. to employ its power and geographical advantages to undermine what remained of the Western position along its periphery. The first of these episodes was the Communist coup d'état in Czechoslovakia during February. After the war

Czechoslovakia held an anomalous position in European affairs. It was, like Berlin, an area of free government behind the Iron Curtain. Soviet influence in Czech affairs was obvious as early as 1947 when that nation refused to cooperate with the Marshall program. For many in the State Department the fall of the Czech government in 1948 was expected, especially since the Communist Party commanded a large plurality in the national Parliament. President Edward Beneš was leader of the National Socialists, the largest of the non-Communist parties, but the Premier and other members of the cabinet were Communists, including the Minister of the Interior who controlled the police. Non-Communist leaders threatened to break up the coalition, which permitted the Communists to control the cabinet, if Communists were permitted to dominate the police establishment. When the Premier refused to comply with these demands, the non-Communist members of the cabinet resigned. The Communist Party, controlling the police, forced the Social Democrats to join them in forming a new government. When Beneš recognized the new cabinet, the coup was all but completed.

Informed Americans reacted violently to the fall of Czechoslovakia, not only because that nation had served as a bridge between East and West but also because they recalled how Hitler, using similar pressures, had seized Czechoslovakia ten years earlier to inaugurate a general assault against his enemies. The Chicago *Tribune* observed late in February, "The American people can very well reflect that this is where they came in. It was ten years ago this fall that the independence of Czechoslovakia was sacrificed at Munich." Former Ambassador to Russia Harriman warned, "There are aggressive forces in the world coming from the Soviet Union which are just as destructive in their effect on the world and our own way of life as Hitler was, and I think are a greater menace than Hitler was."

If this could happen to Czechoslovakia, why not elsewhere? "There is no reason to expect," declared *The New York Times* on February 26, "that Czechoslovakia will be the last target of Russo-Communist expansion." Truman reminded the nation that the Soviet Union and its agents had "destroyed the independence and democratic character of a whole series of nations in eastern and central Europe." Now it was clear that they intended to extend their ruthless course of action "to the remaining free nations of Europe. . . ." The fall of Czechoslovakia to Communist leadership seemed to prove the adage that no nation could do business with the Kremlin without signing its own death warrant. It not only made the U.S.S.R. appear strangely insidious but also created the illusion that the unknown force—communism—had the power to topple governments and convey nations into the Soviet camp. It aggravated the fears and enforced the convictions of those who viewed the East-West struggle in purely ideological terms.

The Soviet blockade of West Berlin in June 1948, severing all land and water communications between that city and the Western zones of Germany, demonstrated the Soviet inclination to employ force to counter the shifts in Western attitudes and policies toward the defeated power of World War II. For the Kremlin, intent on keeping Germany a cipher in European politics, the only acceptable Allied policy toward that nation was one that would preserve the four distinct zones of occupation and limit the growth of the German economy. But increasingly after 1945 the Western occupying powers determined to reconstruct the Germany under their control both economically and politically. In his speech at Stuttgart in September 1946, Secretary Byrnes had suggested a change in American policy. "The time has come," he declared, "when the zonal boundaries should be regarded as defining only the areas to be occupied for security purposes by the armed forces of the occupying powers and not as self-contained economic and political units." He implied that if the Soviets refused to cooperate in a new policy toward Germany, aimed at the political and economic unity of that country, the Western powers would merge their own zones. He even suggested the establishment of a provisional German government. In December 1946, the British and American governments joined their zones economically and assigned increasing numbers of Germans to important administrative posts. In this new era of East-West conflict the wartime policy of unconditional surrender appeared remote and ill-advised.

At the Council of Foreign Ministers meeting at Moscow in March 1947, the Soviets attempted to prevent the merger of the Western zones into one political entity outside their control by offering a unified Germany on the basis of partial Soviet control of the Ruhr. When Marshall countered with the proposition that the Big Four maintain joint control over both the Ruhr and Upper Silesia, Molotov withdrew his proposal, preferring thereafter to rebuke the West for attempting to rebuild a West German republic as an ally against Russia. At Moscow the Soviets clarified their conditions for German unification. It would come only when the Western powers had withdrawn their occupation forces from that nation.

Unable to control the trend toward the rebuilding of an independent and powerful West Germany, the Kremlin in the spring of 1948 began to restrict the traffic between Berlin, the West German outpost one hundred miles behind the Iron Curtain, and West Germany itself. General Lucius D. Clay, the American commander in Germany, warned the administration in Washington that any retreat from Berlin would expose the West to Soviet blackmail until communism would run rampant. "I believe that the future of democracy," he said, "requires us to stay." Continued Soviet restriction culminated in June with the establishment of a complete blockade. Rather than concede their right of access to the city, the Allies resorted to a massive air lift to supply the beleaguered population. This permitted the West to maintain its position in West Berlin without resorting to armed force. During the negotiations that followed, Stalin assured the Western Allies that Russia respected the Western right of access. It was clear, however, that the Kremlin hoped to prevent the establishment of a West German government by making this the price for lifting the blockade. But the West responded by expanding the air lift until it became evident to the Soviets that the blockade gave them little bargaining power. By February 1949, Stalin withdrew his opposition to the establishment of a West German government. During May, after several weeks of secret negotiations, he lifted the blockade. But Stalin countered Western success by creating the East German Republic as a member of the Soviet bloc. The division of Germany, economically and politically, was now complete. In Germany, as in Slavic Europe, the United States had failed to achieve its goal of an open, unified, and tension-free Europe.

THE NORTH ATLANTIC TREATY ORGANIZATION

These demonstrations of Soviet aggressiveness magnified Western European fears of Soviet power. For many European leaders the question no longer was one of pushing the Soviets out of the satellites; it was now a matter of preventing Soviet encroachment on free Europe. During March 1948, in their quest for greater military security against the Soviet danger, Great Britain, France, the Netherlands, Belgium, and Luxembourg signed the Brussels Pact of mutual defense. Thereupon these nations approached the United States for the required military support. President Truman, thoroughly committed to the defense of Western Europe, framed an immediate appeal to Congress: "This development deserves our full support. I am confident that the

United States will, by appropriate means, extend to the free nations the support which the situation requires." Congress endorsed the President's views by passing the Vandenberg Resolution of June 1948, by a vote of 64 to 4, thus preparing the nation for a formal military alliance with the countries of the Atlantic world.

Less than ten months later, in April 1949, the five members of the Brussels Pact, with the United States, Canada, Denmark, Iceland, Italy, Portugal, and Norway signed the North Atlantic Treaty with ceremonies in Washington. Article 5 set forth the primary obligations of the signatories:

The Parties agree that an armed attack against one or more of them in Europe or North America shall be considered an attack against them all; and consequently they agree that, if such an armed attack occurs, each of them, in exercise of the right of individual or collective self-defense recognized by Article 51 of the Charter of the United Nations, will assist the Party or Parties so attacked by taking forthwith, individually and in concert with the other Parties, such action as it deems necessary, including the use of armed force, to restore and maintain the security of the North Atlantic area.

Strategically, NATO was dependent on the sword and the shield— a combination of massive air retaliatory power and active troops designed to withstand any initial aggression against Western Europe. To secure the necessary air and naval bases for deterring Soviet aggression, the United States, in cooperation with its allies, prepared to reactivate the American bases in Britain, rebuild the wartime bases in North Africa and West Germany, and establish new bases within the territorial jurisdiction of other NATO members.

Dean G. Acheson, who succeeded Marshall as Secretary of State in January, 1949, seized the burgeoning policies of the administration and proceeded to mold them into one immovable defense against the U.S.S.R. What mattered to him was essentially the power and unity of the Atlantic community. If the Kremlin, he repeated, ever succeeded in breaking up the Western coalition, it would have a free hand in dealing with all the nations of the world. In April the new Secretary appeared before the Senate Foreign Relations Committee to defend the newly formed North Atlantic Pact. NATO, he said, was a defensive alliance—an agency designed primarily to carry out the purpose of the United Nations Charter. But he refused to dodge the issue of involvement. "If you ratify the Pact," he told the Senators, "it cannot be said that there is no obligation to help, but the extent, the manner, and the timing is up to the honest judgment of the parties." After considerable debate, the Senate ratified the treaty in July.

Next Acheson argued vigorously for the expansion of the NATO military establishment. "The first line of defense is still in Europe," he told the nation in August 1949, "but our European allies today do not have the military capacity to hold the line. The shield behind which we marshaled our forces to strike decisive blows for the common cause no longer exists. In that sense, the United States is open to attack on its own territory to a greater extent than ever before." Since Europe's vulnerability increased the danger of war, military assistance to the NATO countries would strengthen international peace as well as American security. Behind the new armament program was the essential purpose of placing more power in the hands of those nations concerned with stability than the Soviets could assemble in support of their aggressive ventures. *(See Document No. 6 on p. 193.)*

Few Americans doubted the wisdom of a strong military posture toward the U.S.S.R. for, in 1950, there was no apparent alternative. To Western Europeans, American policies alone sustained the Atlantic Alliance. First, the leadership of the United States in atomic weapons was a genuine source of security against the enormous Russian military capacity on the ground. Second, the economic weakness of Western European nations made United States economic aid a serious necessity. Third, the intransigence of Stalinist policies made Russia appear a dangerous and constant threat to the independence of Western Europe. Either the nations of the West would accept the support of the United States or they would face national suicide. NATO was built on the solid foundation of common interest in building defenses against a known antagonist.

Yet any anticipation that the Western alliance would force a rapid change in Soviet purpose had evaporated before the organization was fully ratified. During 1949 the Soviets broke the United States' atomic monopoly. Thereafter the task of bringing overwhelming power to bear on the Soviet Union to force concessions short of war became totally impossible. At best Western military policy might limit Soviet expansion and gain time during which any internal dilemmas within the Soviet system might either produce a total collapse or at least force some accommodation with Western purpose.

THE NEW FAR EASTERN BALANCE OF POWER

At mid-century, when the nation had adjusted in some measure to the Russian challenge in Europe, it discovered suddenly that postwar events in the Far East had terminated the perennial American effort to create a stable Orient around the China of Chiang Kai-shek. During the war the United States had saved Chiang from the Japanese; after 1945 it seemed incapable of saving him from his internal enemies, the Chinese Communists under Mao Tse-tung. Faced with a bitter civil war in China, Ambassador Patrick J. Hurley resigned in November 1945, charging that the Foreign Service career officers were sympathetic with the Chinese Reds and that the administration had failed to make public its purpose for China. Byrnes replied to Hurley's charges on December 7. "During the war," he recalled, "the immediate goal of the United States in China was to promote a military union of the several political factions in order to bring their combined power to bear upon our common enemy, Japan. Our long-range goal, then as now . . . is the development of a strong, united, and democratic China."

To bring the desired peace and unity to China, Truman dispatched General George C. Marshall to China in December 1945, to seek a coalition government. Thereafter the administration turned over the direction of American Far Eastern policy to this soldier-statesman. Throughout 1946 Marshall pursued the illusive objective of achieving some reconciliation between the Chinese Nationalists and the Chinese Communists. Until the time of his return to the United States early in 1947, when he succeeded Byrnes as Secretary of State, Marshall had found both groups in China hopelessly intransigent. Democracy in China, he concluded, required the triumph of that nation's liberal elements.

Marshall's failure to secure American interests in China exposed the administration to partisan attack, for China policy had been the creation of the Executive, not Congress. By 1947 Republican leaders, cognizant of Chiang's declining fortunes, termed American China policy bankrupt and demanded stronger action. Republican pressure led to the mission of General Albert C. Wedemeyer to China in the summer of 1947. His report, which both recommended additional aid to the Kuomintang and admitted that the Nationalist government had little chance of success, was so confusing that Marshall, now Secretary of State, repressed it. Some critics demanded the extension of the Truman Doctrine to China, but Marshall refused to budge from his purpose of limited involvement in the Chinese civil war. China, he reminded the nation, was 45 times as large with 85 times as many people as Greece. To maintain Chiang in power, he predicted, would require billions of dollars and millions of American lives. Democrats in Congress sat mutely, hoping that Marshall's prestige would carry their party through the threatening political battle over the alleged loss of China. Finally, the administration in 1948 accepted a heavy Congressional appropriation for aid to Chiang under the Marshall Plan and, terminating its effort to achieve a coalition government, tied American policy firmly to the Kuomintang. Still Marshall rejected both Republican demands for intervention and Madam Chiang Kai-shek's eleventh-hour plea for help in December 1948.

When Chiang's collapse appeared imminent in February 1949, the President called Acheson, Vandenberg, and Vice President Alben Barkley to the White House to formulate a policy that would forestall Congressional criticism. Vandenberg opposed desertion of the Nationalists for fear that the United States would "never be able to shake the charge that we [were] the ones who gave poor China the final push into disaster." Unable to formulate a long-range policy for China, the administration continued to ship moderate quantities of aid to the nationalists but in every other respect maintained a free hand.

Chiang's final defeat and withdrawal to Formosa during the late months of 1949 loomed so large on the immediate diplomatic and political horizon that the administration felt compelled to explain it to the American people. In August it published the famous China White Paper, a bulky document which attempted to prove that the upheaval in China was the result of massive internal changes over which the United States had no control. Acheson summarized the administration's defense of its policies in one terse statement: "Nothing that this country did or could have done within the reasonable limits of its capabilities would have changed the result, nothing that was left undone by this country has contributed to it." Before the National Press Club in January 1950, the Secretary again summarized his concept of the upheaval within China: "The Communists did not create this condition. They did not create this revolutionary spirit. They did not create a great force which moved out from under Chiang Kai-shek. But they were shrewd and cunning to mount it, and to ride this thing into victory and into power." *(See Document No. 7 on p. 197.)* Many Americans who knew something of events in China found Acheson's analysis reassuring. The object of American policy in the Orient, declared the Washington *Post* on January 10, "should be to drive a wedge between authentic nationalism and aggressive communism. This is a job that is essentially diplomatic, requiring the pooling of American wisdom and effort, for Asia is going to be the problem of the century."

In Congress, however, the Nationalist China bloc mobilized to force its program on the nation. On January 2, 1950, Senator William

F. Knowland of California released a letter from Herbert Hoover which declared that the United States should support the Kuomintang on Formosa and develop a policy to return China to the road of freedom. Truman countered three days later with the statement that the United States had no intention of becoming involved further in China's civil war by establishing bases on Formosa or by utilizing American armed forces to protect the Nationalist government. Chiang would receive economic but not military aid. Acheson warned the nation that the persistent effort to tie American policy to Chiang would isolate the United States diplomatically and "mobilize the whole of Asia's millions solidly against [it]."

Senator Joseph McCarthy of Wisconsin quickly submerged the China question even more deeply in the mire of partisan politics. In February 1950, without presenting any evidence, he captured the headlines with the charge that the State Department was "thoroughly infested" with Communists. The Senator's sensational accusations at Wheeling, West Virginia, supplied the rationale which tied the unlimited expectations of a counter-revolution in China to the concept of limited American expenditures. By placing the responsibility for Chiang's failure on American leadership, he discovered the argument that would permit a show of aggressiveness in Asia without the corresponding assumption of any expensive military commitment. If the United States had failed to control the Chinese revolution, it meant simply that the State Department was full of Communists. With their removal from office the nation could anticipate the return of the Nationalists to power over all China. Supported by this rationale as well as by much of the Republican Party, the supporters of Chiang Kai-shek in the United States suddenly found themselves in an unshakable position to determine American China policy. Such relentless pressures within the nation permitted the Truman administration no more freedom to recognize the new balance of power in the Orient than it had been permitted, in its European policies, to recognize the new balance of power in Europe.

WAR IN KOREA

North Korean aggression across the 38th parallel in June 1950 brought the entire problem of containment into focus. To the administration this aggression was nothing less than the beginning of a general Communist assault on the free world. "The attack upon the Republic of Korea," the President warned the nation, "makes it plain beyond all doubt that the international Communist movement is prepared to use armed invasion to conquer independent nations." Everywhere Washington officials accused the Kremlin of initiating the attack. If aggression succeeded in Korea, it would be repeated elsewhere until it rendered a third world war inescapable. To prevent attacks in Southeast Asia, the President increased American military assistance to the Philippines and Indochina, and ordered the Seventh Fleet to defend Formosa.

This fear engendered by the Korean War permitted the administration to extract from Congress defense measures which it had urged repeatedly throughout the previous year. In June 1950, Acheson had appeared before Congress to request one billion dollars to strengthen the defenses of Western Europe. In August the administration added almost four billion dollars to its requirements. Congress, having stalled at the first request, approved the second with one opposing vote in the House and none in the Senate.

Simultaneously, the Truman administration brought its program for rearming West Germany, established as the Federal German Republic in June 1949, to a successful conclusion. In May, 1950, John J. McCloy, retiring High Commissioner for Germany, declared bluntly that German troops were required for the defense of Europe. In September the Foreign Ministers of the United States, the United Kingdom, and France, responding to the shock of the Korean War, agreed that the recreation of a German national army would serve the best interests of both Germany and Western Europe. They authorized the new German government at Bonn to establish its own foreign office and enter into diplomatic relations with foreign countries.

China's entry into the Korean War in November 1950 tended to prove the administration's assumption that the Communist threat of aggression was worldwide. If the new assault was successful in Korea, ran a White House press release in December, "we can expect it to spread through Asia and Europe to this hemisphere. We are fighting in Korea for our own national security and survival." Because the danger was worldwide, it was all the more essential that Congress increase the combined military strength of the free nations. In December, the NATO Council unanimously asked the President of the United States to select a Supreme Commander. Truman responded by naming General Dwight D. Eisenhower, then president of Columbia University, to the task of translating military plans into armed forces in being. Despite its importance in official thought, the Korean War did not alter the Europe-first orientation of the Truman administration. It saw the chief deterrent to Communist expansion in the collective forces of the North Atlantic community, not in any all-out involvement of American power in the struggle against Communist forces in the Far East.

During its initial phases the Korean War had been popular in the United States and claimed vigorous bipartisan support. But when the mainland Chinese propelled the war into a long, dreary, military stalemate, critics of the Truman administration found the arguments which rendered the war the unnecessary consequence of past decisions. The United States, they charged, had invited the aggression in Korea both by failing to create an army in South Korea capable to matching the power of the Communist-led forces of North Korea and by excluding both Korea and Formosa from the perimeter which the United States would defend against military attack. The North Koreans, declared Senator Robert A. Taft of Ohio, merely took the administration at its word. "They knew that we had permitted the taking over of China by the Communists," he added, "and saw no reason why we should seriously object to the taking over of Korea. The Korean War and the problems which arise from it are the final result of the continuous sympathy toward communism which inspired American policy."

Under the pressure of events in Asia and partisan attacks on past decisions in China, the American attitude toward Peking began to harden into one of extreme antagonism. In February 1951, the United States managed to push a resolution through the U.N., by a vote of 44 to 7 with 9 abstentions, which branded the mainland Chinese aggressors in Korea. The intensity of the Republican attack on the Korean War increased markedly in April 1951, when President Truman recalled General Douglas MacArthur from his Pacific command for criticising publicly the limited war policies of the administration. During the Congressional hearings which followed the General's return to the United States, the Senators extracted from Secretary Acheson the promise that he would not recognize the Peking regime or permit the United Nations to do so. This promise followed, ironically, the Secretary's long and brilliant defense of American policy in China which no one challenged. Acheson never intended that the policy of nonrecognition should continue indefinitely beyond the termination of the war.

For the Truman administration the Korean War gradually became a political liability of incalculable proportions. Yet there was no escape from its burdens. Any armistice required some recognition of the military stalemate which would leave Korea divided and the Chinese successful in preventing United States armed forces from reaching the Chinese frontier. Politically the President was too weak at home to negotiate such a peace. But any struggle for victory would mean enormous casualties and the danger of a general war in the Far East. To most Americans this decision was equally unacceptable. Only the election of Dwight D. Eisenhower to the presidency extracted the nation from its dilemma, for in July 1953 he was permitted to accept an armistice on terms which Truman could not have accepted without being termed an appeaser.

Not until the Korean War demonstrated the strength and aggressiveness of mainland China did American leadership accept the necessity of building an alliance system in Asia. In August and September of 1951, the Truman administration negotiated mutual defense treaties with the Philippines, Australia, and New Zealand. Also in September 1951, it signed a similar pact with Japan which, although it placed no obligation on the United States, conveyed to this nation the right to maintain land, air, and naval forces in and about Japan.

MEANS WITHOUT ENDS

Despite the considerable success of the Truman leadership in building a response to the challenge of Soviet power, the general trend of national policy continued to disturb many students of diplomacy. Some who accepted the need of Western rearmament rejected the customary definition of the Soviet danger employed to justify it. By mid-century it had become habitual for American officials to depict the Soviet problem in ideological rather than imperialistic terms. Former Ambassador to Russia Walter Bedell Smith, for example, warned the nation in June 1949: "It is extremely important for the democracies, and especially the United States, never to lose sight of the fundamental fact that we are engaged in a constant, continuing, gruelling struggle for freedom and the American way of life that may extend over a period of many years."

Such observations on the Soviet threat properly recognized the unprecedented magnitude of the external challenge to Western security, but it was never made clear how this danger, if largely ideological, could be resolved by policies of military containment. To impose such obligations on American policy encumbered it with added burdens of fear and recalcitrance in a situation that under the best of conditions would have been difficult enough. For some frightened Americans who accepted the notion of limitless struggle, the world conflict, especially after the outbreak of the Korean War, had reached the state of intensity in which successful coexistence with the Soviet Union was no longer possible. One editor demanded that the President remove from his administration those "who have sold and fed him on the pap of 'co-existence' with Soviet Communism."

Kennan was among those who challenged the singleminded national concern with military strength, especially after the deepening of the military response with the North Korean aggression. To him the assumptions regarding Soviet intentions and methods appeared to accept the certainty of general war. If it was true that the Kremlin was secretive and hostile, it had been that way since 1917. If it overshadowed Europe with its armed might, it had done so since 1945. The United States, he pointed out, had coexisted with the U.S.S.R. for 33 years; it had no choice but to do so in the future. It seemed doubtful, moreover, if there was anything particularly new or sinister in the Soviet decision to use North Korean puppets in the assault on South Korea. Few students of Russia believed Korea the beginning of another world war. Writing in *The New York Times* of February 25, 1951, Kennan accused those who condemned coexistence of assuming that there were inexpensive means available for undoing the power revolution of the previous decade. He reminded them of the price their intolerance really advocated. "They should not try," he said

to comfort themselves and their readers with the flimsy pretense that this counsel of despair does not mean war. It does; and if this is the view they are going to take, let them have the forthrightness with themselves and with others to come out and say that what they are talking about is war and tell us how and to what ends and with what resources they propose we conduct that war, and how we are to assure the agreement of the members of a great coalition to a course founded on preconceptions which they do not share, and how a better world is supposed to emerge from the other end of this entire process.

Those who saw limited significance in the Korean War questioned American policy toward Germany. The inclusion of West Germany in the NATO treaty commitment, warned James P. Warburg in May 1949, would not only involve the West in the rearming of Germany but would also solidify the Eastern bloc. Nothing, he predicted, would cement the Warsaw Pact alliance as the fear of a rearmed Germany. To arm West Germany, warned Kennan, would create an unacceptable threat to the Soviet Union and would divide Germany permanently into a Western and Soviet sphere. Never, said the critics of German rearmament, would the Kremlin tolerate a united Germany armed and free to pursue its own destiny. To the British and French who accepted the need of rearming Germany, American policy simply eliminated for them the necessity of facing the German problem at all.

Whatever the magnitude of its military structure, it was doubtful if the West could obtain a settlement with the U.S.S.R. on its own terms. To the extent that the new posture of strength vis-à-vis the Soviet Union had the limited purpose of containment it comprised a viable policy. But the persistent refusal of the Truman administration to define American objectives in terms other than self-determination placed the nation's goals beyond the capabilities of Western preparedness. To explain the ultimate purpose of American military power, especially after Truman's decision of January 1950 to develop the hydrogen bomb, Acheson created the notion of negotiating from strength. Yet negotiation requires not superior power, but objectives than can be resolved through diplomatic bargaining. Negotiation from strength was meaningless as the foundation of policy: nations with the requisite power need not negotiate; those lacking such power will refuse to negotiate. Thus American policy had been reduced to a package of means without ends. "Foreign policy in [Acheson's] regime," complained the Washington *Post* in April 1951, "has become merely a carbon copy of Pentagon strategy without regard to policy or principle. A military man has to think in terms of war tomorrow, but not the diplomat."

Without some American willingness to accept the Russian gains of World War II there seemed to remain only the prospect of eventual war. One Washington *Post* editorial declared: "If it is assumed that every proposal coming from the other side is made in bad faith, then obviously no negotiation is possible. But negotiation is the essential business of diplomacy." Arthur M. Schlesinger, Jr., attacked what he regarded as a fundamental moralism in American foreign policy in the *Foreign Policy Bulletin* of February 23, 1951:

. . . The policy of abstract moralism is an honorable and high-minded policy; but it is so concerned with being right in the abstract that it forgets to be effective. . . . The function of foreign policy is not to provide an outlet for moral indignation, however warranted that indignation may be. The function of foreign policy is to produce desired results.

European spokesmen, concerned with their region's security, lauded the vigorous leadership of Truman and Acheson in building the Western defense structure. But to Winston Churchill and British students of Russia it made considerable difference whether Western capacity was being designed to negotiate a suitable division of interests in Europe or to secure the unconditional surrender of the Soviet Union. If successful negotiation was its purpose, then delay might be futile. Western power vis-à-vis Russia appeared as strong in 1950 as it was likely to become. Churchill argued for a negotiated settlement in January 1948, in an address before the House of Commons:

I will only venture to say that there seems to me to be very real danger in going on drifting too long. I believe that the best chance of preventing a war is to bring matters to a head and come to a settlement with the Soviet government before it is too late. This would imply that the Western democracies . . . would take the initiative in asking the Soviet for a settlement.

Two years later Churchill put his case before the House of Commons with even greater urgency. The Western position, he warned, was becoming weaker. "Therefore," he concluded, "while I believe there is time for further effort for a lasting and peaceful settlement, I cannot feel that it is necessarily a long time, or that its passage will progressively improve our own security. Above all things, we must not fritter it away."

But official Washington was not prepared, intellectually or politically, to follow such advice. The very notion of a global conflict in a fluid power structure rendered all diplomatic settlements illusive and meaningless. The limitless attacks on the Truman record, especially in the Far East, helped to solidify the American response in the cold war into a peculiarly American pattern. The administration's fundamental refusal to recognize the power revolution of the 1940s, either in Europe or Asia, carried with it an illusion of omnipotence which seemed to guarantee the ultimate victory of the West over its Communist enemies. Yet the nation could erect no force commensurate with the principles and pressures that determined its objectives abroad. It could neither settle its outstanding differences with Moscow or Peking through diplomacy nor dispose of them through war. It could only drift along behind its moral principles while the persistent failure of those principles rendered them diplomatically impotent. Unable to employ either its power or its diplomacy, the nation could escape its diplomatic and intellectual dilemma only by assuming a world of unrelenting hostility in which diplomacy had no place.

Self-Determination and
European Security

Russia's enduring hegemony over East-Central Europe comprised the central issue of the cold war. It was here that Stalin first challenged the illusion of Allied wartime unity when, in defiance of his wartime promises, he refused to relinquish Soviet control over the regions occupied by the Red Army in the closing months of World War II. Through the fifteen years which followed, the Soviet rulers resisted every Western effort to negotiate, in the name of self-determination of peoples, the diminution of Soviet military and political preponderance in the regions behind the Iron Curtain. Instead, the Kremlin pursued the antithetical goal of forcing the United States to agree to a division of Europe into two major spheres of influence, each nation guaranteeing the other primacy in its sphere. Together, ran the Soviet argument, the two super powers would prevent other nations from disturbing the equilibrium thus established. Premier Nikita Khrushchev phrased this Soviet expectation clearly in July 1959: "We want to live in peace and friendship with Americans because we are the two most powerful countries and if we live in friendship these other countries will also live in friendship."

This Soviet vision of postwar Europe seemed wholly anachronistic. Its emphasis on naked power politics disturbed those who placed their hopes in the United Nations. The policies of repression in Eastern Europe appeared curiously out of place in an era when men and nations struggled successfully to be free. Indeed, Soviet conduct took its toll in the perennial defiance of national will and in the constant threat of rebellion. But if the political and military price which the maintenance of the Iron Curtain exacted of the U.S.S.R. was enormous, it did not strain the Soviet economy or modify Soviet purpose. This reality narrowed the alternatives for United States policy almost to the vanishing point.

FROM CONTAINMENT TO LIBERATION

Essentially, the U.S.S.R. gave the United States two realistic choices in Europe. Either this nation could bring overwhelming power to bear on the Soviet Union to force some compliance with the wartime agreements, or it could recognize the new Soviet hegemony and accept its existence as the basis of future negotiations. For American leadership, both Democratic and Republican, neither course was acceptable. Quite obviously the United States and its NATO Allies had no intention of destroying the Russian position in Eastern and Central Europe by force. On the other hand, they feared that any diplomatic recognition of Soviet aggression would appear to be an abandonment of clearly stated wartime principles and an admission that victory in 1945 had not ushered in a new era free from power politics. Strangely, the United States viewed the new Russian hegemony less as a threat to Western security than as a threat to Western ideals. It responded to the challenge of the Iron Curtain, not with power or diplomacy, but with an effort to escape the responsibilities of both. The resort to the rhetoric of disapprobation, so characteristic of American behavior throughout the fifties, often created the popular illusion of a vigorous policy vis-à-vis the Soviet Union whereas it actually served as a device to avoid the necessity of creating a policy at all.

Powerless to alter the status quo behind the Iron Curtain, the Truman administration sought to stabilize the line of military demarcation. To that end it employed American military and economic aid to rebuild the power of Western Europe and prevent further Russian encroachment on European soil. But this recognition of the Iron Curtain's existence was provisional, for American leaders assumed that successful containment would produce tensions within the Soviet structure and force modifications of Soviet purpose. Containment implied an eventual rollback of Soviet occupation. This ruled out the necessity of negotiating with the Soviet Union on the basis of spheres of influence in Europe.

When military containment soon demonstrated that it would not bring freedom automatically to the Iron Curtain countries, critics charged that the Truman policies merely relegated the captive peoples of Europe to permanent suppression. John Foster Dulles, who became Secretary of State in January 1953, represented the burgeoning conviction that the United States could do better. He possessed a deep sense of the importance of moral force in international affairs and supreme confidence in the ultimate triumph of principle. In his article, "A Policy of Boldness," published in *Life*, May 19, 1952, he developed the concept that the nation had available moral resources that could topple the Soviet imperial structure. He cast aside the Truman-Acheson belief in limited power and long-range expectation as inadequate for the nation. Mr. Dulles charged that American policy was not even designed to win a conclusive victory in the cold war. It was conceived less to eliminate the Soviet peril than to live with it "presumably forever." The time had come, be wrote, to develop a *dynamic* foreign policy that conformed to *moral* principles. American policy must move beyond "containment"; it must anticipate the "liberation" of those who lived under compulsion behind the Iron Curtain. *(See Document No. 8 on p. 202.)*

Again in the Republican platform of 1952 Mr. Dulles promised a program that would "mark the end of the negative, futile and immoral policy of 'containment' which abandons countless human beings to a despotism and Godless terrorism which in turn enables the rulers to forge the captives into a weapon for our destruction." Mr. Dulles made clear his program as Secretary of State in an address before the Four-H Clubs Congress in November 1954: "Liberation normally comes from within. But it is more apt to come from within if hope is constantly sustained from without. This we are doing in many ways." The concept of liberation demanded above all that the United States shun any settlement that would recognize Soviet control over alien peoples.

Unfortunately, the rhetoric of universal freedom created national goals based on aspirations that had no relation whatever to American power or American security interests. In at least three important respects the announced purpose of liberation could endanger the welfare of the United States, for governments must ultimately bear responsibility for their words as well as their actions. First of all, because there was really no issue in Soviet-satellite relations that was vital to the United States, it was clear that any revolt behind the Iron Curtin could lead only to embarrassment. If the nation pressed its moral commitment to liberation, it might become involved in an unwanted war. If, in a crisis, it denied its commitment, announced continually through a determined and anxious phraseology, the nation would demonstrate to the world that its pronouncements were meaningless as policy. The clear evidence that the declared purpose would not be backed by force would destroy even the diplomatic power of recognition.

Second, the national adherence to the goal of liberation, by permitting the United States to claim every challenge to the Soviet hegemony as a victory for American foreign policy, could only fasten the status quo more firmly on the satellites. It was doubtful if the Soviets would concede anything to the continuing pressures of nationalism if American officials heralded every concession as a Soviet admission of guilt. American policy could have no higher aim than to encourage the Russians to correct their own wrongs without appearing to be losing the game of diplomacy to the United States. Third, the verbal commitment to liberation entailed a claim to guardianship that could involve the nation in war against its interests. As long as the United States identified itself openly with self-determination, the Soviets could well interpret any pressure against their control as the result of American interference. Should that pressure ever become acute enough to endanger Soviet security, American involvement, if only verbal, would endanger the peace of this nation. Liberation, as the London *Economist* asserted, meant the risk of war or it meant nothing. If Western survival required the liberation of the satellites, why did the nation not prepare itself to pay the necessary military price? If such objectives were not worth that price, why had their fulfillment been made the *sine qua non* of a formal peace?

THE FUTILITY OF LIBERATION

Mr. Dulles faced his first test in 1956. For a decade the behavior of Communist dictatorships in Eastern Europe had produced currents of resistance. By the time of Stalin's death in 1953 it was obvious that the intense repression of the Soviet system was beginning to produce diminishing returns. Facing the liability of surly populations, the Khrushchev-Bulganin regime, confident of its strength, gambled on the proposition that it could secure greater allegiance to communism by easing the Soviet grip. In line with this conviction, Khrushchev in February 1956 denounced the cult of leadership and stimulated the critical thought already released by the death of Stalin. Quickly the criticism encompassed the very structure of the Soviet system itself. There could be no limit to criticism once the principle that it could exist in any form had been established.

After the East Berlin riots of 1953, it was evident that the satellites were becoming restless under the new freedom. Everywhere there erupted a ferment of popular excitement, demanding better living conditions, a freer press, more representative government, and national independence similar to that enjoyed by Tito's Yugoslavia. In most nations local Communist leaders kept the new pressures within bounds by making concessions. In Poland the demand for changes quickly outran what the local regime could deliver. The result was the famed Poznan riots of June 1956.

If such challenges to the Soviet monolith were the high purpose of American policy, it was essential that Washington not pour scorn and ridicule on the Kremlin because it appeared to be losing its grip on its own structure. When the tendency to chide developed in the summer of 1956, George F. Kennan pleaded in *Harper's:*

Let us not, in particular, discourage evolution in this new direction by receiving it with wild boasts that it represents the triumph and vindication of our policies and the ignominious defeat for the Soviet leaders who have introduced these changes. The victories of democracy occur not when men are destroyed, but when they are illuminated and made wiser and more tolerant. If greater liberality now comes to the Soviet world, the victory belongs not to us but to the forces of health and hope that live—thank God—in men everywhere. . . . Let us have the humility to recognize these things, let us remember we are the agents, not the authors, of the eternal verities in which we profess to believe, and let us not take personal credit for what is in reality the power of these verities themselves.

When the rioting occurred in Poland, the United States government rightly disclaimed all responsibility. To the Poznan marchers American aspirations for liberation meant nothing. It was hunger and repression that drove them beyond desperation. In defying Poland's Communist regime they looked only to their own resources.

But when the growing instability of the Soviet sphere produced the riots in Hungary, the United States became too deeply implicated to escape all responsibility. Secretary Dulles from the beginning identified American purpose with the aspirations of the revolting Hungarians. On October 27, 1956, he explained to the Dallas Council on World Affairs why this nation had taken the issue of Hungary to the U.N. Security Council. "These patriots," he said, "value liberty more than life itself. And all who peacefully enjoy liberty have a solemn duty to seek, by all truly helpful means, that those who now die for freedom will not have died in vain." He declared that the spirit of patriotism and the longing for freedom was at last breaking the Soviet grip on the lands behind the Iron Curtain. "The weakness of Soviet imperialism," the Secretary continued, "is being made manifest. Its weakness is not military weakness nor lack of material power. It is weak because it seeks to sustain an unnatural tyranny by suppressing human aspirations which cannot indefinitely be suppressed and by concealing truths which cannot indefinitely be hidden." Mr. Dulles invited the Hungarians, as they now achieved their independence, to draw upon the United States for aid in adjusting their economy to serve the needs of their own people.

Such boasts that the American-encouraged aspirations for freedom were now rending the Soviet hegemony asunder were drowned out within a week by the crash of Soviet tanks as they slowly ground down the revolutionary forces of Budapest. Some Hungarian leaders cried out for aid, assuming that this nation's purpose of liberation was more than a moral preachment. They were informed, with stark realism, that any American effort at assistance would precipitate World War III. In admitting at the moment of greatest urgency that Hungary's independence was not required by the security interests of the United States, American officials rendered the concept of liberation a mockery. Those who expected help from the West recalled in their bitterness the words of the American delegate at the U.N. declaring that the United States would never desert the people of Hungary. As one Budapest factory foreman said of Western broadcasts into Hungary, "The speakers in their studios in Munich had it easy: just talking, talking, talking. We did the fighting." One Hungarian at Eisenstadt spoke for many of his fellow refugees when he said, "After listening all these years to Radio Free Europe, we can never believe the West again." Hungary demonstrated that policy not guided by national interest becomes irresponsible when put to the test.

In its dilemma the United States turned to the U.N. The basic condemnatory resolution, introduced into the Security Council by the American delegate early on November 4, was eliminated by a Russian veto. Immediately the General Assembly was called into emergency session. That afternoon the Assembly passed the resolution, calling on the U.S.S.R. to stop its armed attack on the people of Hungary and to withdraw its forces from that nation without delay.

Prime Minister Nehru of India warned the West that condemnation would only intensify the conflict, for under moral pressure the

Kremlin could not relent without some admission of immorality. As the U.N. passed resolution after resolution, the neutralist spokesmen of India, Indonesia, and Burma remained unalterably opposed to the Assembly's efforts to turn the Soviets out of Hungary with words. V. K. Krishna Menon of India declared realistically that it was "not possible, except by military intervention, to alter the course of affairs in Hungary, unless we bring into relationship of things, whatever authority, whatever government, exists in Hungary." To him the revolution was a matter to be negotiated between Hungary and the Soviet Union. U.N. interference would merely magnify the cold war between the United States and the U.S.S.R. without achieving any useful purpose. United States Ambassador Henry Cabot Lodge, observing that the neutralist nations were always the first to resist external interference when it applied to Asia, accused them of maintaining a double standard of international morality. That the U.N. resolutions saved no Hungarians seemed to make no difference as long as the Soviet Union stood properly condemned.

By mid-December the Assembly had adopted ten resolutions rebuking the Russians for their actions in Hungary. What they had achieved for the defeated and disconsolate Hungarian rebels was not clear. In July 1957, James J. Wadsworth, deputy United States delegate to the U.N., admitted sadly that the U.N. had not secured the freedom of the Hungarian people, but he found solace in the fact that the resolutions had mobilized the conscience of the world. "Never has a revolution been so widely known," he informed members of the American Bar Association in New York, "never has an oppression been so completely condemned. The fires of moral condemnation lighted at the U.N. are plaguing the Soviet rulers today and will continue to plague them for years to come."

American abstention in the Hungarian revolt demonstrated that even with the support of a major uprising this nation could not and would not change the 1945 line of demarcation. Yet Washington officials refused to accept even this lesson from the Hungarian debacle. American policy statements continued to condemn the Russians for their domination of Hungary. On the second anniversary of the Hungarian revolt the State Department announced: "These actions of the Soviet and Hungarian Government in defiance of the U.N. . . . have occasioned deep concern in the U.S. as elsewhere throughout the world. *They cannot and will not be ignored.*" In December 1958, Ambassador Lodge declared at the U.N. that the Hungarian people "must be relieved of that scourge of terror. . . . If the existing tension is to be relaxed and the danger of still another tragic explosion ended, it will be necessary to end the injustice which causes the tension." After 1956 the U.N., under pressure from the United States, repeatedly called upon the Hungarian puppet regime to comply with the resolutions adopted so often and so overwhelmingly. But by 1960 the rapidly declining percentage of nations willing to engage in the annual censure of the U.S.S.R. looked less and less like an impressive moral judgment.

American declarations of indignation toward the Soviet posture in Eastern Europe perpetuated a utopian response to the challenge of Soviet behavior. Whereas they held out the promise of freedom, they scrupulously avoided any reference to means. They created the illusion that American moral purpose still comprised a substitute for containment, and encouraged Americans to forget that in their purpose of freeing the satellites it was not their relations with Eastern Europe that mattered, but their relations with the Soviet Union. What the verbal adherence to liberation could achieve other than the continued disillusionment of those who took it seriously was not apparent. And yet if no one took it seriously, the rhetoric of freedom had no purpose at all.

In its failure to control events behind the Iron Curtain, the United States eventually conceded everything but principle. Yet in refusing to concede principle, the nation admitted only its unwillingness to act under the conditions which existed. The continuing appeal to principle conveyed the warning that the nation might, under altered circumstances, attempt to undo what it had not accepted. It was for this reason that the decision to sustain a perennial rebuke toward a situation of power entailed a vast danger, for in a crisis an impatient and fearful Russia might give the United States the clear-cut and sudden choice between principle and war, just as did the Japanese in 1941. When a nation's goals, anchored to aspirations, encompass more than its interests, it must in a crisis either fight for what is less than vital or beat an ignominious retreat. Neither reaction can serve the true interests of the nation.

THE CONFLICT OVER GERMANY

Germany presented the second stubborn problem in Soviet-American relations. Whereas the disposal of this issue, like that of Eastern Europe, remained firmly in Soviet hands, the Kremlin was forced to assume a more costly and uncontrollable commitment in its

German policies than elsewhere within the Soviet sphere. For here it defied the will not only of the 17 million Germans under its control, but also of the 52 million that resided outside its hegemony. It was the Soviet Union alone that paid the price of maintaining the division of Germany and of sustaining the Allied wartime objective of curtailing the military power of the defeated nation.

For the Soviets the price was not too high, for control of East Germany was the keystone of the entire Soviet structure. Even the tenuous Soviet proposals for unification insisted on a German confederation which would leave the political status of East Germany unaltered. To Russians over thirty the Nazi invasion of June 1941, was still the most significant date in their memory; Russians much younger could recall the thousands of destroyed cities, towns, and villages that bore mute testimony after 1945 of the violence of the German invasion. If Russia's own postwar development and its military establishment removed the immediate danger of another German invasion, there existed in Russia the fear that Germany, to gain its national objectives, might embroil the Western powers in a war against the Soviet Union. A united and free Germany, moreover, would endanger the entire Communist structure of Poland and Czechoslovakia. The central purpose of Soviet foreign policy was to prevent the destruction or subversion of the Russian hegemony by German ambition.

For that reason the Russians feared and resented the Western decision to rebuild German power. When Eisenhower and Dulles demonstrated their inability to dismantle the Iron Curtain, they carried the program of containment in Europe to its logical conclusion. During February 1953, Dulles visited six western European countries and Great Britain to urge their governments to perfect the organization of the European Defense Community (EDC), designed to bring West Germany into the European defense structure. At issue was French ratification of EDC. Secretary Dulles's warning that French failure to approve the plan would compel Washington to reappraise its policies toward Europe brought a resounding French rejection of EDC. This left the West scrambling for some new formula that would permit the introduction of German power into an integrated Western defense. In the crisis British Prime Minister Anthony Eden committed four British divisions to the continent; at the same time he placed curbs on Germany which satisfied the French. In London during September 1954, the Western allies adopted the British-French formula; at Paris a month later the Foreign Ministers approved the new agreements with Germany. Germany received independence and membership in NATO.

If the prospect of a rearmed West Germany within NATO was a defeat for Soviet purpose, it was scarcely more acceptable to those peoples of Eastern Europe who had experienced the German conquests. The Czechs and Poles especially had not forgotten the bestiality of the Nazi occupation and regarded every new German division as a potential force for Irredentism. By the late 1950s Eastern European intellectuals pointed to the fact that Germany was again printing atlases that showed part of Czechoslovakia and Poland as belonging legitimately to a unified Germany. For them the thought of an armed and aggressive Germany held more terrors than did postwar Russia.

American policy simply denounced Soviet efforts to curb German power, through the forced division of the country, as another infringement on the principle of self-determination. In applying this principle to Germany, the United States demanded nothing less than unification under free elections. American purpose for Germany was synonymous with its purpose for the satellites. It sought the dismantling of the Soviet sphere in Europe by demanding the fulfillment of Russia's wartime promises, unmindful of the fact that such a proposal asked Moscow to abandon all the advantages that nation had won by its close-run victory in World War II. It would, in effect, transform the enemy of the United States in that war into the victor, the major ally into the loser. American purpose, in short, demanded that the Soviets agree to the maintenance of an opposing alliance which included not only their wartime allies, but their wartime enemies as well. It was not strange that the Russians never took the Western proposals seriously.

American objectives in Germany appeared so eminently satisfactory because they combined this nation's principles with its interests, for both would be served by a Soviet retreat to its boundaries of 1939. Yet the American preference for the triumph of German over Russian will appeared less the result of a studied evaluation of Western interests than the result of an immediate ambition to undermine the postwar position of the Soviet Union. Russia's perennial fear of Germany had always given its policies toward that country a certain consistency. American policy toward Germany moved in twenty years from militant neutrality to intense enmity to undisguised approbation. Indeed, after 1950 the villain of 1945 could do no wrong. The effort to contain Russia, in large measure with German power, was reminiscent of the Western diplomacy toward Hitler that came crashing to the ground with the Nazi-Soviet Pact of 1939 and Hitler's subsequent attack on the West. Western diplomacy tended to resurrect the hope of the thirties—that an armed and united Germany would somehow resolve the Russian problem. It was not clear that such a policy would serve the West any better in the future than it had in the past.

Both to prevent the Soviets from stabilizing the division of Germany and to sustain the German sense of unity, the Western powers recognized only the Western Federal Republic. Even the U.S.S.R. exchanged diplomatic representatives with the Bonn government; the importance of West Germany in European affairs gave it no logical alternative. Chancellor Conrad Adenauer of West Germany made the denial of legitimacy to the puppet government of East Germany a cardinal policy, convinced that any recognition of that regime by the West would undermine his own government and lead to a permanent division of his country. So strongly was the government at Bonn opposed to recognition that it broke off diplomatic relations with Yugoslavia when Tito offered diplomatic recognition to East Germany.

WESTERN EUROPE'S ATTACHMENT TO THE STATUS QUO

This nation's perennial failure to undermine the Soviet hegemony did not destroy the popularity of its policies in Western Europe. It was not that Europe's conservative spokesmen had any interest in this nation's moral purpose of liberating Eastern Europe. As one European diplomat, after praising American cooperation in saving the Western coalition, remarked at the London Conference in September 1954: "This is fine, we will accomplish what we came here for; but please, let us not try to do more, let us not embark on any American 'paper' to turn the Russians out of Poland." What mattered to Western Europe was the determination of the administration of President Dwight D. Eisenhower to perpetuate the Truman policy of military containment. To Allied leaders containment was always a viable and laudable objective, for they never expected more of American power than the maintenance of the status quo of 1945.

For many Europeans the division of the continent into two huge military camps was their guarantee against uncertainty. Despite their words to the contrary, they doubted the wisdom of any diplomatic settlement that would achieve a united Germany with a will of its own. Countless numbers of Western Europeans had no intention of facing a powerful, free, and ambitious Germany again. They, like the Russians, would regard its creation as the final measure of their defeat in World War II. Rather than face such a hazard, they accepted willingly policies which, because they demanded too much, had the effect of perpetuat-

ing a divided Europe, guaranteed in its stability by American and Soviet forces. Even few West German leaders believed that unification
was vital enough to pursue on any terms which the Soviets might accept.

Western conservatives had no greater desire to replace oppression
with instability in Eastern Europe. Before their submergence into the
Nazi empire in 1939 and 1940, these nations were neither orderly nor
democratic. With the exception of Czechoslovakia, they were weak,
authoritarian, without balanced economies, and torn by minority problems. They could not manage their internal affairs or play any reassuring role in world politics. If Soviet occupation defied the principle of
self-determination, it at least eliminated one dangerous aspect of the
perennial German-Russian conflict. As independent nations lying
between a rejuvenated Germany and a security-conscious Russia, the
Slavic states would again invite aggression and war as they did in 1939.

Thus many Europeans regarded the status quo too acceptable to
be endangered with change. They believed that the hard military line,
symbolizing a divided Europe, was the continent's best guarantee of
peace. No nation could challenge it without the deliberate intention of
starting a war. Since the military stalemate was the best of all achievable worlds, any policy that endangered Western security in pursuit of
a German settlement or an ephemeral new deal for the satellites would
be, in their estimation, utterly irrational. As Alan Bullock, Censor of
St. Catherine's Society, Oxford, declared in 1958: "However much,
and however sincerely, we may wring our hands, we are not going to
endanger the status quo in order to help the peoples on the other side of
the Iron Curtain. The fact that Europe is divided, and Germany too, is
no doubt deplorable, but I do not believe that this fact by itself will lead
to a disturbance of the status quo."

This widespread devotion to the stability afforded by a militarily
divided Europe separated Western interests almost imperceptibly from
those of the U.S.S.R. That this broad area of agreement was not
reflected in Western diplomacy resulted partially from West German
intransigence, partially from a general disinclination to concede the
principle of self-determination. Any diplomatic acceptance of the division of Europe would force the West to share with the Kremlin the
responsibility for thwarting German and East European nationalism.
By defending principle, the West tied German interests to NATO and
placed the onus of repression squarely on the Soviets. What the West
gained, in short, by denying the legitimacy of Soviet action was the
force that nationalism could exert on the Soviet structure.

Unfortunately, this advantage had real meaning only in the context of a determined Western effort to unite Germany and free the captive nations—a purpose that did not exist in Western policy at any time after 1945. The West had no more interest in the resurgence of German or Slavic nationalism than did the Soviet Union. Every expression of self-determination within the Soviet sphere would be as much an embarrassment to the West as a danger to the U.S.S.R. The identification of Western interest with German and East European nationalism—supposedly the principal assurance of the West's ultimate triumph over Soviet repression—was a relationship that would be denied in any crisis.

Nationalism could endanger the Soviet structure only at the price of war. For that reason Western policy could fulfill its purpose for the captive nations only to the extent that it preserved their environment from anarchy and destruction. It could not serve the oppressed before it had established better and more relaxed relations with the Kremlin, for the evolution of the satellites toward freedom—and Germany toward unification—could result only from an increase in Soviet security. It was ironic that the West's verbal devotion to self-determination, because it was inimical to Soviet security interests, was the chief guarantee that self-determination would have little chance of success. Whatever the verbal assault on the Iron Curtain, it was so meaningless within the context of European politics, and yet so dangerous in its ultimate implications, that the West's fundamental policies were forced to accept either the status quo or war.

THE PROBLEM OF WEST BERLIN

Successful as the Kremlin leaders had been in forcing a practical acceptance of the status quo on the West, they could not view past stability as the fulfillment of Soviet diplomacy. They could neither relax nor enjoy their advantage as long as the Russian hegemony defied the aspirations of Germany and much of the West. Ultimate Soviet security required Western recognition of a divided Europe, for this alone would commit the West as well as the U.S.S.R. to the limitation of German authority. To force this concession from the West, the Soviets attempted again after 1958 to exploit Western vulnerability at its exposed outpost of West Berlin.

Actually, West Berlin's status threatened Soviet security as well. This city of 2.2 million West Germans, garrisoned by token forces from the West in accordance with wartime agreements, and located a hundred miles east of the Iron Curtain, prevented the consolidation of the Soviet hegemony. Its symbolism as the capital of a united Germany impeded the crystallization of the concept of two Germanies. West Berlin, moreover, was an escape hatch through which thousands of East Germans—many of them valuable citizens—fled to the West. Even West Berlin's prosperity was a source of embarrassment for the Kremlin. During the 1950s the city sprouted handsome buildings, elegant shops, and obvious comforts. Nowhere was the contrast between the progress of West Germany and the slow and painful development of the unwieldy East German economy more apparent. West Berlin, with the easy atmosphere of free minds, demonstrated the achievements of a free economy and refuted in a thousand ways the Communist theories of Western stagnation and decay. As a showcase of freedom and prosperity, the city was a constant irritant to the Soviets and a source of discontent to the East German and satellite peoples. Yet its chief significance in European diplomacy lay in the fact that it was a point at which the Soviets could apply pressure to secure what was fundamental to their purpose—the recognition of a divided Germany.

In November 1958, Premier Khruschev touched off a crisis when he challenged the Allied status in West Berlin in a note to the Western powers:

The Soviet Government has resolved . . . to abolish the occupation regime in Berlin. . . . At the same time the Soviet Government is ready to open negotiations with [the West] on granting West Berlin the status of a demilitarized free city . . . It is obvious that some time is needed. . . . In view of this the Soviet Government proposes to make no changes in the present procedure for military traffic [to West Berlin] for half a year. . . . If the above period is not used for reaching a relevant agreement, the Soviet Union will effect the planned measures by agreement with the German Democratic Republic.

Khrushchev assured the West that he had no intention of communizing the city. But his warning was clear. Either the West would accept his program or the U.S.S.R. would sign a separate peace with the East German regime and give it control of the access routes into West Berlin.

During the Geneva Conference of Foreign Ministers, which convened in May 1959 to consider the Berlin question, the Western powers refused to concede their legal rights of access to West Berlin. Having pledged themselves to the defense of the city's inhabitants, they would agree to no compromise that might infringe upon their responsibility for the status of the free Berliners. Nor would they recognize the East German regime. Dean Acheson wondered why the Western powers consented to negotiate at all. The Western position in Berlin, he said, was quite satisfactory.

Throughout the Geneva deliberations, which again turned on the fundamental question of Germany's future, the Western position reflected its devotion to the principle of self-determination. Andrei Gromyko, representing the Soviet Union, based his position on power rather than principle. He denied the validity of self-determination for Germany. He recalled repeatedly what Hitler's Germany had done to Europe when it enjoyed self-determination. The total failure of the negotiations at Geneva, which terminated finally in August, illustrated the crucial importance of Berlin and Germany to the continuing struggle in Europe. In the basic conflict between Western principle and Soviet security interests lay the continuing cold war.

That the West moved through the Berlin crisis of 1959–1960 without either conceding anything or preparing for any action simply reflected the status of big power diplomacy in the postwar world. Behind the mutual restraint in action, if not in rhetoric, was the fundamental caution encouraged by the nuclear capability on each side. Second, the continued absence of armed conflict suggested that the unresolved issues between East and West were considerably less than vital. The stability of Europe reflected the realization among Western and Soviet leaders that the issues of the cold war were better left unresolved than disposed of by war. Third, behind the continuing lack of diplomatic settlement lay the notion, held equally by Americans and Soviets, that time was on their side. For some the avoidance of serious negotiations was the surest guarantee that world politics would some day square with their own purpose. The crisis would come when one side discovered that it had expected too much of time. It was then that the world would produce statesmanship of the highest order or pay the consequences of drift.

To recognize the East German government for an equivalent benefit would comprise a serious affront to German nationalism, but it would not infringe on any vital interest of the Western world. Indeed, by 1960 the West had coexisted with the East German regime quite satisfactorily for fifteen years. American interests, moreover, were not identical with those of Germany. Germany's national objectives required the total exclusion of Soviet interests from Central Europe; those of England, France, and the United States did not. This nation had no obligation to pursue the illusion of German unification under free elections merely to satisfy German nationalists, especially when such purpose required a Soviet capitulation. Every Russian government since Peter the Great had asserted its primary interest in Central Europe and had been willing to fight for it. Quite obviously European diplomacy would remain barren until it began to balance the interests of Germany with those of all the wartime Allies. The status quo—the only point of commencement available—had served the interests of the Western powers, including West Germany, quite as much as it had the Soviet Union.

EUROPE'S UNRESOLVED PROBLEMS

Through the first fifteen postwar years the containment policies of the United States had stabilized a divided Europe. This fundamental arrangement, supported by mutual, if unacknowledged, interests and a military stalemate, left all of Europe's long-term challenges unresolved. Statesmen and scholars were still concerned with the evolution of the continent toward some new condition which better represented the national aspirations of all European peoples. If Europe's political structure was stable, it was obviously not permanent. Soviet repression consigned the satellites to an anomalous position. They were neither independent states nor blocks in the Soviet structure. Time would free them or destroy their national entities. There was danger that continued repression would create a general apathy and despair which would undermine all national ambition. The failure of Western diplomacy to mitigate Soviet retaliation in Hungary read a powerful lecture to the satellite peoples. In retrospect it was clear that the simple Western appeal to self-determination had been a device for avoiding rather than facing the hard problems posed by the captive nations. Yet how could Europe achieve self-determination without stumbling into war? The West's vast military establishment had served only one purpose—to guarantee security in a divided continent. It had, in fact, accentuated the division of Europe. Unless Western power could contribute to the disintegration of the Iron Curtain, it assured nothing but the continued separation of the Continent into two spheres of influence.

German nationalism continued to threaten the Iron Curtain and with it the peace of the world. As Secretary of State Christian A. Herter warned the Soviets at Geneva in May 1959:

It is the teaching of history that the artificial partition of a strong and vigorous people can only result in disaster for those that stand in the way of their reunification. Only the whole German people can be entrusted with the task of determining the future of the German nation. Until the Soviet Union recognizes these self-evident facts and cooperates to this end, there will never be a solution of the German problem or the problem of European security.

For the West the danger lay not only in the possibility that resurgence of German nationalism might lead to war, but also in the fact that Germany, in its disillusionment with Western policy, might one day negotiate unilaterally with the Kremlin to achieve unification.

Such fundamental and unanswered questions as these gave rise in the late 1950s to the burgeoning concept of "disengagement." George F. Kennan first gave it form and synthesis in his Reith Lectures over the BBC in the late autumn of 1957, later published under the title of *Russia, the Atom, and the West.* Kennan accepted the traditional goals of Western diplomacy—the achievement of greater self-determination for the captive peoples, including those of East Germany. Any evolution toward self-determination, he pointed out, required nothing less than the voluntary withdrawal of Soviet occupation forces from the Iron Curtain countries. But since the question of Soviet occupation could not be divorced from that of Russian security, he suggested that NATO also disengage its forces from West Germany and agree to the neutralization of that country. Lastly, he recommended the establishment of a nuclear-free band across Central Europe, an idea popularized in January 1958 by Adam Rapacki, the Foreign Minister of Poland. Disengagement, in short, questioned the fundamental decisions of the past which had assumed that desired changes within the Soviet sphere could best be achieved by perpetuating a hard military line of demarcation across Europe.

Kennan doubted that the withdrawal of NATO forces from Germany and the elimination of that country from the alliance would endanger Western security. If the Soviets reoccupied the vacuum created by mutual agreement or even attacked the West, NATO could respond as quickly and successfully as any other arrangement would permit, for nuclear power had long comprised the West's basic defense structure. Kennan's impact on European liberals was profound. The German Social Democrats immediately came up with a phased program of their own. Indeed, they advised the Bonn government to negotiate unilaterally with the U.S.S.R., charging that the West had nothing to offer but more intransigence.

Dean Acheson's sweeping criticism of Kennan's thesis appeared in *Foreign Affairs,* April 1958. His arguments reaffirmed NATO's traditional commitment to military containment. He doubted that the

West could ever pay the requisite price for a Soviet military retreat without weakening its own security, for the Kremlin had consistently demanded the liquidation of NATO. Acheson challenged the notion that the U.S.S.R. could afford to evacuate the satellites as part of an agreement on disengagement. Retiring Soviet forces would leave in their wake a group of unstable Communist regimes whose collapse the Kremlin could not tolerate without risking the overthrow of its entire system. It was equally improbable, Acheson wrote, that the Soviets would accede to the absorption of East Germany into the economy and political structure of West Germany. Such an eventuality, he warned, would bring the Soviets back into Central Europe in force.

Lastly, Acheson, ever mindful of the basic American purpose of breaking up the Iron Curtain, found the means for achieving this objective in NATO itself. A powerful and united Western Europe, he wrote, exerted a radiating influence on the Soviet sphere. It had prevented the total repression of Poland and Yugoslavia; in time it would subvert the entire Soviet structure. A thriving Western economy would produce vast economic change behind the Iron Curtain. How this would affect the political structure of Soviet sphere he explained in *Foreign Affairs:*

With the rise in the standard of living in the Soviet Union, and as some broader participation in the direction of affairs was made essential by their very magnitude and complexity, the Russian need for forced communization and iron control of Eastern Europe would diminish. Then negotiations, looking toward a united Germany, under honorable and healing conditions and toward the return of national identity to the countries of Eastern Europe while preserving also the interests of the Russian people in their own security and welfare, could for the first time be meaningful and show buds of hope.

European conservatives shared Acheson's deep commitment to NATO, for security held top priority in their scale of values. They regarded the Atlantic Alliance as the primary achievement of postwar diplomacy, and attributed the amazing economic recovery of Western Europe to its existence. Thus they opposed any change in its structure. To them the Rapacki Plan for a nuclear-free zone was nothing less than a Soviet trap. Second, they feared that any withdrawal of Allied forces from Germany would terminate in the complete elimination of American troops from Europe. "It would be folly," declared Paul-Henri Spaak, Secretary General of NATO, in June 1959, "and I venture to say criminal folly, to follow a policy which might lead to the departure of American troops from Germany." Disengagement would eventually remove the United States, the keystone of Western security, from the European scene, warned Spaak, and reestablish the conditions that led to war in the thirties. Third, the neutralization of Germany, ran the conservative argument, would withdraw German forces and space from NATO, curtail the alliance's effectiveness, and forever limit its operations to nuclear weapons. "Deadlock and stalemate are certainly hard to endure," admitted one British official, "but to yield would be worse. We should all of us do well not to forget that lesson of the nineteen-thirties."

CONTAINMENT WITHOUT DIPLOMACY

Containment remained a program of sanguine expectation. For its creators, its mission had not changed. It would not only prevent Soviet expansion, but would eventually produce the long-desired changes within the Soviet sphere. In contrast to the concept of disengagement, military containment promised the ultimate triumph of self-determination without any loss of security or without the need of recognizing Soviet interests in Eastern and Central Europe. It promised a triumph of German over Russian purpose without war. The continuing arms race was merely the price required for security; it was the assurance that the play for time would result in self-determination before it would result in open conflict. Unfortunately, the quiet anticipation of change avoided the central issue of European politics—the future of Russo-German relations. The Soviet hegemony was, in large measure, the Kremlin's answer to a problem born of long and painful experience. That East Germany was the keystone of the postwar Soviet political structure suggested an immutable purpose. How time alone could resolve the German question without benefit of serious diplomacy was nowhere in evidence.

This nation's response to the Iron Curtain was characterized during the 1950s by a disturbing dichotomy. Its policies of containment, brilliantly conceived to counter the threat of Soviet imperialism, revealed the power to stabilize a divided Europe. They never revealed the power to do more. This fact alone established the limits of successful national action. The United States could have achieved no more vis-à-vis the Soviet Union in Europe before 1960 than it did. But Secretary Dulles, having promised the liberation of the captive peoples, not through the quiet passage of time, but through the application of moral principles, became imprisoned by the public opinion he helped to create. His limited power would not permit him to achieve what he had promised; domestic pressures would not permit him to accept less. In this self-imposed dilemma he could sustain his personal popularity before Congress and the nation only by placing the blame for his failure on Soviet intransigence. This reduced his conduct of foreign policy to a futile incantation of principles that had no relationship to Europe's power structure. It subordinated American diplomacy to the requirements of domestic politics.

Eventually such meaningless and inconsistent behavior exacted its price on the country. Dulles admitted readily that it left no room for diplomatic maneuvering. "We must avoid war," he said, "and still stand firm and affirmative for what we deem to be just and right." When a nation treads such a narrow course, two questions are always pertinent: Is the course demanded by the national interest? Does it bring rewards commensurate with the dangers being courted? In Europe Dulles's achievements, other than the continued containment of the Soviet sphere which was in no way anchored to his perennial condemnation of Soviet repression, were negligible. But his refusal to concede any legitimacy to the Soviet quest for security, while it gained nothing, transformed every American demand to the high realm of unshakable purpose. It kept the American people on a war footing emotionally, if not militarily. It did not prepare them to accept the only kind of peace available to them. Herein lay the deep tragedy of the concept of liberation. It taught the American people to expect through peaceful means what they could actually have only through war. It created a dangerous habit of mind which chained American leadership to the everlasting and futile pursuit of the unachievable.

Any break in the European deadlock required a retreat from both principle and the heavy reliance on arms. Both requirements involved risks; they did not demand trust of the Soviet Union. The essential purpose of diplomacy has always been to discover and adjust conflicting interests. That the mutual interests of East and West in Europe were legion was obvious from the continent's very stability. What European peace demanded above all was the diplomatic recognition of those national commitments, East and West, which could be infringed upon only at the price of war. By definition this conceded only what was vital to the opposition. Successful peacetime negotiations had never done less. Whatever arrangements the Soviets claimed were already supported by ample military power. The United States could hardly give away what it did not have.

Five

The Postwar Challenge of Asia

Like Caesar's Gaul, the world is divided into three parts. That this was not obvious in the immediate postwar years was attributable to the dominance of the Soviet-Western conflict in international affairs. World War II had witnessed the rise of two superpowers on the ashes of five other great nations that had been badly weakened by the demands of unconditional surrender—England, France, Italy, Germany, and Japan. With the establishment of the Soviet hegemony in Eastern Europe, a bipolar world replaced the traditional world of multiplicity and constantly shifting alignments. The United States and the U.S.S.R., like two huge magnets amid crumbling military structures, pulled the key nations of Europe like steel filings toward the poles. Those countries which continued to hover in orbits of their own were unimportant individually and collectively. Until mid-century the vast Afro-Asian world, still tied in large measure to Europe's faltering empires, played no active or recognizable role in international affairs.

NATIONALISM AND COMMUNISM IN ASIA

As divided Europe moved toward a new stability, enforced by unprecedented peacetime military establishments, Asia and Africa unleashed another disquieting cold war on the world—a world against their own colonial past. This struggle had no relationship to the conflict in Europe, for it rested on foundations slowly formed since the dawn of the century. This awakening of the vast underdeveloped continents, which would eventually revolutionize world politics and buttress all postwar tendencies against bipolarism, resulted initially from the dichotomy, growing throughout the century, between the wealth, education, and intelligence of foreign-trained native élites and their subordinate political and racial status imposed by a history of colonial and white rule. These leaders, in their struggle for recognition and power, searched for those popular appeals which might excite in their backward populations the fundamentally European emotion of nationalism. This emotion they could then employ in the name of the masses to strengthen their onslaught on the old order, whether that order were identified with European colonialism or indigenous feudalism. Always the new nationalism was anchored ideologically to three essential principles of Western civilization—racial equality, self-determination of peoples, and social justice. As late as World War II native leaders had achieved little against the reluctance of the Western powers to part with their imperial structures.

Japan's successful invasion of Southeast Asia in 1941 and 1942 instilled new courage in native nationalists and brought the underlying revolution to a new stage of insistence. As one Malay leader declared, "Yes, I worked for the Japanese during the war. They did more to awaken my country than all the years of English rule. They showed us what Asians could accomplish." One month after the fall of Singapore the astute London *Economist* warned: "There can be no return to the old system once Japan has been defeated. . . . The need is for entirely new principles to which lip service has long been paid." Asian leaders warned the West that the settlements following the war would embody the concept of Asiatic equality or there would be no security for the West in the Orient; any white armies on Asian soil fighting to maintain the status quo against native forces, whatever the justice of their cause, would be regarded *ipso facto* as the aggressors.

After 1945 the old empires, now subjected to unprecedented pressures, began to disintegrate. Most colonial powers, exhausted by war and encouraged by the United States, conceded to the inevitable. Through an orderly transition the regions of South and Southeast Asia under British and Dutch rule achieved self-determination. In Indochina French intransigence quickly involved that dying empire in a costly and futile civil war. Within a half dozen years over 600 million people had achieved their independence; over a billion Asians had changed their form of government, expelling regimes that had appeared unshakable when war came to Asia in 1941.

But the revolutionary pressures against the status quo were merely gaining momentum as the emotions which they unleashed threatened after 1950 to tear down every imperial vestiage of the past. Increasingly millions of Asians and Africans discovered, through modern instantaneous communication, that elsewhere the world had undergone dramatic improvements in living standards. The pervading conviction that their own poverty and backwardness had been imposed by misrule stimulated the so-called "revolution of rising expectations." No government, whatever its nature, could ignore it with impunity. As the demands of self-determination gripped the more poverty-stricken and autocratically-governed regions of Asia, the Middle East, and Africa, the voices of native leaders became more strident and hysterical in their demands for change. In Africa the jungle backwardness of black populations emphasized the question of racial inequality and led Premier Nkrumah of Ghana to observe, "There will be no peace until the world has learned to put its relations with Africa and the man of color on a new basis of freedom, equality, mutual respect and dignity."

In a world of unprecedented ideological conflict, Asian and African nationalism was neither right nor left. As an indigenous movement, its leadership and intent were molded largely by local conditions. For Afro-Asian nationalists, therefore, Western political and economic organization had limited appeal. Their distinction as national heroes permitted no significant political or military concessions to foreign powers. Nor was their perennial resort to violence any evidence of Communist or Facist indoctrination. If they preached dogma and discipline, it was because in a non-democratic order the road to power was revolution, not the ballot. Communist success, wherever it occurred, resulted from the ability of its leaders to capture the mood and the program of the nationalists.

What the new nations required was time and opportunity to establish themselves as viable political and economic entities. Such ambitions motivated them against involvement in world politics. But sophisticated national leaders quickly discovered that the United Nations gave their countries a voice in international affairs completely disproportionate to their power and responsiblities. As the Afro-Asian nations swelled the U.N. membership in the late fifties, they played an increasingly important role in the organization's activities.

At the U.N., as in all their foreign activities, the new nations stood firm on the issues that affected them; toward those that divided the world they remained uncommitted. First, they were determined to defend their individual sovereignties. President Sukarno of Indonesia reminded a joint session of Congress in May 1956, that whatever the aid which Asians received from others, they would permit no material advantage to buy from them any part of their hard-won freedom. In their foreign policies the Afro-Asian nations would settle for nothing less than eventual self-determination for their continents. As Sukarno declared before a New York audience during his 1956 tour of the United States, "In this age, the age of Asian and African nationalism, there can be no final peace or security until the last vestiges of colonialism have been swept into the ash can of history along with Fascism, feudalism, slavery, and other rubbish of the ages. . . ."

Second, the new nations defended repeatedly their right to remain aloof from the East-West struggle. As early as October 1949, in an address at Columbia University, Nehru of India outlined the program of neutralism, "The main objectives of that policy are: the pursuit of peace, not through alignment with any major power or group of powers, but through an independent approach to each controversial or disputed issue. . . ." Because official doctrine of the neutralist nations regarded both power blocs responsible for the Cold War in Europe, to join either one would endanger the interests and the self-respect of the new sovereignties. Nehru observed at Bandung in April 1955, that it was "an intolerable humiliation for any nation of Asia or Africa to degrade itself by becoming a camp follower of one or the other of the power blocs. . . ." For many neutralists this refusal to take sides became an end in itself. One African diplomat remarked at the 1960 session of the U.N. General Assembly: "Neither side has won us, and we are determined that neither will."

THE SOVIET RESPONSE

This fundamental instability of the non-European world produced a clear dichotomy in Soviet purpose abroad. In Europe Russia had a vested interest in stability. Any war in Europe would erase the achievements of the past and terminate the slow and painful evolution of Soviet society toward its goal of peace and plenty. Increasingly the Russian emphasis on coexistence revealed a deep commitment to the European status quo. Communism was the means by which Moscow maintained control of its satellite empire. Almost totally removed from that ideology was the Russian nation itself, pursuing historic objectives of national interest vis-à-vis the powers of Western Europe.

But outside the Western World the U.S.S.R. identified its interests with turbulence and change. Soviet leaders, the product of revolution themselves, accepted without equivocation the basic tendencies of the age. They saw as early as World War I that the arrogant and tranquil world, erected and maintained by the superior power and organization of Western Europe, was growing increasingly unstable. V. I. Lenin, the founder of the Soviet state, declared in 1921 that the "millions and hundreds of millions [of the colonial countries] . . . are now coming forward as independent, active, revolutionary factors. It is perfectly clear that in the impending decisive battles in the world revolution, the movement of the majority of the population of the globe, which is first directed towards national liberation, will turn against capitalism and will, perhaps, play a much more revolutionary part than we expect." After World War II the revolutionary fervor, which Lenin anticipated a quarter century earlier, could no longer be contained. All that remained for Soviet leaders was to scavenge it—to stimulate, guide it, and exploit it.

Soviet advantage in a revolutionary world was apparent everywhere. If the older imperial world belonged to Western Europe alone, the Russians had only to identify themselves with the anti-Western forces to capture some of the West's lost prestige. Always they sought to provide aspiring societies with alternative concepts and methods for achieving their goals. The U.S.S.R. had demonstrated that a nation could build its economy through controlled production and consumption rather than awaiting the slow accumulation of capital through the profits of free enterprise. The Soviet system accepted the sacrifice of life and comfort, even tyranny, as the price of material progress. It emphasized cooperation and national purpose rather than individual wealth and individual freedom. The Communist way presented a model to nations in a hurry, motivated by an awakening national consciousness, but with insufficient resources to permit capital accumulation through private economic activity alone. Unfortunately for the West, in much of the Afro-Asian world the fundamental attributes of Western civilization were irrelevant, for it was not clear how either democracy or capitalism could take root in that environment. Individual freedom often seemed less essential than collective freedom from alien rule. The Soviet emphasis on national achievement rather than individual rights, on efficiency rather than democracy, gave the Soviet system a pertinence which the Western example did not have.

To expand Soviet influence and to carry the ideological conflict into the underdeveloped continents, the Russian leaders moved into most revolutionary situations of the 1950s, peddling goods and offering money, markets, advice, and even guns. After 1956 the U.S.S.R. invaded the field of foreign aid and quickly expanded its piecemeal beginnings into a grand strategy. The Soviet economy appeared capable of sustaining an ever-widening scale of activity abroad. In their effort to penetrate the former Western hegemony through policies of trade and aid, the Soviets again possessed several clear advantages. Russia, unlike the United States, could actually use large quantities of whatever the underdeveloped countries could place on the world market. With no tradition of "colonialism" in the turbulent continents to the south, the Kremlin could make its pretense of "disinterestedness" appear exceedingly plausible.

With nothing to lose in the revolutionary efforts of Asia and Africa to dispossess the West, the Soviets encouraged the new nations in their neutralism. Anushan Agafonovich, Director of the Soviet Institute of World Economic and International Relations, assured the delegates to the Afro-Asian conference at Cairo in December 1957, that Russian aid carried no military or political obligations. "We do not ask you," he said, "to particiapte in any blocs, reshuffle your governments or change your domestic or foreign policy. We are ready to help you as brother helps brother. . . . Tell us what you need and we will help you and send, according to our economic capabilities, money needed in the form of loans or aid . . . to build for you institutions for industry, education and hospitals. . . ."

If the Soviets had little to lose in the Afro-Asian revolutionary movements, they also had little to gain. It was not clear that the Kremlin could move revolutionaries—even Communist revolutionaries—as pawns into wars of liberation designed to further Soviet influence and authority in a divided world. The Soviets, with a minimum of effort, could identify their interests with a revolutionary cause. They could encourage it with assertions that Russia favored wars of national liberation. They might, on occasion, even supply revolutionaries with arms and equipment and thereby, at little expense to themselves, frighten the West into unpromising counter-revolutionary involvements. But conscious of the limits that nationalism placed on any possible Soviet gain in even the most favorable situation, the Kremlin would behave cautiously and minimize the risks of direct confrontation with the United States on issues and in areas of limited global significance. Whatever the Soviet contribution to revolutionary change, Asians would ultimately serve no interests but their own.

THE AMERICAN COMMITMENT TO STABILITY

American purpose at mid-century stood in sharp contrast to that of the U.S.S.R. Whereas the Kremlin sought to maintain the status quo within its own sphere and encourage change in Africa and Asia, American policy was designed to create maximum change behind the Iron Curtain and to prevent it elsewhere. On both counts, this nation placed itself in opposition to the fundamental political and military realities of the age. This explains with some precision the perennial frustration of American ambitions throughout the Eastern Hemisphere.

That this nation should have revealed so little comprehension and appreciation of Afro-Asian nationalism was astonishing, for the anti-colonial upheaval owed its philosophical genesis more to Woodrow Wilson than to Lenin. It was little but the twentieth-century version of this nation's struggle for freedom and equality. The Declaration of Independence served to rationalize both revolutionary movements. But the United States in the twentieth century was no longer the tiny Republic that had identified its search for security and recognition with the progress of liberal revolution. By 1900 the American people discovered that they had achieved the best of all possible worlds. Thereafter they opposed any fundamental alterations in the worldwide. political and economic structure as it had evolved under the aegis of the Western powers. To perpetuate that structure, the United States had entered the two world wars of this century. This nation's growing commitment to law and order came as well from its own democratic past which permitted it, with one notable exception, to resolve its great internal challenges with a minimum of disorder. The violence and hysteria of Afro-Asian nationalism after 1950 was strangely disturbing to a satisfied and complacent people, especially when that pressure for change tended to undermine the stablity of a Western-dominated world which had served this nation so well. The logic which conceded all advantage in a turbulent and revolutionary world to the U.S.S.R. was simply the final motivation in dictating a status quo policy for the United States.

Perhaps the precise response of official Washington to the Afro-Asian upheaval was conditioned by events in China. Those who attributed the collapse of Chiang Kai-shek's regime to some combination of American subversion and Soviet aggression were forced to deny the very existense of nationalism as the determining force behind change in that country. This placed them and the nation in crucial dilemma. For how could they ignore the indigenous nature of revolution in China and still recognize its role in the general upheaval of Asia and Africa? Certainly no one attributed to the United States Department of State the independence of India, Ceylon, Burma, Pakistan, or Indonesia, or the civil war in Indochina. But with an iron logic, the American posture toward China forced American leadership, from fear or from conviction, to disregard in most of its fundamental decisions the tides of Afro-Asian nationalism. The nation's policy toward China corrupted beyond measure its attitudes toward revolutionary change.

Chiang Kai-shek's retreat before the Communist-led revolutionary forces of China persuaded many Americans that Soviet communism was a special threat to Asia and Africa. What made the danger of expanding Communist penetration into the underdeveloped continents appear so acute was the theory that Marxism was antithetical to national sovereignty and that communism would gradually destroy all national entities in Asia and create one vast community under Communist domination. To some American officials Soviet imperialism was merely the Asiatic agent for the new universalism. "The Soviet leaders, in mapping their strategy for world conquest," Secretary of State Dulles warned in November 1953, "hit on nationalism as a device for absorbing the colonial peoples." The danger, continued his argument, rested in the ability of Communist agitators to aggravate the nationalist aspirations of people so that they would rebel violently against the existing order. Before a new stability could be created, the Communists would gain control of the nation and convey it into the Soviet orbit. So pronounced became this interpretation of pressures against the status quo in Asia that American policy tended to credit communism, emanating from Moscow, rather than nationalism with stimulating revolutionary action against governments friendly to the West.

PERCEPTIONS OF DANGER IN INDOCHINA

In Indochina the pattern of American response to Asian communism was equally clear. When in 1946 Ho Chi Minh, that country's noted Marxist revolutionary, began his long military struggle for the independence of Indochina from French rule, observers on the scene, as well as Washington officials, agreed that the strength of Ho's revolution lay in the nationalist fervor of the countryside and the general desire of the population to rid the region of white colonialism. But Paris, determined to maintain its Southeast Asian empire, warned official Washington that any American support for self-determination in Indochina might, as Charles de Gaulle expressed it in March 1945, make France "one of the federated states of the Russian aegis." Key State Department spokesmen, responding to that threat, argued effectively that American success in opposing Russia would be measured in Europe, not Asia. Thereafter the Truman administration refused to acknowledge Ho's appeals for help. In his memorandum of February 3, 1947, to the Embassy in Paris, Secretary of State George C. Marshall explained why the United States would support the French in Indochina. "We do not," he wrote, "lose sight of the fact that Ho Chi Minh has direct Communist connections and it should be obvious that we are not interested in seeing colonial administrations supplanted by philosophy and political origin emanating and controlled by Kremlin." Marshall admitted that he had no evidence of Ho's subservience to Moscow, but his rationalization of American behavior transformed Ho, as an alleged Soviet functionary determined to bring Indochina into the Russian orbit, from a nationalist to the chief enemy of his country's independence.

In the Elysee Agreements of March 1949, the French promised independence to the three Indochinese states of Cambodia, Laos, and Vietnam. When they named Bao Dai, former king of Annam, spokesman for the new state of Vietnam, the United States quickly recognized the French puppet regime as the pro-Western, anti-Communist answer to Ho Chi Minh. During the fateful spring of 1950 Loy W. Henderson, State Department official, expressed the new American faith:

The United States is convinced that the Bao Dai Government of Vietnam reflects more accurately than any rival claimants to power in Vietnam the nationalist aspirations of the people of that country. It hopes by its policies with regard to Vietnam, to contribute to the peaceful progress of Vietnamese people toward the realization of the fruits of self-government. My government is convinced that any movement headed by a Moscow-recognized Communist such as Ho Chi Minh must be in the direction of subservience to a foreign state, not in that of independence and self-government.

Still Bao Dai won few defectors from Ho's League for Vietnam Independence, the Vietminh.

With the outbreak of the Korean War in June 1950, Indochina no less than Korea emerged as a key to the independence of all Asia from Soviet encroachment. The French, increasingly hard-pressed in Indochina, supported their claims for greater American aid by insisting that they too were containing international communism in Asia. Under that assumption the United States underworte some 80 percent of the financial cost of the French military effort in Southeast Asia. No longer was the American interest in opposing Ho subject to official questioning. As one National Security Council document of early 1952 declared, "Communist domination, by whatever means, of all Southeast Asia would seriously endanger in the short term, and critically endanger in the longer run, United States security interests." How Ho's success would undermine those security interests neither this document nor any which followed bothered to define. The NSC document warned simply that the loss of any Asian country to communism would quickly result in the loss of the rest of South and Southeast Asia, as well as the Middle East. Ultimately the loss "would endanger the stability and security of Europe."

It was not strange that Dulles and much of the Eisenhower administration reacted dramatically during the spring of 1954 to the critical French preparations for the showdown at Dienbienphu. Dulles told the Overseas Press Club of New York on March 29: "Under the conditions of today the imposition on Southeast Asia of the political system of Communist Russia and its Chinese Communist ally . . . would be a grave threat to the whole free community." Having warned that the French province was the key to all Southeast Asia, Dulles had no alternative, in the absence of British support, but to revise downward the American estimation of the region's strategic importance or to commit the United States to a unilateral defense of the province. Early in January 1954 he had announced to the world his new policy of "massive retaliation." *(See Document No. 9 on p. 205.)* Many Americans lauded the new doctrine as an inexpensive device to stop Ho Chi Minh and prevent unwanted change in Asia. Ho called the bluff and proceeded, in late April, to destory French resistance at Dienbienphu. Because external aggression was not at issue, the United States found no occasion to enter the struggle. Even as the French used the Geneva Conference that summer to extricate themselves from Vietnam, both Paris and Washington recognized as the legitimate spokesmen for the independent, but temporarily divided, Vietnam, not the victorious revolutionaries of the north, but those Vietnamese losers who had aligned themselves with the French. Thereafter the United States, unlike the French, underwrote the new Saigon regime with military and economic aid and identified the American interest in a stable Orient with the success of that regime. Thus from its inception the American commitment to South Vietnam carried the seeds of disaster.

ADDICTION TO THE STATUS QUO

Wherever in Asia Communist regimes triumphed or threatened to do so, their leaders spoke the language of nationalism. Yet official Washington, in its concern over Communist expansion, continued to deny the essential role of nationalism in any genuine Communist success. Walter Robertson, Assistant Secretary of State for Far Eastern Affairs, for example, declared in a speech at Hampden-Sydney College in June 1958, that communism, instead of riding the crest of nationalism, actually warred against it and, if successful, would bring the entire continent of Asia under the control of Peking and Moscow. So completely did such argument anchor American interest to the status quo that one well known Indian leader declared that if his nation had not achieved its independence as early as 1947 the United States would have opposed it.

At times the American addiction for the status quo forced it to deny its own principle of self-determination of peoples. This doctrine asserts that every society has the right to establish its own objectives and to decide for itself which method is appropriate. It grants the right of revolution, and the right of revolution assumes the right to employ force. Speaking for another age, Thomas Jefferson advised that "a little rebellion, now and then, is a good thing, and as necessary in the political world as storms in the physical." Again he wrote: "The tree of liberty must be refreshed from time to time with the blood of patriots and tyrants." Whereas the Western world of the twentieth century abhorred the resort to political violence, it could suggest no alternative course of action for disposing of non-democratic governments.

To limit change in the contemporary world, the United States adopted the concept that change, to be legitimate, must be peaceful. President Dwight D. Eisenhower declared before the U.N. General Assembly in August 1958 that the status quo was not sacrosanct and that change was the law of life and progress. "But when change reflects the will of the people," he added, "then change can and should be brought about in peaceful ways." How political change in much of the Afro-Asian world could be achieved peacefully was not clear. This strange doctrine that change was legitimate only if peaceful was illustrated by the cartoon depicting an emaciated Arab tribesman held to the desert sand by a well-fed sheik. At the side stood Mr. Dulles, shaking his finger in the face of the prostrate tribesman and informing him that it was permissible to revolt provided that he did so peacefully. Such dogma insisted that other peoples and societies really had no right to make essential decisions for themselves. And to the extent that the United States employed its resources to prevent change in other nations, it defied its own fundamental principle of self-determination. V. K. Krishna Menon, after challenging the American concept of legitimacy before the U.N. General Assembly in 1960, invited the United States delegation to read the Declaration of Independence. "Legitimism," he declared, "cannot be defended, and if you object to revolutionary governments, then you simply argue against the whole of progress."

That rationale which attributed change to Communist aggression rather than indigenous nationalism gave the United States no intellectual choice but to place its emphasis on military alliances to prevent that change which it did not want. The Korean War tended to substantiate the validity of the military response in the Far East, for here indeed the threat to the status quo was one of military aggression. But the Korean War remained an isolated example. Elsewhere the pressures for change, whether Communist-led or not, responded to indigenous conditions.

To strengthen the regimes along the Chinese periphery against pressure from Peking and Moscow, now regarded by Washington officials as the primary and at times the only cause of Asian instability, the United States constructed its Asian policy around a series of alliances aimed at the containment of communism. These pacts included, in addition to the earlier treaties with Japan, the Philippines, Australia, and New Zealand, a mutual defense agreement with the Republic of Korea, in October 1953, and the Southeast Asia Treaty Organization, negotiated in the fall of 1954. SEATO, the basic treaty structure in Asia, comprised the United States, England, France, Australia, New Zealand, Pakistan, Thailand, and the Philippines. These eight nations agreed to act jointly against "any fact or situation which might endanger the peace of the "area" south of Formosa. As a military arrangement it was of doubtful value, for the only nations that could have made it a success in building the needed balance of power in the Orient to offset the expanding strength of China—India, Burma, Ceylon, and Indonesia—refused to join it. These four nations preferred to maintain their neutralist position in the conflict that centered in the United States and mainland China.

For the United States, SEATO was aimed at stopping the spread of international communism through armed force. But because such a threat of open aggression was remote and common action almost impossible, the pact required little of its Asian members but a verbal commitment to anti-communism. On the other hand, the Asian signatories could make special claims on the United States for financial and political support. Whatever compatibility of interest flowed from the American desire for allies and the Asian desire for American aid, it did not cover the specific and crucial question of the future of China. For its inconsequential military support the United States was willing to pay a high political price. By furnishing arms to Pakistan, for example, it placed an enormous military and financial burden on India, a nation of even greater concern to the United States.

In December 1954, Secretary Dulles completed the American alliance system in Asia by negotiating a mutual defense treaty with the Republic of China on Formosa. The agreement with Chiang Kai-shek prevented any Nationalist Chinese forays against the mainland by establishing the requirement that all use of force in the Formosan Straits be a matter of joint agreement unless the question were self-defense. Japanese internal development throughout the 1950s, plus the conviction that the nuclear stalemate made an alliance with the United States increasingly dangerous, prompted the Japanese government to demand greater voice in the alliance. In the new treaty of January 1960, the United States again secured the use of Japanese facilities and areas for its military forces. But the Japanese reserved the right to determine how American troops on Japanese soil would be deployed, for the Japanese were determined not to be drawn into a war, especially against mainland China, by the support which the United States would require of its Japanese bases.

For the active defense of Southeast Asia the United States carried a unilateral burden, for budgetary considerations limited the defense of the region of massive retaliation. To create a military establishment for Asia, Mr. Dulles admitted before Congress, would be "an injudicious overextension of our military power. We do not have the adequate forces to do it," he explained, "and I believe that if there should be an open armed attack in that area the most effective step would be to strike at the source of the aggression rather than to try to rush American manpower into the area to try to fight a ground war."

What value the alliance system would have in repelling attack was not clear, for the Asian nations possessed only conventional weapons and Mr. Dulles warned that this nation would not support another local war. By his admission there were no ground forces within the alliance structure that would be effective against the armies of mainland China or even of North Vietnam. In the event of aggression the forces in Southeast Asia could serve only as a trip wire to bring the nuclear weapons of the United States into play, unless this nation, despite Dulles's repeated assurances, chose to fight again on the Asian mainland. Such a defense system required no alliances at all. If this nation's interests, moreover, were actually challenged by Chinese aggression, American power would be brought to bear as readily in defense of Burma or India as for Thailand or Pakistan.

ALLIANCES VS. NEUTRALISM

Alliances became the measure of American success in building centers of resistance toward the Soviet bloc. This perennial search for allies was predicated on the assumption of a divided world in which no nation would choose neutrality. Mr. Dulles, referring to the agreements which had built the American alliance system, made this clear at Iowa State University in June 1956: "These treaties abolish, as between the parties, the principle of neutrality, which pretends that a nation can best gain safety for itself by being indifferent to the fate of others. This has increasingly become an obsolete conception and, except under very exceptional circumstances, it is an immoral and shortsighted conception. The free world today is stronger, and peace is more secure, because so many free nations courageously recognize the now demonstrated fact that their own peace and safety would be endangered by assault on freedom elsewhere." That freedom of choice on which this nation relied as recently as 1941 was now denied to others as immoral behavior.

But this purpose of bipolarizing the world soon demonstrated its limitations. Most nations rejected the concept of a divided world. They refused to enter any military arrangement with the West at all, for they regarded the postwar structure of world politics as neither stable nor permanent. The very notion of a world divided into two all-encompassing spheres, in which nations could be accurately categorized as friends or enemies, was unrealistic, for national interests were too varied and fluid. Indeed, in every Asian crisis of the 1950s, this nation's allies, both European and Asian, behaved as neutrals. This reluctance of most nations to identify themselves with the United States in world affairs, especially in time of crisis, gradually forced American officials to adopt an ambivalent view toward neutralism. Frederick W. Jandrey, Deputy Assistant Secretary of State for European Affairs, expressed the newer American attitude with some precision in May 1958:

We fully respect the right of any state to choose neutrality. We would never try to compel a nation to join a collective security system against its will. But this does not mean that we are obliged to agree with its reasoning. It would have been comparatively easy for the United States itself to have retreated to a policy of neutrality and isolation after World War II. . . . Fortunately . . . we took a more far-sighted view. . . . But just as we ourselves have recognized our inability to "go it alone," so do we believe that, in the long run, *no* free nation can successfully go it alone. . . . The Soviet Union and its Communist handymen have never respected either neutrality or nationality. To them, a neutral is simply a potential victim.

For many statesmen and students of world affairs the powerful trend toward neutralism comprised the world's best hope of avoiding World War III. It promised after 1950 to replace the immediate postwar movement toward bipolarism with a countering movement toward an older and more normal multiplicity and flexibility in world politics, and to permit nations outside the power blocs to blunt the sharp edges of the East-West military conflict. Indeed, in every major crisis of the fifties—Korea, Indochina, and Formosa—it was neutralist pressure as much as any other factor that kept the struggle limited.

A nation's security is determined less by its formal alliances than by the sheer quality of its foreign policies. Merely furnishing military equipment to allies requires neither imagination nor specific knowledge of competing national interests. No nation concedes its rights of decision to another simply through the act of signing a document. Its allegiance to any understanding can be won only through the constant wisdom of policy, for in any conflict it has but one obligation—to seek out its own interests. It is mutual interest, not formal alliance, that determines whether nations will stand together in a crisis. If this nation's allies failed to support it in any controversy vis-à-vis the Chinese mainland, it was because their attitudes toward Peking's position in Asiatic affairs did not coincide with those of the United States. The challenge of change demanded policies anchored less to ephemeral agreements, however formal and impressive, than understanding and tolerance.

Unfortunately the indiscriminate search for receptive, pro-Western factions in Asia and Africa prompted United States officials at times to support narrow-based and irresponsible governments, incapable of stimulating the patriotic devotion of their peoples. Poorly-governed states could hardly be useful as allies, especially when the arms they received were employed largely to sustain their avowedly anti-Communist regimes from their internal enemies. "As a consequence of our concentration on military pacts and doctrines," Senator J. William Fulbright observed in July 1958, "there are few of the newly independent countries in the world in which we have an understanding of the motivations of the common man. In most countries, the United States has dealt with princes, potentates, big business, and the entrenched, frequently corrupt, representatives of the past.'' Yet in official American policy there was no recognition of legitimacy in revolutionary pressures against even such regimes.

To achieve domestic stability, new nations required both the opportunity for genuine self-determination and sufficient economic expansion to assure some progress toward the satisfaction of domestic requirements. Sukarno denied that military aid contributed anything to Western security, either in building effective military establishments or in assuring responsible governments. Nations receiving military equipment, he warned Congress in 1956, merely became more dependent on the United States and less worthwhile as partners. It was essential for Asian security, he said, that the countries of that continent disposed of their domestic challenges with some efficiency, for the greater their internal achievements and sense of national pride, the greater would be their determination to defend themselves against external enemies.

THE EISENHOWER DOCTRINE

This established habit of evaluating all revolutionary tendencies in the Afro-Asian world in purely cold war terms forced the nation's leadership to ignore the myriad of non-Communist forces at work in every crisis of the 1950s. Behind every political upheaval of the decade was the desire for a higher stage of governmental efficiency and responsiveness to the needs of long-oppressed peoples for a better life and a greater measure of self-realization. In every revolution or riot there was the search for the substance as well as the promise of a more democratic order. Throughout Asia dissident elements requested of their governments more determined efforts to avoid big-power alignments. But official Washington, in its continuing effort to resist change, attributed the growing instability of many American-backed governments to communism rather than the demand for greater national self-determination in both domestic and international affairs. This stereotyped American response was clear in every major upheaval of the late 1950s. It lay at the heart of the famed Eisenhower Doctrine.

Middle Eastern instability, following the Suez crisis of November 1956, required some declaration of United States policy. To meet the new responsibilities occasioned by the momentary deflation of traditional British and French influence in the region, President Eisenhower, on January 5, 1957, requested that Congress sponsor a joint resolution which would offer economic aid to the Middle Eastern nations "desiring such assistance in the development of economic strength dedicated to the maintenance of national independence." To guarantee the integrity of such nations, the resolution added that "if the President determines the necessity thereof, the United States is prepared to use armed forces to assist any such nation or group of such nations requesting assistance against armed aggression from any country controlled by international communism." Middle Eastern instability, the President charged, had been heightened by Soviet efforts to dominate the region. The resolution recognized no challenge to the status quo in the Middle East except that of Communist aggression or subversion. It designated the Middle East specifically as a battleground of the cold war. Denying the strength of neutralism in the Middle East, Vice President Nixon observed that the outcome of the crisis in the Arab world would be determined "by what happens to the millions of people who are trying to decide whether they will align themselves with the Communist nations or with the free nations."

Critics everywhere agreed that the Eisenhower Doctrine contained two basic fallacies. First, it obscured the legitimate role of nationalism in Middle Eastern instability. Moreover, it was Israel, Britain, and France, not international communism, that had threatened the status quo in the Suez crisis. Second, the Eisenhower Doctrine committed the United States to the status quo in a region where there were few if any viable political entities. Some of the Middle Eastern states, such as Lebanon and Jordan, were hardly "nations" at all. Conditions were ripe for revolt in Iraq, Lebanon, and Jordan. In Iraq revolution had been smoldering for a decade. When Nuri-es-Said, its pro-Western premier, dissolved the Parliament in 1954, in which the opposition was less than thirty out of 144, his opponents were convinced that change would require a revolution. In Lebanon, President Camille Chamoun enjoyed only limited popularity after the elections of 1957. His opposition did not necessarily represent "anti-Western" elements, but in significant degree simply the "outs." The Jordanian government was renowned for its nepotism and corruption. So unstable was his throne that King Hussein was forced to entrust his life to white Russian bodyguards. Increasing this deep-seated instablity within a number of pro-Western governments resulted from Colonel Gamal Abdul Nasser's Pan-Arab movement, centering in Cairo, which warred on the governments of the individual Arab states in the interest of creating a greater Arab unity.

Within weeks of the announcement of the Eisenhower Doctrine the United States was called upon to defend its commitments. In April 1957, a coup threatened to overthrow King Hussein. Syria, Egypt, Iraq, and Israel stood ready to intervene and, if necessary, partition the country. The President, acting under the new doctrine, despatched the Sixth Fleet to the Eastern Mediterranean. This demonstration of force, plus a huge grant of $10 million, bolstered the regime and gave it some stability. Several months later pro-Nasser forces in the Syrian army took control of that country. This new elite rejected American interference and in February 1958 linked Syria to Egypt to form the United Arab Repulic. In July, pro-Nasser elements in Iraq unleashed a revolt which terminated in the murder of King Faisal and Premier Nuries-Said and in the seizure of the Iraqi government. Convinced that the new regime was not pro-Communist, the United States quickly recognized it.

Strengthened by this successful coup, the Pan-Arab movement threatened to overturn the governments of Lebanon and Jordan. Both states appealed to the United States. An American army brigade, flown into Lebanon from West Germany, and a regiment of British paratroopers, dropped into Jordan, saved the two pro-Western governments. But this commitment to maintain all Middle Eastern regimes in power, whatever their quality or popularity, threatened the United States with permanent involvement in Middle Eastern affairs. There was no guarantee that many governments of the region could survive the withdrawal of foreign military support. Indeed, in 1960 the pro-Western Menderes government of Turkey, under serious indictment for repression, waste, corruption, and even atrocities, fell before a military junta. Pan-Arabism, with its appeal to the grandeur of Arab history, remained a powerful force, especially among Arab intellectuals. The boundaries which it sought to erase were largely artificial and meaningless. American officials seldom explained how Pan-Arabism threatened Western interests in the Middle East, but they knew that it endangered the status quo. This fact suggested why, under the Eisenhower Doctrine, the movement was not only opposed but also identified with Soviet expansion.

THE PERSISTENCE OF REVOLUTION

By 1960 one American-backed regime in Asia after another began to falter under the internal pressures for greater self-realization. The political and moral price exacted from the perennial denial of self-determination, in the interest of sustaining purely anti-Communist regimes, was demonstrated clearly in a succession of revolts and riots in pro-Western countries.

Throughout the postwar period President Syngman Rhee of South Korea was second only to Chiang Kai-shek as the favorite of American diplomacy in the Far East. The United States had fought the Korean War in large measure to save him and his regime. His Liberal Party, supported by a police force of 300,000, enjoyed a monopoly in South Korean politics. After controlling a series of elections, Rhee attempted in March 1960 to hand-pick his potential successor by maneuvering the victory of his longtime intimate, Lee Ki Poong, as Vice President. This initiated a wave of student protest which culminated on April 19 in a mass uprising of more than 100,000 persons in Seoul, the Korean capital. In the rioting 140 people were killed. Rhee summoned his American-trained army to rescue his regime, but it refused to fire on the student-led mob. Rhee attempted simultaneoulsy to bring the United States government to his support by instructing the Korean ambassador in Washington, You Chan Yang, to announce that the riots were Communist-inspired. Learning that he had been purposely misinformed, Yang submitted his resignation.

Eventually, under American pressure, Rhee agreed to go into semi-retirement and secure the resignation of Lee. But on April 25 another riot forced his total capitulation. That his government had never been democratic was known to American officials, but stability seemed a better defense than democracy against the Communist enemy. President Eisenhower, at his news conference of April 27, simply deplored the resort to violence in Korea.

With the failure of massive retaliation to save Indochina for the French in 1954, the United States government determined to build up the neighboring kingdom of Laos into a "bulwark against Communism." During the next five years that country received more aid on the basis of its three million population than any other country in the world. Those funds were used to support an anti-Communist regime, admittedly undemocratic, whose only obligation to this nation was to use its army to fight the Communist Pathet Lao forces of northern Laos. The election that brought the right-wing government into power was blatantly rigged. It denied both the Communist and neutralist elements of the country a single electoral seat. The perennial failure of the Laotian government to stabilize the country was evidence of its inability to create any popular support among the village populations.

When this regime was overthrown by a military coup engineered by Captain Kong Le, a rebel leader, in August 1960, the Asian press termed the uprising another failure of American policy in the Far East. The Bangkok *World* pointed to the anti-Americanism of the new regime as "another aspect of . . . the dilemma of funneling aid through unpopular and possibly corrupt governments." Kong Le accused the deposed leadership of warring on the Pathet Lao merely to obtain money from the United States, for obviously the war had been conducted with little enthusiasm. The new premier, Prince Souvanna Phouma, promised to call off the civil war and make Laos a neutral in the cold war. But he failed in this purpose. The right wing, under pro-American Phoumi Nosavan who controlled the army, overthrew the neutralist government and continued to fight the Communist guerrillas. By the end of 1960 the Soviet Union had begin to support the Pathet Lao forces openly with military equipment, threatening to bring another Indochina-type struggle to that land-locked country.

Again in Japan the United States was victimized in 1960 by its refusal to recognize any opposition, except communism itself, to its purpose of building one vast anti-Communist bloc in the Far East. The Kremlin warning, following the U-2 incident of May, that Russia would retaliate against any base used to launch further spy flights across Soviet territory, ignited a violent neutralist reaction among Japanese students especially. Such deep-seated convictions reflected, in part, the uniqueness of the Japanese experience. Many citizens of Japan had no intention of forgetting the atomic destruction of Hiroshima or the long American occupation; they had no interest in another war. They resented the defiance of the spirit of the Japanese constitution in the rebuilding of the Japanese military establishment. They observed that many Japanese officials, including Premier Nobusuke Kishi himself, had been part of the old order. Long before the U-2 flights Japanese neutralists had challenged their government's military arrangement with the United States.

This growing opposition to Japanese military policy culminated in bitter attacks on the renewal of the mutual defense pact. Premier Kishi rammed the new treaty through the lower house of the Diet late on the night of May 20 after the Socialist opposition had been removed bodily from the chamber for creating a disturbance. Under the Japanese constitution the treaty would be ratified automatically in thirty days whether approved by the upper house or not, provided the Diet was not dissolved in the meantime. Much of the rioting of May and June was designed to force the resignation of the Kishi government.

Eventually the Japanese demonstrations were directed at

President Eisenhower's scheduled visit of early June, for Kishi's opponents interpreted the visit as an effort to bolster his regime and save the treaty. When the President reached Manila on his Far Eastern tour, 20,000 rioters stormed the Japanese Diet in the most violent demonstration yet staged against the treaty, the Kishi regime, and the President's visit. During a wild night of rioting one person was killed and almost a thousand, including 600 police, were injured. Kishi met with his cabinet and announced to reporters that he would ask the President to cancel his visit. In Manila Mr. Eisenhower accepted the decision of the Japanese government with sympathetic understanding. The Kishi government withstood the siege until the treaty went into effect and then resigned.

In his report to the nation late in June, the President said: "It seems apparent that the Communists some time ago reached the conclusion that these visits were of such positive value to the Free World as to obstruct Communist imperialism. . . . With their associates in Peking, they went to great lengths and expense to create disorders in Tokyo that compelled the Japanese government to decide . . . that it should revoke its long-standing invitation for me to visit that sister of democracy." Undoubtedly Japanese Communists were out in force during the riots. But the President's report not only absolved United States policy of all responsibility for the Tokyo demonstrations, but also refused to acknowledge the existence, much less the legitimacy, of neutralism as a factor in Japanese thought.

THE PROBLEM OF SELF-DETERMINATION IN A DIVIDED WORLD

For the new nations of Asia and Africa the great problem of the 1950s was that of preserving their struggle against the past without becoming involved in the great contest of power between the U.S.S.R. and the West. Why this proved to be difficult was obvious. In every revolutionary situation extremists of right or left, with little interest in popular government, were willing to seek the moral and physical support of the outside world with their stereotyped appeals to communism or anti-communism. Because the big powers, always in search of some ideological advantage, were usually ready to intervene, every major upheaval of the fifties tended eventually to expose the conflict of interest between the United States and the U.S.S.R. Self-determination was generally the loser. It was not strange, therefore, that the authentic and established leaders of Asia and Africa bitterly opposed those who managed, through their rhetoric even more than their actions, to excite the anxieties of the great cold war rivals.

American efforts to preserve the status quo outside Europe overreached the nation's resources and interests as much as did its goal of liberation inside the Soviet sphere. Through a wide variety of involvements the United States committed itself to a state of siege along the entire southern periphery of the Soviet bloc under the conviction that the actions of Peking and Moscow prevented the peaceful evolution of the Afro-Asian world. Actually not one revolution in Asia or Africa throughout the postwar period presented a simple struggle between freedom and tyranny. Yet the United States, from its underestimation of the world's revolutionary fervor, continued to define the cold war in both moral and global terms and to deny officially that the Afro-Asian nations had interests and ambitions quite separate from those of the United States and the Soviet Union—that the world was, in fact, divided into three parts.

It was ironic that this nation generally ignored the principle of self-determination in Asia and Africa where it had some chance of success and promoted it behind the Iron and Bamboo curtains where it had no chance of success at all. But too often Americans behaved as if communism were the host rather than the parasite of change. Adlai Stevenson challenged this tendency when he declared, "The beginning of wisdom in the West, I think, is to have our own creative policy—not just a negative policy to stop the Communists, but one that reflects our own vision of a viable world society and our own understanding of the revolutions through which we live." Only when the United States recognized officially that past changes, whatever their magnitude, were not synonymous with Communist aggression would it discard its feeling of universal obligation, eliminate the nagging character of its diplomacy, and cease to respond to every episode in Asia as if it endangered the security of the nation.

Ends Without Means:
The Eisenhower Years

When Dwight D. Eisenhower left the White House in January 1961, fifteen years had passed since Soviet repression in Eastern Europe and the American effort to counter it first destroyed the promise of great power unity in the postwar world. Despite the continuing magnitude of the resulting Cold War, the United States as a nation was more divided than ever before on the meaning of the Russian challenge. In a sense this confusion was understandable, for there were elements in the conflict that had no clear precedent in history—the sheer destructiveness of modern weapons, the huge military establishments, and the multiple nature and persistence of international pressures. But increasingly the East-West conflict widened the dichotomy between two American concepts of the Soviet threat: first, that the struggle continued to be circumscribed by traditions of power politics and national interest; second, that it had evolved into a limitless contest between freedom and tyranny on a global scale, a totally revolutionary phenomenon propelling history down its final, dangerous course. American reactions to the cold war varied from absolute dread that nuclear destruction might terminate civilization itself to the utter impatience that the West continued to tolerate the existence of the Communist system at all.

Policies required to span such a chasm of thought and concept could only be indecisive, confused, and inconsistent. Eventually any nation, if it would conduct itself responsibly in world affairs, must determine with some precision the peril which it faces. The persistent overestimation of danger provokes the nation to demand too much of itself and of the enemy simply to guarantee that enough will be demanded; the persistent underestimation of danger undermines its determination to protect even what is essential. The first tendency produces within the adversary the emotion of fear; the second, of overconfidence. Either reaction contains within itself the seeds of aggression and war. Any rational and consistent response to the Russian challenge required, therefore, some reasonably accurate evaluation not only of Soviet intention but also of Soviet power available to achieve it.

There was much in the United States-Soviet conflict that flowed logically from the past. Such extended struggles have been common enough in history, for great nations have usually found themselves in competition for prestige and security, sea lanes and resources, markets and even empires. That such a rivalry would eventually embrace the United States and Russia had been predicted for over a century. In the 1830s Alexis de Tocqueville, the brilliant French critic of American democracy, pointed to the two nations as the great powers of the future, and observed that "each of these seems to be marked out by the will of heaven to sway the destinies of half the globe." In the next decade Alexander Herzen, the Russian liberal, denied that human destiny was nailed to Western Europe. He saw in the United States and Russia two young, vigorous nations which were preparing themselves to wield the power that once belonged to Europe. It seemed inescapable that these two aspiring giants, with their extensive territories, temperate climates, energetic populations, and abundant resources, would come to the forefront of world politics as major contestants for prestige and power. In a sense the cold war had been a traditional struggle, conducted in a historic context, the mere fulfillment of prophecy.

THE CONCEPT OF GLOBAL CONSPIRACY

Throughout the decade of the 1950s this limited concept of the cold war received scant attention in the United States. Most American officials, political leaders, and writers accepted the notion that the Soviet Union represented a global conspiracy. They argued that the Kremlin was concerned less with stabilizing its postwar position than with dominating the free world. What mattered fundamentally to them was the irreconcilable conflict between freedom and an ideology that aimed at the complete subjugation of the individual through the rule of terror. They regarded Soviet communism as a virus that could not be contained; if permitted to exist, it would destroy freedom everywhere. The Communist movement, Charles Malik of Lebanon, former president of the U.N. General Assembly, warned in 1960, sought "to overthrow every existing government, regime, system, outlook, religion and philosophy and bring the whole world—all human thought, aspiration, action and organization—under its absolute control." For some American writers the cold war was merely the continuation of a vast ideological assault on the free world that began with the Bolshevik triumph of 1917 and had been perpetuated by the absolute faith of Lenin, Stalin, and Khrushchev in the ultimate victory of the Communist system.

In this context of total conflict Soviet maneuvering could not be accepted as traditional Russian behavior but only as an integrated scheme to divide and confuse the free world, to throw it off balance, to promote its collapse. There was much in Soviet action to substantiate such conclusions. The Kremlin introduced uncertainty and abused the normal privileges of diplomacy; it violated flagrantly previous agreements and turned high-level conferences into political forums. Toward regions outside its sphere the Soviet Union maintained a varied offensive that combined military, political, economic, and psychological methods. It exploited violence to further its ends; it kept the world under constant tension by maintaining its armed might, by blustering and threatening. Senator Barry Goldwater, in his book, *The Conscience of a Conservative,* summarized the Soviet challenge in such terms: "We are confronted by a revolutionary world movement that possesses not only the will to dominate absolutely every square mile of the globe, but increasingly the capacity to do so. . . ." The Senator pointed specifically to the Soviet military power which rivaled that of the United States, the superior propaganda skills of the Kremlin, and the Communist ideology which imbued its adherents with a sense of historical mission. These powerful resources, he added, were "controlled by a ruthless despotism that brooks no deviation from the revolutionary course."

Soviet leaders did little to dispel such fears. They announced repeatedly their purpose of world domination. Nikita Khrushchev's words especially were characterized by a disturbing arrogance. At a Kremlin reception in November 1956, he stated the oft-quoted but not exceptional phrase, "Whether you like it or not, history is on our side. We will bury you." The Soviet leader used every occasion to stress the superiority of the Communist system. Capitalism will perish, he warned, just as feudalism perished earlier. "All the world will come to communism," he declared in June 1957. "History does not ask whether you want it or not." The Soviet Premier warned the West that the underlying Soviet purpose transcended the policies and actions of the moment. "People say our smiles are not honest," he once observed. "That is not true. Our smile is real and not artificial. But if anyone believes that our smile means that we have given up the teachings of Marx, Engels, and Lenin, he is badly mistaken."

Khrushchev's new economic policies appeared at once more hopeful and more threatening. These policies, anchored to an expanding Soviet economy, were designed to bring Soviet action into conformity with Soviet purpose. They were, in the words of the Soviet Premier, a device for dominating the world without military conquest. The new Russian imperialism moved forward on three fronts. It offered the Soviet model to the underdeveloped world; it sought to spread Soviet influence through programs of trade and aid; and, lastly, it threatened to reduce the United States to a second-rank power through the achievements of the Soviet economy itself. Soviet productive power was thus to become a massive political weapon which would elevate Russian prestige and power throughout the world.

Anticipating the eventual triumph of the Soviet system through industry and technology alone, the Kremlin leaders attempted to call off the cold war in Europe if not in Asia and Africa. Their insistence that the struggle between communism and capitalism henceforth be peaceful reflected a realistic judgment of the destructiveness of modern war. If this was a denial of Marxist dogma on the inevitability of war, it meant that Khruschev, unlike Marx, had some knowledge of hydrogen bombs. The relaxation of tension had the dual advantage of permitting a greater concentration of productive energy and resources within Russia itself and of producing greater complacency in the Western world. The Soviet plea for "peaceful coexistence" did not promise any reduction of goals; it illustrated simply the Kremlin's burgeoning confidence in nonmilitary means in its continuing, if partially concealed, offensive against the non-Communist world.

THE GOAL OF TOTAL VICTORY

American leaders warned the nation repeatedly against the acceptance of a Soviet-inspired peace. Such an acceptance, Secretary of

State Dulles declared in April 1955, would lead to the degradation of the human race. The Secretary added: "The Communist leaders know that, if pacifism becomes a prevalent mood among the free peoples, the Communists can easily conquer the world. Then they can confront the free peoples with successive choices between peace and surrender; and if peace is the absolute good, then surrenders become inevitable." The Soviet challenge was so insidious and pervading that it simply permitted no relaxation or compromise. Similarly Andrew H. Berding, Assistant Secretary of State for Public Affairs, appraised Soviet intentions following the Khrushchev visit to the United States in September 1959, in these words:

We have noted a partial change in Soviet tactics. The Soviets have seemed somewhat more amenable, less aggressive, more relaxed, less provocative. . . . But, while Soviet tactics seem to have changed, we have been able thus far to detect no change whatever in Soviet ultimate ambitions–the creation of a Communist world. . . . They know that in a major war the Soviet Union would suffer devastation many, many times greater than the terrible losses they experienced in the last war. Therefore the thesis of Lenin that war is necessary to overcome capitalism has evidently been modified. But the conflict will be waged just the same, and with the same intensity as if it were military. The battlefields will be political, economic, psychological. There is every reason to believe that the Soviets will employ all means possible to triumph in all these fields.

Traditionally peace was the absence of war. Unfortunately, by 1960 it was no longer that simple, for the concept of a global Soviet conspiracy dictated that peace, to be genuine, had to be total. If one assumed that the Soviet Union would never concede its goal of dominating the globe, then the cold war would continue until either freedom or communism was destroyed. Either Russia would be driven back, its victims liberated, or it would steadily and inevitably take over the free world. It was essential, therefore, that American policy pursue not coexistence, but ultimate victory. "Like it or not," Eugene Lyons wrote, "the great and inescapable task of our epoch is not to end the Cold War but to win it." Peace would be tolerable only when it followed a victory over communism. Meanwhile the West dared not accept the status quo behind the Iron Curtain because it represented a necessary triumph for international communism in its career of world conquest.

But by the standards of total victory successful policy demanded more. Some writers and politicians suggested that the United States seek no less than the liberalization of the Kremlin and the granting of freedom to the Soviet peoples, for only the destruction of one-man rule could guarantee the ultimate security of the West. To protect Asia from subversion and conquest, some demanded more hostile and aggressive policies toward Peking for the purpose of eliminating that regime entirely. According to the doctrine of global conflict the nation really had little choice. The cold war, Secretary Berding declared, is a "constant battle for victory, of one over the other, ultimate total triumph, and ultimate total defeat."

Peace between the United States and the U.S.S.R., then, could not exist until all problems were solved and all men had been freed. Only when freedom and justice prevailed would Soviet power cease to threaten the world. Peace, declared President Dwight D. Eisenhower at Paris in December 1957, is not "an uneasy absence of strife bought at the price of cowardly surrender of principles. We cannot have peace and ignore righteous aspirations and noble heritages. The peace we do seek is an expanding state of justice and understanding. It is a peace within which men and women can freely exercise their unalienable rights to life, liberty, and the pursuit of happiness." In his Christmas message of December 1959, the President again made it clear that the United States did not regard mere coexistence as a satisfactory arrangement for mankind. "After all," he said, "an uneasy coexistence can be as barren and sterile, joyless and stale of life for human beings as the coexistence of cell-mates in a penetentiary or labor camp." The United States, he added, anticipated the day when all the world would be free and enjoy a peace in which all peoples could engage in an open exchange of goods and ideas and contribute fully to the progress and prosperity of the world.

By the late 1950s the notion that the United States dared settle for nothing less than victory appeared capable of capturing the entire nation. One group of distinguished clergymen declared, quite characteristically, in national convention: "Without freedom under God for every man and for every nation there can be no peace." Similarly Vice President Richard M. Nixon, observed during the 1960 campaign that "as long as any man or woman is not free any place in the world, freedom is threatened where it exists. . . ." David Sarnoff, conceiving of national purpose in terms of universal principles, added dramatically in a noted essay of 1960, "Our message to humankind must be that America has decided, irrevocably, to win the cold war." Any lesser purpose would merely consign the United States and its principles to oblivion.

ENDS WITHOUT MEANS

What the postwar generation had witnessed in world politics was essentially the manifestations of an unprecedented power revolution. It was the effort of Russia and China to establish a new order in international affairs that placed such an enormous burden on American foreign policy. Successful diplomacy demands the constant evaluation of changing power relationships among nations and the resulting shifts in national interest, for any revolution in the force which other nations can bring to bear on world politics must either prompt a general, if reluctant, concession to the new realities or actuate the creation of a countering force to undo the change. At heart the American dilemma in the cold war was the nation's inability to choose either alternative. For many national leaders the power revolution wrought by the rise of the Soviet Union was too threatening and too immoral to be accepted diplomatically. What remained was either inaction, supported by the rhetoric of disapprobation, or the establishment of policies designed to roll the Soviet Union back to its boundaries of 1939 and to recreate the power balance of the thirties. Unfortunately the many Americans who proclaimed the exceedingly ambitious ends of total victory neglected almost entirely the question of means.

This nation's basic response to the Soviet challenge was military. At one time it was assumed that the West, with its capacity to outperform the U.S.S.R. in industrial production, could, through successful containment, give the inconsistencies within Russia time to undermine the entire Soviet structure. The experience of a decade of almost exclusive attention to nuclear armament demonstrated, however, that Western military preparedness would never be sufficient in itself to force any agreement on the Kremlin. The high hopes of American policy slowly disintegrated under the constant search for military strength which always seemed to elude the nation. The West did not win the race for military power, and it was clear after the launching of Sputnik in 1957 that no conceivable Western military establishment could achieve any declared purpose of American policy without war. Perhaps the satellites could not be freed even through war, for the resulting destruction would leave little worth liberating. Western military strength, despite its unprecedented magnitude, was still limited. And it was the vast discrepancy between ends and means that produced both inaction and embarrassment in the recurring crises of the postwar years. But the persistent failure of the nation to dismantle the Soviet empire did not reduce the ends of policy; it merely sent men in a frantic search for other, more effective, means to close the gap between the goal of total victory and the experience of limited power.

In general those who continued to search for the means that would assure the ultimate Western triumph over communism found them in various forms of psychological warfare. This strategy became the foundation of the policy of boldness that sought to bring liberation to those behind the Iron Curtain through the rhetoric of freedom disseminated largely through massive radio towers. Upholding such methods of psychological warfare, Representative O. K. Armstrong of Missouri declared in February, 1952: "Let us realize this great and fundamental truth: That the struggle against communism is the struggle for minds and hearts of mankind. It cannot be won by bombs and guns alone. The strongest weapon that we hold in our hands is truth itself." Such a policy of liberation would succeed, Senator Thomas J. Dodd of Connecticut wrote in the summer of 1959, because it was "in harmony with the moral principles on which our faith and civilization are based."

This tendency to concede almost limitless power to words conformed to the deep-seated habit of attributing everything dangerous in the postwar world to Soviet ideology, not Soviet power. It was international communism that was the root of all evil. It was this insidious movement that created the monolithic Soviet bloc which included Red China, that stimulated and guided the revolutionary currents of Asia and Africa, that built the industrial and scientific bases of Soviet achievement. Having started at zero four decades earlier, it had by mid-century gained control of one-third of the world's population and was still reaching outward. But to those who discovered in communism, not in the force unleashed by Soviet productivity and Afro-Asian nationalism, the fundamental threat to traditional Western security, the danger never represented more than a body of ideas. Countering policy, therefore, demanded largely competing thoughts and words, not competing economic and military strength. This explained why those who accepted the notion of world revolution never placed any strain on the national budget.

If bold words were the essential element of power, critics of coexistence wondered why the West did not throw the Soviets back on their heels by making the same boasts that one day capitalism would conquer all Communist values and drive them from the face of the earth. They charged that those who denied the efficacy of such methods were conceding the inevitability of Soviet domination. To them any preference for traditional methods of diplomatic behavior, amid the progress of world revolution, merely illustrated the extent to which communism had undermined the will of the free world.

Still another approach to the problem of total victory was suggested by William S. Schlamm in his book, *Germany and the East-West Crisis: The Decisive Challenge to American Policy* (1959). Rather than bargain with the Soviets over the future of Germany, he wrote, the West must grasp the offensive. In partnership with a heavily armed West Germany, the United States, employing threats of violence, must force the Russians out of East Germany. This would succeed, he predicted, because the Soviets had to avoid war. The West, having rolled the Soviets out of one strategic position, would gain the momentum and soon drive the Russians behind their prewar boundaries. Any Soviet resistance would indicate merely that the Kremlin had changed its strategy and would have attacked the West anyway. Such risks the West must assume, he warned, for the mere desire to avoid conflict would guarantee the eventual triumph of communism. Senator Goldwater, proposing a similar course of action, insisted that the United States support any future revolution behind the Iron Curtain with the threat of massive retaliation if the Russians attempted to suppress it with force. The Soviets would concede to Western demands, he assured Americans, because they would not risk the destruction of their whole system merely to prevent the loss of one region.

Whatever the nature of Soviet global strategy, somehow the postwar hegemony of the Kremlin in East-Central Europe remained the key to the entire East-West conflict. As Senator Dodd observed, "if the Soviet Union could have the wisdom to withdraw to its prewar frontiers, tensions would disappear overnight and the whole world sleep better." What happened to the world revolution under such conditions was not clear. If the issue between the United States and the U.S.S.R. was world domination, as the Senator insisted, then how could the cold war be resolved merely by freeing Hungary and Poland? If the conflict centered in the misuse of Soviet power in Europe, then the global challenge was quite limited after all.

For Secretary Dulles the superiority of freedom over despotism alone assured the ultimate triumph of the West. To him the free world, given time, could win the cold war totally at no great cost to itself, for the Soviet weakness lay fundamentally in the human spirit. By combining its military, economic, and moral assets, the West could exploit that weakness. The time would come, Mr. Dulles declared in December 1957, "when inevitably, the Soviet rulers will have to change their attitude toward their own people, toward the rest of the world." If the United States remained strong and at the same time made its own freedom and liberty a flaming example to the world, the people behind the Iron Curtain would feel it and sense it and demand more of it for themselves. That, he said, was the "strategy of victory." The Secretary voiced his conviction again in September 1958, when he said, "If there is any one thing in the world that is inevitable, it is that human beings want for themselves a degree of personal freedom and liberty which is denied by communism. So I believe that it is inevitable sooner or later, that that desire for personal freedom will manifest itself. Therefore we do not accept the type of Communist rule that now prevails as a permanent situation anywhere in the world." It was this conviction that virtue would triumph over evil that encouraged Mr. Dulles to pursue goals that had no relationship to the power he wielded.

Herein lay the fallacy in the concept of total threat and total response. Its adherents, from their morbid conviction that the West could not resist Soviet ideology or subversion, demanded the eventual destruction of the Communist system. Then they discovered the promise of ultimate victory over Russian communism in the pervading weakness of the Communist system itself. This inconsistency explained the total lack of balance between ends and means in national action. For the ends of policy were predicated on the assumption that the adversaries were omnipotent, omniscient, monstrously efficient, unhampered by any problems of their own, in possession of frightening power, and bent only on the destruction of the free world. But the means of policy were based on the antithetical assumption that the Soviet system was a hollow shell, incapable of governing its own people, subject to destruction by weapons no more elaborate than words and radio transmitters. Either the Soviet Union was no threat at all, or such weapons for victory were totally inadequate.

This same absence of any serious balance between ends and means characterized the American posture toward China. With the accession of Mr. Eisenhower to the presidency, the nation's commitment to Chiang Kai-shek became one of unshakable determination. Such key leaders of the new administration as John Foster Dulles, Walter S. Robertson, and Arthur W. Radford perpetuated an attitude of uncompromising antagonism toward the mainland regime and created a rationale to justify it. *(See Document No. 1 on p. 171.)* They rushed into every Far Eastern crisis with strident appeals to the anti-Chinese sentiment which they had helped to create, but neither they nor the nation had any desire to pay the price of war to destroy the Chinese enemy.

Nonrecognition expressed their faith that one day the Peking regime would cease to exist. American action, Mr. Dulles explained, was based on the assumption that "international Communism's rule of strict conformity is, in China, as elsewhere, a passing and not a perpetual phase." It was the intention of the United States, he said, to speed that passing.

Those who anticipated the total elimination of Peking through a firm posture of disapprobation were never troubled by doubt. If the Communist threat to Asia was so pervasive as to require that regime's ultimate destruction, the American formula assured that result without war or diplomacy. The continued recognition and support of the Kuomintang on Formosa, a State Department memorandum assured the nation in August 1958, "enables it to challenge the claim of the Chinese Communists to represent the Chinese people and keeps alive the hopes of those Chinese who are determined eventually to free their country of Communist rule." However powerful and threatening the enemy, its obliteration was always assured by the very ideological and moral aberrations which constituted the original danger itself. By such doctrine every challenge to the national will, once it had been designated repressive and thus a defiance of the human spirit, could not escape ultimate self-destruction. It was not clear how such expectations of victory, demanding no price at all, could serve as the basis of serious policy.

The assumption that the free world could triumph over the Communist enemy everywhere without war had no clear historic precedent. Certainly the weapons of coexistence, disturbing as they were, had less the power of conquest than did the weapons of war. Yet many Americans, admitting the limits of nuclear war, anticipated total victory through crusades of liberation alone. Such action would either remain meaningless or require more or less fighting, for it was doubtful if the Soviets would concede to a verbal assault what they would not concede to a military threat. If it ever appeared that the United States might free the satellites, for example, through nonmilitary techniques, war would be imminent indeed. For certainly the Soviets would not leave their weapons unused while they went down before a barrage of words. Peaceful liberation remained a possibility only as long as it demonstrated its utter futility.

THE LIMITS OF SOVIET POWER

Obviously the Soviet offensive was varied and disturbing, but nowhere after 1945 did it reveal the overwhelming power attributed to its Communist structure. Communism failed as an exportable commodity; its success even in Russia was doubtful. The Soviet empire had been built, not through the revolutionary doctrines of Marx and Lenin, but through the power of the Red Army under Stalin. Not one square foot of territory was delivered to the Soviet Union through Communist revolution alone. Even in Czechoslovakia the massive weight of Soviet armies helped to demoralize the nation and aid the Communist coup of 1948. In none of the Soviet satellites did communism demonstrate any power to destroy national sentiment and tradition.

Direct Russian control extended only as far as the reach of the Red Army. Marshal J. B. Tito of Yugoslavia, the devoted Communist, defied Marxist internationalism so thoroughly that he withdrew his nation from the Soviet bloc. Hungary's Kadar-Münnich regime, established as a puppet by the Kremlin after the revolution of 1956, was subservient to Russian influence. During its first four years in power, however, it sought to bring internal unity to Hungary. The Hungarian people, tired of the cause of liberation after the United States' failure to support the revolution, resigned themselves to the new regime. But they were still Hungarian, and fifteen years of Soviet control did not diminish their patriotism. If the U.S.S.R. was unable to corrupt Hungary between 1945 and 1960, it was difficult to see how it could corrupt the entire world. Only through sheer force did the Soviets maintain their hegemony over East Germany, Poland, Hungary, and the other satellites.

Wladyslaw Gomulka of Poland was as dedicated to communism as were the Kremlin leaders. Yet he remained a true Polish patriot, concerned solely for the welfare of his country. Polish communism was cast in his image. Gomulka was often distressed at his nation's refusal to accept his doctrines, and his efforts to impose them as a national program often went beyond what the Kremlin believed expedient. If he carefully avoided differences with Moscow, it was because he feared that Soviet interference might destroy his program completely. Under Gomulka communism remained a Polish, not an international phenomenon.

Undoubtedly there was something exploitable for Russia in a revolutionary Afro-Asian world. If earlier in this century Western Europe alone maintained that vast colonial hegemony that blanketed much of Africa, the Middle East, and Asia, any nationalistic pressure against that status quo could only weaken Western power and influence. But the anti-Western revolutions themselves did not belong to Russia, and the Soviet triumphs were exceedingly limited. That very nationalism which contributed to revolution at once placed limits on the control which the Soviets were permitted to exert. Western prestige and influence, moreover, did not necessarily decline with the independence movements; in some countries, such as India, it actually increased. The Soviets gained nothing militarily and little politically (China was a temporary exception) from the vast change that swept the Orient and Africa after 1945.

The reason was clear. Communism in Asia, as in Europe, remained subservient to nationalism. It gained the ascendancy in China and Indo-China, and threatened to do so elsewhere, but only by capturing control of some aspect of an indigenous nationalistic movement. Even in the Communist countries of Asia nationalism remained the chief determinant, and no quantity of Soviet arms would undermine its primacy unless they were accompanied by significant numbers of Russian troops. Mao Tse-tung was devoted to Chinese, not Russian, interests. That China, unlike Yugoslavia, remained in the Soviet bloc revealed simply a current mutuality of interest. But China, under the impact of its new nationalism, was more determined to pursue its own destiny than ever before in its history. For that reason, China in the twentieth century comprised a greater threat to the Soviet Union than at any time after the days of the Mongols. The moment could well come when the Soviets would rue the day that Communists gained control of China. Ho Chi Minh's possible triumph over all Vietnam would scarcely serve any Soviet interest, for he was fiercely independent of all external control. Indian Communists, if successful, would still be Indians, concerned with the future of India. Applying this type of analysis to the non-Soviet world in general, Louis J. Halle wrote: "A Communist United States might be no less hostile to the Soviet Union than a liberal democratic United States. Because its total resources could be more easily mobilized, it might, in fact, be distinctly more threatening." Subversion and revolution were not triumphant methods of external conquest in Asia because successful Communist revolutionaries, riding the tide of nationalism, were intense patriots, not traitors.

THE LIMITS OF ECONOMIC IMPERIALISM

It was even less clear how the Soviet Union could dominate the world with its new economic offensive. What mattered was capability, not intent. Soviet policies of trade and aid could elevate Russian prestige, create opportunities for strengthening the Soviet economy, build attitudes of friendship, and perhaps render some weak economies vulnerable to Soviet pressure. They could not do more. Throughout the previous four decades the foreign trade and investments of the United States were unprecedented. Whatever this vast economic activity brought to the United States, it did not include conquest or even much friendship. More often American economic preponderance was a source of resentment, and the more vulnerable it rendered other economies, the greater that resentment had been. No nation can annex another or even gain control of its external policies through trade and investment alone, any more than one nation can destroy the sovereignty of another through revolution. In either case the power of decision remains within the weaker nation.

Soviet industrial and technological achievement was a genuine threat to American prestige and greatness. But the concept that Soviet economic productivity alone could command the power to dominate much of the world was an exaggeration. First, few American economists accepted Khrushchev's prediction that communism would bury capitalism. They agreed that the Soviet economy had grown more rapidly than that of the United States; they admitted that this growth in itself gave a boost to Soviet prestige; but they did not agree that the Soviet economy could outstrip that of the United States in the long run. Henry Cabot Lodge, when United States Representative to the U.N., commented realistically on the challenge of the Soviet economy:

I . . . do not dispute Chairman Khrushchev's right to challenge us. Nor am I worried by improving the lot of the Russian citizen. In fact I welcome it. But I do dispute the accuracy of his prophecy. If we do what we are capable of doing, the Soviet Union will never surpass us. A country which thrives on competition as we do—in business, in politics, in sport—should not shrink from the idea of competition. A nation which sees what tens of thousands of plans of independent producers can create in the way of new wealth need never worry about competition from a state which is run by a central bureaucracy.

Second, it was difficult to see any relationship between productive capacity and world domination. For fifty years American productivity faced no serious competitor abroad. That fact lowered the prestige of nations such as England and France; it even curtailed their industrial expansion and limited their prosperity. If it reduced them gradually to second-class powers, it did not destroy them. Nor did past decades of American economic supremacy destroy or even weaken the Soviet economy. It seemed illogical to assume that once Soviet production exceeded that of the United States, this nation would falter and collapse. To accept Soviet words as a clear prediction of history was to accept the strange doctrine that communism was superior even when it was behind. What mattered in the cold war, unfortunately, was the relationship between industrial capacity and national power. It was this that created a danger of incalculable proportions to the Western world. Were there no cold war between the United States and the Soviet Union, the question of the Russian economy would hardly have been an issue between them at all.

Third, if the United States chose to accept the Soviet boasts of conquest through productivity as serious, there was still no clear answer to the challenge in the realm of diplomacy. What kind of foreign policy could have guaranteed the curtailment of the Soviet economy? The United States had contributed comparatively little to its continued evolution. Any effort to destroy it through war would have sacrificed much of this nation's own remarkable economic structure. Soviet industrial expansion was a matter of historical change which had little connection with Khrushchev's words. If the U.S.S.R. had the necessary resources, energy, and efficiency to surpass the United States, this nation could no more stop the process than could a troubled Britain stop the onrush of the American productive system sixty years earlier. The new Soviet challenge could not be ignored, but the answer rested within the American industrial system itself.

Perhaps more troublesome to Western concepts of democratic progress in the world was the Soviet and Chinese example. For backward and crowded countries, lacking resources and capital funds, the United States could hardly serve as a model at all. This nation grew up in a spacious and richly-laden continent; its system and achievements could not be duplicated elsewhere. Walter Lippmann saw the dilemma clearly: "We cannot beat the Soviet example by our example. For we are not an example that backward peoples can follow, and unless we can manage to create an example which they *can* follow, we shall almost certainly lose the Cold War in Asia and Africa, and perhaps elsewhere."

Fortunately, national autonomy was still the key to the Afro-Asian world. If nations there chose communism, it was doubtful if the resulting economic structure would have any more similarity to Marxism than would an economic system based on liberal democracy resemble that of the United States. Whether they built on Western capital or on some modification of the Chinese system, they would remain African and Asian. Wherever they might secure their aid, they would grant no more than limited jurisdiction to any external power. As allies they would be liabilities; they would contribute little to their defense and demand miracles that no one could perform.

There remained the Marxist interpretation of history to which the Kremlin leaders paid verbal homage. Their persistence in intoning the Marxist incantations perpetuated tension and fear in a divided world. Westerners pointed to the nearly fulfilled predictions of Adolf Hitler's *Mein Kampf,* forgetting that Hitler's success was based on military power which the West refused to counter, not on nonmilitary devices and ideology which supposedly gave meaning to the Soviet purpose of world domination. The Kremlin leaders were politicians. Unlike Hitler, they faced military force sufficient to prevent any drastic miscalculations. And their day-to-day decisions reflected a host of immediate problems, many of them of a defense nature, rather than any deep-seated conviction that the world would one day belong to them.

THE LIMITS OF AMERICAN POWER

Soviet power confronted the West with continuing pressures against its unity, its prestige, and even its security. The challenge did not rest in communism "and the governments its controls," as Mr. Dulles often insisted, for the Communist governments of Poland and Yugoslavia were not hostile to the United States at all. The danger centered in the persistence of big nation rivalry. Russian policy pursued primarily its long-standing intention of establishing the largest possible hegemony for that nation in Eastern and Southeastern Europe. Amid the revolutions of Asia and Africa it sought, in addition, the political retreat of the West. What made the Soviet Union more threatening than in the past was not its idelogy, but its relative power to achieve its goals. But if basic Soviet purpose was traditional, it still required more than spiritual strength to contain it within its historic precedents. Even this limited objective was vastly more dangerous than the rhetoric of world conquest and crusades for liberation suggested. The persistent effort to anchor American purpose to nonmilitary devices encouraged the nation to underestimate the means required to preserve the West's precarious status in world affairs.

Unfortunately the military containment of Russia and China failed to achieve the vague but grandiose expectations attached to it. The moral and physical power required to frustrate Soviet intention proved to be illusive indeed. The search for military superiority through the creation of weapons of mass destruction brought no dilemma of the postwar era nearer settlement on Western terms. Much of the lack of realism in the national effort to counter the Soviet challenge stemmed from the general assumptions that the existence of thermonuclear weapons rendered war either impossible or so destructive that it would destroy civilization itself. The popular doctrine that war had been eliminated seemed to guarantee the time required for freedom to achieve its ultimate triumph over Communist tyranny. Meanwhile it encouraged the nation to live dangerously, to neglect its diplomacy, to respond to every threat of Communist expansion with "brinkmanship." At the same time the conviction that war could not be limited, or a nuclear war survived, ruled out the need of planning the conduct of future war to its conclusion, of maintaining conventional forces powerful enough to contain limited aggression with chemical explosives alone. Together these conclusions reduced military requirements to the mere possession of nuclear weapons and the means of their delivery. They satisfied the traditional American concern with tax reduction without forcing any diminution of national expectations. And they permitted the nation to ignore the sword of Damocles that hung over it, for there was no guarantee that war would not return to the world through deliberate attack, accident, or provocation.

Every trend of the 1950s warred on the old bipolar concept of international power and weakened the Western alliance. England and France, no longer dependent on the United States for their existence, reasserted their former indepenent courses in world affairs. Charles de Gaulle, possessing his own atomic weapons, calmly defied the will of NATO. Germany and Japan, despite their verbal devotion to established military arrangements, threatened increasingly to move out on their own. Long-range missile development weakened the mutual interest of the United States and its Allies in the maintenance of European bases. The growing vulnerability of this nation to direct nuclear attack undermined much of Europe's confidence in the willingness of the American people to involve themselves in a European war. Somehow the United States seemed much more reliable when it was less vulnerable. The burgeoning concern of Europeans with their own nuclear arsenals reflected in some measure their conviction that they required their own deterrents against Soviet aggression.

IN LIEU OF DIPLOMACY

Measured by the limits of national power, American foreign policy served the country well during the first fifteen years of the postwar era.

United States leadership, both Democratic and Republican, accepted the warning of Winston Churchill that the Soviet Union, heavily armed and traditionally aggressive, posed a danger to Western security. If those who determined national policy never agreed on the character and extent of the Russian threat, they chose to build and maintain the Atlantic Alliance as the surest guarantee against Soviet expansion and the recurrence of war. That Europe remained remarkably stable through fifteen years of sometimes bitter disagreement and tension must be attributed in large measure to the national effort of the American people. The repeated acceptance of change in the Afro-Asian world, seldom in accordance with this nation's will, was not in itself a measure of failure. Soviet gains in the turbulent subcontinents were decidedly limited; none of them challenged the vital interests of the United States. Through fifteen years of crises, neither side in the cold war experienced any major gains or losses.

This relative stability in the balance of power demonstrated the need as well as the feasibility of coexistence between East and West. Fifteen years of continuous conflict illustrated repeatedly the finite character of both American and Soviet strength. But at no time between 1945 and 1960 did United States officials confine this nation's intentions abroad to the obvious limits of the power at their disposal. The language of American diplomacy, admirably designed to reassure a citizenry at home, promised no less than the gradual erosion, before the superior appeal of freedom, of those forces in the world that defied American purpose (a purpose identified generally with the exclusion of Communist influence from international politics). Such broad ideological goals, while popular in themselves, eliminated the considerable power of the United States from any precise role in guiding its diplomacy. It was never made clear how any acceptable national effort could extend the base of freedom around the globe or even curtail the power and ambition of either of the nation's major cold war antagonists. Thus, United States policy in 1960 existed at two levels. Whereas day-to-day decisions permitted the Republic to coexist with the U.S.S.R. on terms that were generally satisfactory, the national preoccupation with goals of universal freedom and justice denied that coexistence with communism was an acceptable arrangement at all.

This clear discrepancy between the nation's transcendent mission and its limited authority repudiated the historic principle that external objectives be circumscribed by available means. This defiance of diplomatic tradition did not pass unchallenged. One question was fundamental to all serious discussion of American foreign policy after 1945: What was the nation attempting to defend? Or phrased in more popular terms: From what was it refusing to retreat? The problem was crucial, for the national leadership, in assigning diplomacy the vague task of deflating the Communist structure, never distinguished between the United States as a nation and the American way of life as objects to be safeguarded. A nation and its ideology are not synonymous. One is a geographical, economic, political, and military entity; the other is a concept that resides in the minds of men. When the two converge, as indeed they may, one policy can serve them both; when they diverge, the country must make a choice. In resolving the inescapable dilemma of choice in its relations with the Soviet bloc, American leadership in large measure placed the nation's destiny on the altar of its principles, assuming that the United States, with its vast resources, would take care of itself. To John Foster Dulles, for example, the Republic during his secretaryship was protecting both its security and its principles. But of these, he declared repeatedly; the principles of the Republic came first.

There were many unrecognized arrangements in the world which defied the principles of self-determination; no American took any pleasure at their existence. But some observers pointed to the nation's lack of power, and therefore of obligation, to serve mankind in general. It seemed apparent after 1945 that any decided attempt to eliminate from the world those factors which appeared immoral would terminate in the destruction of the considerable good that still remained. Some writers wondered if the verbal acceptance of an obligation to universal freedom, when specific policies were not created to assure its fulfillment, was even moral. Such commitments saved no one and rendered improbable the settlement of any cold war issues through negotiation alone.

American leadership recognized the world's need for some evolution toward a more stable peace. President Eisenhower declared repeatedly that ''we will always go the extra mile with anyone on earth if it will bring us nearer a genuine peace.'' Despite his sincere devotion to the cause of peace, the President really could not lead the way toward any cold war settlement. Having agreed with Soviet leaders on the need of peace at the Geneva Summit Conference of July 1955, he refused a month later to accept ''a status quo in which we find injustice to many nations.'' On the following day Vice President Nixon demanded that the Russians dismantle the Iron Curtain, free the satellites, and unite Germany and Korea under free elections. At the Foreign Ministers' Conference in October 1955, Mr. Dulles refused emphatically to accept Europe's status quo as the basis of negotiation.

Nor did the demands of official Washington recede at any time during the next half decade. The President and his advisors had simply promised too much. They could make peace only on their own terms.

For that reason the President's specific proposals always substituted procedure for political settlement. In his message to Congress in January 1958, for example, Mr. Eisenhower declared it essential that the world translate its desire for peace into action. The works of peace which the President then sought comprised the breaking down of unnatural barriers between nations, international cooperation in projects of human welfare, programs of science for peace, disarmament, and the establishment of a body of world law which would defend the strong against the weak and affirm the equality of nations. Actually all such proposals, uttered in the name of peace, promised no progress toward the organization of peace at all. For nowhere did they include the fundamental necessity of coming to terms with the postwar status of Russia and China in world affairs.

This neglect of diplomacy amid a growing weariness with the cold war eventually forced both Eisenhower and Khrushchev to introduce high-level summitry and tourism as permanent rituals in international life. These were the only means remaining whereby responsible leaders could assure a drifting world that it was not drifting toward war. Unfortunately these procedures were developed in lieu of diplomacy; they reduced peacemaking to pure symbolism. Were settlement the real objective, it could have been obtained more cheaply and efficiently through established diplomatic procedures. Mr. Eisenhower's tours of 1959 and 1960, for example, equated the cause of peace with the enthusiasm of the crowds which greeted him abroad. Yet it was this nation's relations with the governments of Moscow and Peking, not the crowds of New Delhi, Paris, and Taipei, that mattered. Despite all this apparent search for peace, the fundamental issues that plagued the world dragged on, unfaced and unsettled.

There remained in 1960 some consequential lessons of history. For a century the repeated involvement of the United States in war had resulted from a well-established pattern of diplomatic behavior. Prior to every involvement the nation's leadership had refused to accept certain conditions beyond its control as immoral, yet not sufficiently dangerous to the national interest to necessitate any preparation for war. Refusing to resolve these challenges to principle either through diplomacy or a show of force, the country drifted without benefit of genuine policy until the fundamental decisions between peace and war were made, to a large extent, by others. Perhaps the perennial absence of national concern at this pattern of faltering leadership in time of crisis was understandable, for in every conflict the country seemed to achieve gains commensurate with the price of victory. Never was this more true than for the Civil War itself. Unfortunately a century later the United States no longer possessed the advantages of geographic insulation and industrial superiority which had always assured victory in the past. Yet the nation, with its interests ill-defined in a general crusade for self-determination, entered a new period of drift after World War II not unlike that of the 1930s. Thereafter through fifteen years of cold war experience American leadership could not prepare the country to accept either the necessity of coexistence with those forces which challenged its principles or the price required for dismantling the world which it could not accept.

Seven

Vietnam: Unanswered Challenge of the Sixties

Never in American history did a single area of conflict dominate the nation's thought on foreign affairs as long and as divisively as did Vietnam during the decade that followed John F. Kennedy's accession to the presidency in January 1961. That this Asian country, recently established and lacking significant military power, could attain such importance suggests a profound dilemma. First, why should the United States have concerned itself for so long and at such heavy cost with the internal affairs of a new Asian state, over 10,000 miles away, without a navy or air force, and with exceedingly limited ground forces when contrasted to those which existed elsewhere even in Asia? On the other hand, why should a small, backward, jungle-ridden country embarrass the United States militarily when this country possessed more destructive power than any nation in history? Even a cursory examination of the 1950s is sufficient to answer the first question; the answers demanded by the second would become clear only with the passage of time.

Spokesmen of the Truman and Eisenhower administrations, by predicting disaster for the globe should South Vietnam fall, transformed that jungle nation after mid-century into a critical area in the struggle against world communism. President Eisenhower, in April 1959, stressed the military importance of Indochina in terms that had long been commonplace: "Strategically, South Viet-Nam's capture by the Communists would bring their power several hundred miles into a hitherto free region. The remaining countries of Southeast Asia would be menaced by a great flanking movement. . . . The loss of South Viet-Nam would set in motion a crumbling process that could, as it progressed, have grave consequences for us and for freedom.'' Such dramatic phraseology, leaving unexplained the process by which the collapse of South Vietnam would actually endanger the United States and freedom, rendered Washington powerless either to give up its commitments to South Vietnam's defense or to create the means required for victory against the demonstrated power and human resources of North Vietnam. Lacking clearly demonstrable interests in South Vietnam upon which they could build a national consensus, successive administrations in Washington attempted to sustain the war by avoiding all the fundamental issues which it raised. The United States drifted into the war, fought it and left it without the benefit of a national decision. It is not strange that the involvement ended in disaster; it could hardly have been otherwise.

THE EISENHOWER LEGACIES IN SOUTHEAST ASIA

President Dwight D. Eisenhower bequeathed to Kennedy not only a deep commitment to the success of Ngo Dinh Diem's Saigon regime but also a dual program designed to gain that objective at a negligible cost to the American people. After 1954 Washington assigned to Diem the major responsibility for containing the ambitions of Ho Chi Minh and the expansion of Communist influence and power into Southeast Asia. To assure Diem's success the administration embarked on a crash program of military and economic aid, including special funds for the resettlement of refugees from North Vietnam. As Diem, with lavish support, slowly brought some order to South Vietnam—in part at the price of sending his political opposition into exile—the enthusiasm of his American adherents exceeded the bounds of propriety. By 1957 Washington officials spoke freely of Diem's "miracle" in South Vietnam. When in May of that year the South Vietnamese president visited Washington, Eisenhower greeted him at the airport and hailed him as one of the truly outstanding leaders of the age. In their subsequent communiqué, the two presidents anticipated the peaceful unification of Vietnam under a freely elected government. Such phrases were intellectually corrupting in both Washington and Saigon, for they created expectations of success that no reasonable expenditure of effort could achieve.

Even then the evidence of the miracle was largely nonexistent. Diem, concerned primarily with the security and well-being of his own regime, had made little effort to democratize his army or to satisfy the demands of the Vietnamese peasants. After 1957 Communist-led guerrillas began to organize the countryside, taking control of village after village until by 1960 they commanded most of the provinces of South Vietnam. The miracle of Vietnam had been a miracle in public relations, but little else. Still Eisenhower wrote to Diem in 1960 on the occasion of the Republic of Vietnam's fifth anniversary:

During the years of your independence it has been refreshing for us to observe how clearly the Government and the citizens of Vietnam have faced the fact that the greatest danger to their independence was Communism. You and your countrymen have used your strength well in accepting the double challenge of building your country and resisting Communist imperialism. . . . Vietnam's ability to defend itself from the Communists has grown immeasurably since its successful struggle to become an independent Republic.

Already terrorism and infiltration had begun to undermine the carefully constructed image of a stable and secure Vietnam. The insurgency spread even more rapidly with the formation of the National Liberation Front (NLF) in December 1960, dedicated to both the liberation of South Vietnam and the unification of the country. Diem continued to play down the Communist threat, for its existence reflected adversely on his leadership and the alleged triumphs of his government. When in 1961 he acknowledged his inability to counter the increasingly open and defiant guerrilla challenge to his regime, he reminded President Kennedy of the long standing American commitment to South Vietnamese independence.

Washington had prepared meticulously for the possible failure of its political strategy, based on Diem's success in eliminating Ho Chi Minh's influence from South Vietnam, by developing a military strategy as well. After September 1954, SEATO carried the military burden of containment in Southeast Asia. The efficacy of that alliance as a guarantor of Southeast Asian stability quickly moved beyond the realm of official doubt. Beginning with the first SEATO Council meeting at Karachi, Pakistan, in 1956, the organization embarked on its program of self-adulation which continued with diminishing restraint into the 1960s. As late as 1962 Secretary of Defense Robert McNamara assured a Congressional committee that SEATO's evolution into a sound military organization had eliminated the need for United States ground forces in any foreseeable Asian conflict. On the occasion of

SEATO's ninth anniversary in 1963 Prime Minister Sarit Thanarat of Thailand recounted the alliance's successes: "At present it may be said that SEATO is an important fortress capable of making the Communists think carefully before committing any aggression against the area under the Treaty [which included South Vietnam]. Since this organization acts as an effective deterrent to potential aggressors, it has increasingly been attacked verbally by the Communists. This indicates how important SEATO is in resisting Communist aggression." Actually SEATO had never functioned; because of internal disagreements over purpose, it could not function as a unit. Nowhere in SEATO was there any force, other than the mobile striking power of the United States, that could resist the encroachments of Ho Chi Minh. But the United States had no greater commitment to action under SEATO than other members of the pact. As the chairman of the Senate Foreign Relations Committee declared on the occasion of the pact's approval: "The Treaty [SEATO] does not call for automatic action; it calls for consultation with other signatories. . . . I cannot emphasize too strongly that we have no obligations . . . to take positive measures of any kind. All we are obliged to do is to consult together about it."

Washington never contemplated a direct American military involvement in Southeast Asia. Still it continued to predict disaster if containment at the 17th parallel should falter. For the moment this chasm between the ends and means of policy mattered little. As long as Ngo Dinh Diem and SEATO guaranteed successful containment at little cost, the administration faced no need to prepare for action or explain what the United States was really containing. But Eisenhower had accomplished none of his purposes in Asia. Diem's regime had not produced the political and economic miracle claimed for it, SEATO did not possess an effectiveness commensurate with the praise that Washington and others heaped upon it, and non-recognition had not eliminated China's Peking regime. When Eisenhower left office in January 1961, the Saigon regime faced disaster everywhere and SEATO had demonstrated its profound ineffectiveness.

KENNEDY'S RELUCTANT RESPONSE TO VIETNAM

Neither President Kennedy nor his foreign policy advisers assumed office with any intention to review critically the policies which they inherited. Anchoring his administration to past assumptions, the new President warned in his inaugural that the United States would "pay any price, bear any burden, meet any hardship, support any friend, oppose any foe to assure the survival and success of liberty." Still he reminded the nation that the instruments of war far outpaced the instruments of peace. If the Eisenhower policies had been popular and apparently peaceful, it was only because those policies held the assurance of success without reference to the price that the United States would pay to render them effective. Confronted with the rapidly deteriorating fortunes of Laos and South Vietnam, the Kennedy administration had either to give up the struggle against Ho Chi Minh or introduce ever larger increments of military and economic support to enable the nation's allies in Southeast Asia to resist the infiltration and insurgency more effectively.

In Laos the situation was explosive. The Eisenhower-backed pro-Western government had no chance against the pro-Communist Pathet Lao guerrilla forces. Still Eisenhower and Dulles refused to compromise the American goal of creating a strong anti-Communist regime in Vientiane. Kennedy recognized the American overcommitment to Laos, but was determined to avoid any humiliation. In March 1961, he warned Peking, Moscow, and Hanoi via television that the United States would not tolerate a Communist conquest of Laos. During April, however, he followed the British and Russian lead in calling a fourteen-nation conference in Geneva to resolve the Laotian question. The conference quickly agreed to a neutralized Laos and instructed Souvanna Phouma to form a coalition government that would include representatives of the right, center, and left in Laotian politics. The new government assumed office in June 1962, but within a year the Pathet Lao elements deserted, driving the neutral center toward the right and subjecting the country to a renewal of the civil war.

Kennedy and his advisers agreed generally that the earlier perceptions of a Moscow-based monolith, which had motivated the initial opposition to Ho, had been inaccurate. But the repeated assertion of an American interest in Vietnam, Kennedy's apologists argued, created a vital American interest which the new President could not ignore. Whether or not the domino theory was valid in 1954, wrote White House adviser Arthur M. Schlesinger, "it had acquired validity seven years later, after neighboring governments had staked their own security on the ability of the United States to live up to its pledges to Saigon." In what had become standard phraseology, Vice President Lyndon B. Johnson, upon his return from Saigon in June 1961, advised the President: "The battle against Communism must be joined in

Southeast Asia with strength and determination to achieve success there—or the United States, inevitably, must surrender the Pacific and take up our defenses on our own shores.'' Vietnam had become symbolic of American trustworthiness and determination. Few Americans, the administration agreed, would accept any diminution of the country's prestige, especially in Vietnam where the perceptions of potential disaster were acute and the possibilities for success were still reassuring. Thus the Kennedy administration refused to question publicly the assumptions and purpose upon which the two preceding administrations had based their commitments to the Saigon regime.

As Saigon's authority continued to deteriorate, Kennedy, in October 1961, dispatched General Maxwell E. Taylor and State Department adviser Walt W. Rostow to Vietnam to gather information for a major reassessment of the American position in Southeast Asia. Taylor, reporting to the President on November 4, accused North Vietnam of aggression and attributed Saigon's military failures to favoritism, inefficiency, and corruption. But to defend the frontier against infiltration Taylor recommended an initial deployment of 10,000 American troops. Taylor's report offered the choice of defeat, reform, or a direct United States military involvement in South Vietnam. Kennedy rejected the first alternative without accepting the third. ''Let me assure you again,'' he wrote Diem, ''that the United States is determined to help Vietnam preserve its independence, protect its people against Communist assassins and build a better life through economic growth.''

With good reason Kennedy hoped to avoid a military solution in Vietnam. From the beginning Secretary of Defense Robert McNamara reminded him that no reasonable American involvement would tip the military scales in Southeast Asia; the United States might well become mired in a land war which it could not win. Kennedy shared that pessimism. He wondered whether the United States would be more successful than the French in winning the support of the villagers, so essential for success against guerrilla forces. ''No one knew,'' Ted Sorenson recalled in *Kennedy,* ''whether the South Vietnamese officers would be encouraged or resentful, or whether massive troop landings would provoke a massive Communist invasion—an invasion inevitably leading either to nuclear war, Western retreat or an endless and exhausting battle on the worst battleground he could choose.'' Responding to Taylor's request for troops, Kennedy complained: ''They want a force of American troops. . . . They say it's necessary in order to restore confidence and maintain morale. But it will be just like Berlin. The troops will march in; the bands will play; the crowds will cheer; and in four days everyone will have forgotten. Then we will be told we have to send in more troops. It's like taking a drink. The effect wears off, and you take another."

Determined to avoid a hard decision, Kennedy committed the nation to victory, but with increments of military and economic aid sufficient only to sustain the administration's objectives, not large enough to require broad national approval. The President had genuine policy choices available; he chose not to exercise them. Politically it was more feasible to entangle the United States gradually, promising with each increment the success which each preceding increment had assured but had failed to deliver. During 1962 the President increased the military aid to South Vietnam from 4,000 American advisers in January to 10,000 by October, while the Secretary of Defense assured the American people that the government had no policy for introducing combat forces into South Vietnam. Thus the Kennedy administration became trapped in a struggle which it dared not lose but could not win. Even such unpromising behavior seemed preferable to any clear alternative. Neither the acceptance of failure nor the pursuit of a decisive victory on Asian soil appeared politically and emotionally bearable. Half-way measures would not bring success, but they would buy time and keep Washington's options open. They would, over the short run, permit the administration to avoid painful decisions; over the long run they might permit some miraculous display of good fortune.

THE SEARCH FOR A STRATEGY

Kennedy required a strategy that would bridge the gap between the goal of victory in Vietnam and the reality of a limited United States involvement. He found it in the political-military program of *counterinsurgency*. During the spring of 1961 the President prepared to increase the effectiveness of the anti-guerrilla activities in South Vietnam. On March 28 he reminded Congress that since 1945 the "most active and constant threat to Free World security" had been guerrilla warfare. To meet the challenge, the United States, he warned, must organize "strong, highly mobile forces trained in this type of warfare, some of which must be deployed in forward areas." The President accentuated the need for responses that would be "suitable, selective, swift and effective." Once the challenge lay in general war. Now the United States required forces that could deal successfully with small, externally equipped guerrilla bands. Reflecting the activist spirit of the New Frontier, counterinsurgency became fashionable, even faddish. Highly skilled and finely trained American units would be more than a match for any competing force, even in the jungles of Asia. Kennedy placed control of the counterinsurgency forces under a Special Group of high-ranking State and Defense officials in Washington. In Vietnam the program achieved little. Washington refused to permit United States troops to move against the guerrillas; despite intensive training the South Vietnamese acquired neither the skills nor the determination required for effective counterinsurgency operations. When United States forces later assumed responsibility for South Vietnam's defense, they reverted to conventional modes of warfare.

Still Washington officials never questioned the capacity of United States conventional forces, with their superior equipment and firepower, to win the battle for the jungles or the cities. In Korea conventional forces had managed to stalemate the war and drive the enemy to the negotiating table. Such military advisers as Maxwell Taylor never doubted their ability to repeat that success, for they assumed that Vietnam, as a battleground between two opposing forces in a divided country, would ultimately be a repetition of Korea, with the enemy succumbing in reasonable time to the power of American arms.

Unfortunately the struggles for power in Korea and Vietnam were scarcely identical at all. When the Eisenhower administration surfeited Saigon with equipment, advisers, and praise after 1954, it assumed that the known South Vietnamese enemies of that regime would either terminate their allegiance to Hanoi or at least, if they chose to resist, do so without any aid or encouragement from the north. At no time did the Eisenhower planning contemplate a war against the North Vietnamese. But the assumption of a limited struggle proved false. Perhaps it is true that Hanoi directed the South Vietnamese insurgency from the beginning. But if true, the fact that the Vietcong would accept the leadership of Ho Chi Minh, declared by Washington to be the enemy of self-determination in South Vietnam, suggested clearly that for them the assault on the Saigon government comprised the continuation of the old nationalist-Communist revolution rather than an external aggression. It is not certain that the Vietcong would court death and destruction in their homeland merely to serve the expansionist interests of another nation. To them North Vietnam was simply not a foreign power.

Thus in at least two important respects the war in Vietnam could not be a repetition of Korea. Unlike Ho Chi Minh, Syngman Rhee, the pro-Western South Korean spokesman for Korean independence and unity, had contributed little to the independence of the Korean people. United States and Russian armies liberated Korea from Japanese control, and following the postwar division of the peninsula at the 38th parallel, Washington handed the government of South Korea to Syngman Rhee. The fact that Ho Chi Minh's revolutionary forces liberated all of Vietnam, North and South, from French rule, dictated from 1954 onward that the 17th parallel could never equal the 38th parallel in significance as a boundary separating two nations. Nor did the quality of war in Vietnam have much relationship to that in Korea. The Seoul government had the fanatical support of the South Korean populace; this permitted the United Nations allies in Korea to establish stable battle lines and to conduct the war as a conventional struggle in every respect. In South Vietnam, however, the enemies of Saigon moved freely through the whole countryside, striking everywhere and anywhere at will, reducing the actual warfare to a primarily civil struggle where success could be measured only by death and destruction, not by territory captured and held. It was not strange that those officials who anticipated a Korea-type war in Vietnam constantly underestimated the nature of the resistance and the difficulties in gaining clear, demonstrable battlefield success.

POLICY WITHOUT END

Kennedy received repeated warnings that the burgeoning United States military involvement in Vietnam would ultimately fail. In July 1962, Nikita Khrushchev observed that the United States had stumbled into a bog in which it would be mired for a long time. Similarly France's Charles de Gaulle, recalling the French disaster in Southeast Asia, warned Kennedy that Vietnam was totally unsuitable for Western tanks and politics. John Kenneth Galbraith, then ambassador to India, argued against the dispatch of American forces to Vietnam or otherwise deepening the American involvement. The New Frontier—Kennedy's domestic program—would drown in the rice paddies of Southeast Asia, he predicted. What encouraged Kennedy and his White House staff to ignore such advice was their common assumption that they could sustain the military operation in Vietnam indefinitely and thereby push a national decision into some unknown future.

Meanwhile Washington exuded confidence, with the private optimism usually following rather than preceding each successive escalation of the American effort. When by 1962 Saigon's progress seemed substantial, official confidence knew no bounds. Following his first trip to Saigon that year, McNamara reported: "Every quantitative measure we have shows we're winning this war." The President summed up the years' success in his State of the Union message of January 1963, "The spearhead of aggression has been blunted in South Vietnam." With the economic and military increments of 1963 the official optimism became even more pronounced. During March Kennedy's Secretary of State Dean Rusk declared that "Government forces clearly have the initiative in most areas of the country." Not long thereafter the Defense Department announced, "The corner has definitely been turned toward victory in Vietnam." Long before the end of the year the war's end was officially in sight. Apparently the long shot was paying off. What sustained this optimism was the army's reporting structure which encouraged every officer at every level to claim nothing but success for the operations under his command.

Still in the absence of any direct United States military involvement in the war, the means for victory lay essentially in Saigon's capacity to organize, staff, and direct a success counterinsurgency campaign across South Vietnam. But it was clear long before 1963 that the Diem regime was the weakest component in the struggle. So determined was Diem's resistance to United States pressure for reform that his regime inspired attacks on the United States in the Saigon press. South Vietnamese leaders in exile warned Washington officials that only some alternative South Vietnamese government, one that better represented the interests of the people, would command the power and respect to stabilize the politics of the country. Kennedy's continued quest for greater political awareness in Saigon received a critical blow when, in the summer of 1963, Diem's repression of the Buddhists threatened the very existence of his regime. In Washington the embarrassed Kennedy admitted, "In the final analysis it is their war. They are the ones who have to win it or lose it. . . . All we can do is help, and we are making it very clear. But I don't agree with those who say we should withdraw. That would be a great mistake." In October, when Diem had alienated the administration in Washington, the Vietnamese generals struck, assassinating Diem and his brother Ngo Dinh Nhu. At that moment the United States had 16,000 troops in Vietnam, with a continuing commitment to victory and no plan of escape.

Whether Kennedy in time would have reversed his policy of escalation remains unclear. One account—that of Kenneth O'Donnell, a White House official—suggests that Senator Mike Mansfield's repeated warnings of disaster in Vietnam had, by 1963, created significant doubts in the mind of the President. According to O'Donnell, Kennedy called Mansfield to his office that spring and acknowledged his acceptance of Mansfield's argument for a complete American military withdrawal. "But I can't do it until 1965—after I'm reelected," Kennedy informed Mansfield. To desert Vietnam's cause early, Kennedy feared, would create a right-wing uprising against his reelection. As he explained to O'Donnell: "In 1965, I'll be damned everywhere as a Communist appeaser. But I don't care. If I tried to pull out completely now, we would have another Joe McCarthy red scare on our hands, but I can do it after I'm reelected. So we had better make damned sure that I am reelected."

LYNDON JOHNSON AND THE MAKING OF AN AMERICAN WAR

Lyndon B. Johnson entered the presidency, following the assassination of John F. Kennedy in November 1963, devoted to both the Kennedy staff and the drifting policies in Southeast Asia. Johnson, like his predecessors, had no interest in defeat. "Lyndon Johnson," he declared emphatically, "isn't going to be the first American President to lose a war." Maintaining a public mood of caution, he warned the nation against any involvement that would tie the United States to a ground war in Asia. "I have not thought," he said, "that we were ready for American boys to do the fight for Asian boys." Nothing would be more disastrous, he added, than to put American soldiers against 700 million Chinese on the Asian mainland. By 1964 those outside the administration who doubted the possibility of creating a successful program for Vietnam from such disparate and conflicting elements were legion. Inside Washington's power structure such voices were few.

Among the inside critics was Under Secretary of State George W. Ball who reminded the new president:

The South Vietnamese are losing the war to the Vietcong. No one can assure you that we can beat the Vietcong or even force them to the conference table on our terms, no matter how many hundred thousand white, foreign troops we deploy. . . . The decision you face now, therefore, is crucial. Once large numbers of U.S. troops are committed to direct combat . . . we will have started a well-nigh irreversible process. Our involvement will be so great that we cannot—without national humiliation—stop short of achieving our complete objectives. Of the two possibilities, I think humiliation would be more likely than the achievement of our objectives—even after we have paid the terrible price.

Johnson preferred the advice of those who argued that the United States had no choice but to pursue the goal of total victory in Southeast Asia. As Senator Richard B. Russell explained to newsmen after a conversation with the President at the LBJ Ranch, "They [the Vietnamese] won't help themselves. We made a great mistake in going in there but I can't figure out any way to get out without scaring the rest of the world." With little hesitation the President determined that any adjustment in the American program would comprise the escalation of means, not the reduction of goals in Vietnam.

During August 1964, following a minor, even doubtful, North Vietnam attack on American naval vessels in the Gulf of Tonkin, Congress, at the President's request, adopted a resolution which seemed to commit that body to any future executive action required to defend the Saigon government. The resolution declared that inasmuch as the security of Southeast Asia was vital, the United States was "prepared, as the President determines, to take all necessary steps, including the use of armed forces, to assist any protocol state of the Southeast Asia Collective Defense Treaty requesting assistance in the defense of its freedom." Johnson's still limited military commitments, no less than his policies generally, reaffirmed his leadership within the Democratic Party and assured his nomination at Atlantic City's Convention Hall. Eventually they won for him and his vice presidential running-mate, Senator Hubert H. Humphrey, an easy victory at the polls in November. At the end of 1964 the administration had 23,000 troops in Vietnam.

Still reluctant to commit American forces to a jungle war, Johnson and his advisers, which now included ambassador to Saigon Maxwell Taylor, decided by late 1964 to await the proper occasion for launching an air war against North Vietnam. That moment arrived on February 7, 1965, when a Vietcong attack on Pleiku, an outpost in the central highlands, killed eight Americans. Even as the President announced the retaliation by air he assured the nation, "We seek no wider war." The bombing, Washington assumed, would undermine the morale of the enemy, halt the infiltration from the North, and encourage resistance in the South. Victory would now be swift and inexpensive; according to official dogma in Washington the bombing would bring Ho to the negotiating table in six weeks, at most ten.

Fundamentally Johnson had commited the United States to a course of military escalation which ultimately would employ United States forces in combat. When the bombing failed to achieve any of its objectives, the President responded by ordering the destruction of more targets. Still the tempo of war increased. It became clear during the spring of 1965 that the United States, to terminate the war, would be forced to destroy the enemy in the jungles. To this end the President discarded the "advisory" role of the 50,000 then under the command of General William Westmoreland in South Vietnam. Finally, at his press conference of July 28 the President announced that the United States personnel in South Vietnam would be increased from the 75,000 already there to 125,000. Should the United States be driven from the field in Vietnam, he warned, no nation again could ever trust the promises of the United States. But he added, "We do not want an expanding struggle with consequences that no one can perceive." The President had again trapped the nation between the need for victory and the abhorrence of fighting a jungle people on the mainland of Asia.

Convinced that American prestige and security were at stake, the President now prepared to escalate the United States military contribution to any level required for victory. At the same time the administration, supported by the computers in the Department of Defense, reassured the country that victory lay beyond each accretion of allied power in Vietnam. The American troop buildup reached 200,000 in 1966 and continued upward until it exceeded 500,000 in 1967. Meanwhile the bombing of enemy targets, north and south, mounted to astonishing proportions. During 1968 the bomb tonnage dropped on Vietnam gradually surpassed by 50 percent that dropped on both Germany and Japan during World War II. That year the price of war exceeded 200,000 American casualties—30,000 dead—and $30 billion a year. What set the limits to escalation even then was the President's informal bargain with the American people that he would conduct the war without asking for increased taxes.

Westmoreland, with little direction from Washington, formulated a plan of operations in Vietnam designed, first, to avert defeat and then to take the offensive with additional battalions. In its final phases, the strategy anticipated victory sometime after 1968 as the United States achieved total military predominance on the battlefield. To achieve victory with reasonable speed Westmoreland assigned the burden of fighting to American forces. Except in the Delta, he used the South Vietnamese forces largely for pacification—the occupation and organization of regions presumably freed of Vietcong control. Washington accepted the notion that Westmoreland's war of attrition, based on air-supported "search and destroy" operations, would break the enemy's resistance. Without battle lines or territorial objectives, American officials resorted to body counts to measure the war's progress and demonstrate the success of allied military operations. Never before had Washington relied so heavily on quantification to judge its battle effectiveness and the probabilities of victory. Still the war continued unabated, with Hanoi, now fully committed to the struggle for the South, matching each new American increment with a continuing escalation of its own. As the war dragged on month after month, the freedom of the enemy, whether Vietcong guerrillas or North Vietnamese regulars, to move through the countryside and strike anywhere and everywhere suggested that the struggle remained generally a civil war in which political, not military, effectiveness was the ultimate measure of success.

Somehow the death and destruction was no guarantee of an independent, non-Communist South Vietnam at all. For that reason McNamara argued for greater efforts to build an effective government in Saigon and improve the pacification effort on the countryside. In 1967 President Johnson gave Westmoreland responsibility for pacification, civil as well as military, and sent Robert Komar to Saigon as Westmoreland's deputy for pacification. Ellsworth Bunker, who replaced Taylor as ambassador in May 1967, refused to distinguish between military and civil pacification. "To me this is all one war," he declared. "Everything we do is an aspect of the total effort to achieve our objective here." At the same time the President sent General Creighton Abrams to South Vietnam to improve the performance of the South Vietnamese military forces. For victory demanded an effective military and political structure in South Vietnam as well as the elimination of all Vietcong and North Vietnamese influence from the country.

THE GREAT DEBATE

Even as the United States embarked on its massive escalation of the war in 1965 some Washington officials suspected that the effort would not succeed. Assistant Secretary of Defense, John T. McNaughton, began his famed memorandum of January 17, 1966: "We have in Vietnam the ingredients of an enormous miscalculation. . . . The ARVN is tired, passive and accommodation prone. . . . The bombing of the North may or may not be able effectively to interdict infiltration. . . . South Vietnam is near the edge of serious inflation and economic chaos. We are in an escalating military stalemate." For McNaughton the only realistic purpose for remaining in Vietnam was the avoidance of humiliation. The United States had remained in

Vietnam to preserve its reputation as a guarantor and thus preserve its effectiveness elsewhere. To avoid damage to its reputation the United States had escalated its involvement to a high level. But McNaughton understood clearly that, in the absence of a national decision, the United States would never bring enough power to bear on Vietnam to terminate the war with any measure of success. Since the issue at stake was the country's reputation, McNaughton warned that the United States not adopt obligations beyond those expected of the nation by those whose opinions comprised its reputation. That reputation required the prevention of Saigon's fall, but not necessarily the prevention of a coalition government or a neutralized South Vietnam.

For the more optimistic—or terrified—McNaughton's goal of reputation-saving was scarcely adequate, although even that limited goal could become frightfully expensive. If Vietnam confronted the world with an incipient global aggression, the United States had no choice but to win totally. President Johnson summarized the basic objective of three previous administrations in his Baltimore address of April 7, 1965: "Our objective is the independence of South Viet-Nam and its freedom from attack. We want nothing for ourselves—only that the people of South Viet-Nam be allowed to guide their own country in their own way." Such a goal, limited as it appeared, demanded no less than total victory over the Vietnamese enemy.

But the United States had a far more pervading objective: the creation at last of a world order free of aggression and all irrational uses of force. John Foster Dulles's doctrine of massive retaliation had been based on the premise that the United States, because of the destructive power which it wielded, could manage or eliminate change in the Afro-Asian world merely by threatening to employ force. Following the Korean truce of July 1953, no high Washington official attached the country's global commitment to Communist containment to the necessity of fighting on the Asian continent. What rendered Dulles's concept of massive retaliation so acceptable to Americans was its guarantee of Afro-Asian stability without the danger of war.

Before 1965 Kennedy and Johnson, no more than Eisenhower, anticipated the need to involve the United States militarily to preserve the Cold War lines of demarcation in Asia. Writing in *The New York Times Magazine* of June 7, 1964, presidential advisor Walt Rostow could claim victory for United States policy in Laos and Vietnam because, he noted, Presidents Kennedy and Johnson had threatened military retaliation to any level necessary to punish those who sought to overthrow the status quo with force. Rostow described the triumph of containment in Southeast Asia in these terms: "The military initiatives with respect to Laos and Vietnam, in pursuit of clearly-defined and limited political objectives, would have had no serious effect on the course of events unless the Communist leaders concerned were convinced that, echeloned behind these limited demonstrations of force, there had been both the capabilities and the will to deal with every form of escalation they might mount in response, up to and including all out nuclear war." Strangely the threat of retaliation to any level, including nuclear war, did not eliminate the subsequent decisions to dispatch over half a million soldiers to Vietnam. Obviously the military formula, based on massive retaliation, did not work.

Herein lay the military burden of Vietnam. Global containment, as it emerged during the 1950s, had never contemplated the destruction of the enemy in a series of wars; rather it sought the prevention of unwanted change through the absolute assurance that any aggression would ultimately fail before the full might of the United States. In short, the objective was the maintenance of the status quo without fighting. But Ho Chi Minh exposed the hollowness of the nuclear deterrent as a controlling element in the politics of Asia. Still the military lessons of Vietnam in no way curtailed the global objectives of the Johnson administration; it merely confirmed the need for some form of victory in Vietnam. The decision to commit the nation's ground forces to Vietnam, thereby destroying the credibility of the nuclear threat, compelled the Johnson administration, if it would maintain the country's global posture, to establish the worldwide credibility of America's conventional power. For a global commitment to the status quo required either global wars or the maintenance of a recognizable threat of retaliation that would eliminate the necessity for demonstrating everywhere the existence of the national will. It was, finally, the administration's search for an effective non-nuclear deterrent that eventually overrode every argument for compromise in Vietnam.

To contain the global pressures of an expansive communism, ran the official argument, the United States would of necessity apply the so-called lessons of Munich. Dean Rusk instructed the American Society of International Law in April 1965 that Western inaction in Manchuria and Ethiopia had demanded the terrible price of World War II. "Surely," he asserted, "we have learned over the past decades that the acceptance of aggression leads to a sure catastrophe. Surely, we have learned that the aggressor must face the consequences of his action and be saved from the frightful miscalculation that brings all to ruin." "In Viet-Nam today," warned Senator Thomas J. Dodd of Connecticut that year, "we are confronted by an incorrigible aggressor, fanatically committed to the destruction of the free world, whose agreements are as worthless as Hitler's. . . . If we fail to draw the line in Viet-Nam, in short, we may find ourselves compelled to draw a defense line as far back as Seattle. . . ." Senator Henry M. Jackson reminded NATO officials in 1966 that "the world might have been spared enormous misfortunes if Japan had not been permitted to succeed in Manchuria, or Mussolini in Ethiopia, or Hitler in Czechoslovakia or in the Rhineland. And we think that our sacrifices in this dirty war in little Vietnam will make a dirtier and bigger war less likely." President Johnson told a New Hampshire audience that men regrettably had to fight limited wars to avoid the need to fight larger ones.

Similarly a Freedom House statement of December 20, 1967, signed by fourteen Asian scholars, warned the nation against failure in Vietnam: "To accept a Communist victory in Vietnam would serve as a major encouragement to those forces in the world opposing peaceful coexistence, to those elements committed to the thesis that violence is the best means of effecting change. It would gravely jeopardize the possibilities of a political equilibrium in Asia, seriously damage our credibility, deeply affect the morale—and the policies—of our Asian allies and the neutrals. These are not developments conducive to a long-range peace. They are more likely to prove precursors to larger, more costly wars." The concept of falling dominoes, placed in the context of Munich, became the most powerful of all governmental appeals for public support during the critical years of military escalation. Yet the enemy so defined, capable, if unrestrained, of bringing war to the world, could not have been Hanoi. It could only have been Russia or China, or both. Yet if the danger lay in Moscow or Peking, the struggle in Vietnam could hardly resolve it. If, on the other hand, the problem lay in Hanoi, whose forces alone did the fighting and dying, what service the language of global disaster could render was equally unclear. Ho, victorious or not, was no Hitler; Hanoi was not another Berlin. How the Vietnamese enemy endangered the peace of the world no one bothered to explain.

Criticism of the war kept pace with official efforts to escalate both the costs and the importance of the struggle. The unleashing of such huge quantities of destructiveness against a jungle population 10,000 miles distant on the mainland of Asia injured the moral sensibilities of millions of Americans and gradually embittered much of the nation as had no previous external experience in its history. Most critics were not pacifists; they agreed readily that the nation had the right to kill those who threatened its welfare or its existence. The domino theory and its variations had defined the enemies of Saigon as dangerous to the security of all Asia and thus of the United States. But those who challenged United States military escalation in Southeast Asia agreed generally that the struggle for Vietnam was largely an indigenous contest to be resolved by the Vietnamese people themselves. Such argumentation reduced the American effort to a largely illegitimate intervention in the internal affairs of another nation and an overcommitment of resources and manpower in an area where United States interests were secondary at best. The critics demanded decisions which varied from a cessation of the bombing of the North to the segregation of all United States forces to enclaves to reduce casualties; to the imposition of a coalition government on Saigon which included all elements involved in that country's struggle for power; or, finally, to a complete withdrawal of all United States forces from Vietnam whatever its effect on that region's political future. Among the war's active critics after 1966 were not only many students, scholars, and writers, but also retired generals of distinction and both Democratic and Republican members of Congress. Many of the war's critics in government and the press had supported the initial United States intervention; they entered the opposition only when it seemed clear that the United States could not win the war in any traditional sense.

THE PARIS TALKS

President Johnson, his advisers and members of his cabinet, defended the war in a massive national effort. Vice President Humphrey, returning in late 1967 from a tour of the western Pacific, announced that United States policy was achieving gains on all fronts. Soon Ambassador Bunker, on a reporting trip to Washington, assured the nation that the allies were achieving steady progress in the war. General Westmoreland added confidently that "whereas in 1965 the enemy was winning, today he is certainly losing." With United States forces standing at a half million, he said, "we have reached the important point where the end begins to come into view. . . ." This optimism mounted until late January 1968, when Rostow informed newsmen in his White House office that captured documents foretold the impending collapse of the enemy in Vietnam. Even as he spoke his staff relayed the news that the Vietcong had unleashed the Tet Offensive, the most destructive enemy attack of the war. General Westmoreland requested an additional 200,000 men while the President's trusted advisers assured him that the Tet losses had finally placed the enemy on the ropes. But for Johnson the end had come. Facing vigorous and determined opposition among Democratic leaders as well as rank-and-file party members, he announced over TV on the evening of March 31, 1968, that he would order a partial halt of the bombing, open negotiations with Hanoi, and withdraw from the presidential race. So thoroughly had been the repudiation of his policies that neither he nor Rusk dared any longer to travel freely and openly around the country.

Late in April the President announced that talks with Hanoi would soon open in Paris, with Averell Harriman acting as chief United States negotiator. Washington heralded the forthcoming exchange as a major breakthrough for peace, but its mood was not compromising. Those who favored the continued escalation of the war in pursuit of victory had not prevented a bombing halt, but they assured the President that Tet had been an enemy disaster and that the improved allied military situation in Vietnam would permit the United States to be demanding in Paris. When the Paris talks opened on May 13, Xuan Thuy, the North Vietnamese negotiator, made clear to Harriman that Hanoi would be no less demanding. He accused the United States of intruding into the affairs of the Vietnamese people and undermining the principle of self-determination by placing its massive military power at the disposition of the Saigon minority. Xuan Thuy repeated Hanoi's insistence that successful negotiations could proceed only after the United States had halted the bombing of all North Vietnam. Clearly the search for peace had scarcely begun.

Recognizing that any political settlement would endanger its existence, the Saigon regime anticipated the Paris talks with considerable anxiety. South Vietnamese Foreign Minister, Tran Van Do, declared in an interview on April 12, "I feel no qualms [about the future] as long as the fighting continues, [but] I look forward to negotiations with serious misgivings." President Nguyen Van Thieu reminded Washington that he opposed any withdrawal of United States forces from Vietnam. Increasingly Saigon made it clear that it would oppose both the recognition of the National Liberation Front (political arm of the Vietcong) as an independent political force and any halt in the bombing short of absolute guarantees from Hanoi. Washington reassured Thieu that the United States would never accept a political settlement for South Vietnam that defied the principle of self-determination. Clearly the answer to the country's dilemma still lay in

Saigon—on Thieu's success in building an effective military and political structure. Secretary of Defense Clark Clifford promised Thieu larger quantities of the best United States equipment. During July Thieu announced that the United States could begin to phase out its forces in 1969; few United States commanders in Washington and Saigon were convinced.

President Johnson's decision to limit the bombing scarcely slowed the pace of war in Vietnam, but it created a mood of euphoria in the United States that all but eliminated the war as a subject of political debate, especially after the Democratic convention at Chicago disposed of the war critics and nominated Hubert H. Humphrey for the presidency. Both Humphrey and Richard M. Nixon, the Republican nominee, promised peace, but both refused to dwell on the means for achieving that purpose. Meanwhile the Paris talks, whatever the hopes which they engendered, did not move the war any closer to a solution. Hanoi refused to compromise its demands for a total bombing halt of the north. Washington, in turn, required some promise from Hanoi of a de-escalation of its war effort in exchange for a bombing halt. Suddenly on November 1 the President announced that new developments (which he failed to explain) had permitted him to halt the bombing of North Vietnam. Simultaneously he declared that within a week the conversations in Paris would be broadened to include the Saigon government and the National Liberation Front.

Washington quickly rediscovered that Saigon was no less a barrier to settlement than Hanoi. Thieu announced that under no circumstances would his government send representatives to a meeting in which the NLF sat as a separate and equal bargaining agent. As he explained to Catholic leaders in Saigon, "[The NLF] will become the winners. . . . Our existence is at stake." Xuan Thuy in Paris insisted that the NLF was the only authentic voice of the South Vietnamese people, but he welcomed a meeting, he informed the press, that included a Saigon delegation. Mrs. Nguyen Thi Binh, heading the new Vietcong negotiating team, arrived in Paris on November 3, warning that the "Vietnamese people will continue their struggle until final victory." The central issue of the war remained unchanged. Who would control Saigon? For the moment, at least, Hanoi and the NLF would accept a coalition government. To Saigon, however, acceptance of the NLF as equals would lead to compromise, and compromise would terminate in disaster.

This deadlock over purpose reduced the Paris negotiations to matters of form, not of substance. United States negotiators rejected

Hanoi's suggestion of a single four-party conference around a single table—whether square, round, or doughnut-shaped. The United States countered with a seating arrangement that suggested a two-sided conference, proposing specifically a green baize barrier taped diametrically across a circular table. The order of speaking, once begun, would rotate around the table. Saigon accepted this proposal, but Hanoi, recognizing in the United States formula an effort to bury the NLF away in a single Communist team, rejected it. When late in November Saigon, under burgeoning United States pressure, agreed to enter the Paris negotiations, one European journalist quipped that the decision would produce "one conference with two sides, three delegations, and four chairs." Vice President Nguyen Cao Ky, heading Saigon's delegation, arrived in Paris only to make clear his refusal to compromise on procedure or protocol.

Finally, in January 1969, the United States and North Vietnamese negotiators in Paris agreed on a seating arrangement for the conference. Their formula consisted of using an unmarked round table, flanked by two rectangular tables for secretaries. There would be no flags or other identifying symbols. The four delegations would sit as two opposing groups, each to be followed in speaking by the other on its side. This seating arrangement permitted Hanoi to claim the presence of four delegations whereas the "AA, BB" speaking sequence permitted Saigon and Washington to claim a two-sided conference.

Even as the Paris confrontation took form, neither side revealed the slightest intention to accept a compromise. The long and costly United States involvement had postponed the necessary political settlement for another half dozen years; it had in no manner created the occasion for an agreement by convincing either Saigon or Hanoi that it could not ultimately emerge victorious. Essentially it was the chasm between the ends and the means of policy that rendered the whole American effort ineffective. The ends of policy upheld the rights and expectations of Saigon while the means, destructive as they were, failed to diminish the goals or the expectations of Hanoi. "The Vietnam story," Adam B. Ulam concluded, "thus brings into full relief the immorality of unrealism in international politics. . . . Much could have been saved in human lives, in human freedom and contentment through the world, if only U.S. policies had been guided by less elevated and more practical goals. . . ."

Within the United States the needed national consensus, favoring either compromise or victory, remained tantalizingly elusive. Ultimately Johnson's Vietnam policies resulted in far more division at home than victory in Asia. The reason is clear. Those policies were anchored to words and emotions, to high promises of success and dire warnings of the consequences of failure, and not to a body of easily-recognizable circumstances, such as the power and ambitions of Hitler, which carried their own conviction and recommended their own responses. It was not strange that the country divided sharply between those who took the rhetoric and admonitions seriously and those who did not. To defend his direct military involvement in Vietnam with a half million men, the President was compelled to exaggerate the importance of that region to the United States and the rest of the world until he had expended more in cost and destruction than the results could justify. Even then the end of the struggle was nowhere in sight.

Eight

The Changing Structure of Peace

To Richard M. Nixon, who assumed the American presidency in January 1969, the world had entered an era of international relations which demanded new initiatives to meet the challenges and exploit the opportunities created by changed conditions. What Nixon detected above all was the increased evidence of national self-assertion which had begun as early as the 1950s. By 1970 its impact on global politics was too pervading to be ignored. Western Europe and Japan had recovered their economic strength and political vitality and pursued policies divorced from and often at odds with those of the United States. The new nations of Asia and Africa, no less than those of Latin America, were determined to find their security and well-being in policies of their own. National self-assertion had shattered the former unity of the Communist bloc as well. All Communist-led countries, in varying degrees, pursued their national interests rather than the ideological goals imposed by the concept of world revolution. By the late 1960s the conflict between the two Communist giants, Russia and China, had become a major factor of international life, creating unforeseen possibilities for United States foreign policy.

Such dramatic changes in the world scene diminished the political and military influence of the United States and the U.S.S.R. in their relations with the outside world. Facing governments increasingly independent, both countries discovered that their early assumptions of an antagonistic, bipolar world no longer conformed to reality. As a result, believed Nixon, the American people desired a more restrained, if still responsible, international role, with other nations assuming a greater portion of the burden of world leadership. The European allies, he insisted, could assume a larger share of their defense. NATO's role would reflect the new multipolarity. "Our alliances," declared Nixon, "are no longer addressed primarily to the containment of the Soviet Union and China behind the American shield. They are, instead, addressed to the creation with those powers of a stable world peace. That task absolutely requires the maintenance of the allied strength of the non-Communist world. Within that framework, we expect and welcome a greater diversity of policy. Alliance does not require that those tendencies be stifled, but only that they be accommodated and coordinated within an overall framework of unity and common purpose."

THE NEW REALITIES OF INTERNATIONAL LIFE

Long before the end of the 1960s the profound changes in international relationships had rendered much of the Cold War irrelevant. The mutual fear of destruction had long dictated the need of the superpowers to avoid direct military confrontation and to liquidate speedily any that occurred inadvertently. The Cuban missile crisis of October 1962 reminded President John F. Kennedy and Soviet leader Nikita Khrushchev alike that such confrontations could inflict civilization with catastrophe; issues which separated them, therefore, dared not be resolved by war. What the perennial pursuit of international objectives which transcended both the power and the interests of the Cold War antagonists achieved was never clear. Perhaps nothing would have demonstrated more clearly the limited choices confronting the great powers than the outbreak of war. Military conflicts in the contemporary world could be limited only by an unequivocal declaration for the continuance of the *status quo* as the object of the involvement—as was done in Korea. But if a nation at war, fighting under the immediate threat of nuclear escalation, faced the simple alternative of announcing the limits of its intentions or inviting a thermonuclear attack, then it was not unreasonable to suggest that it regard negotiable in time of peace what it would, in time of war, regard as negotiable or suffer general destruction. Such limited choices, if seldom acknowledged, accentuated the price that both the United States and the U.S.S.R. paid for their perennial antagonism.

Soviet relations with the Communist bloc had eroded badly, creating problems for the Kremlin that transcended the Cold War. During the 1960s, it became clear that the earlier assumptions of unity in world communism had never been very accurate. The loss of Yugoslavia in 1948, the repression of Hungary in 1956 and of Czechoslovakia in 1968, demonstrated that the authority of the U.S.S.R. reached as far as its military power. That the Soviets could sustain a Communist monolith on free consent was an expensive illusion. The decision of Leonid Brezhnev, Khrushchev's successor, to repress the Czech government verified the power of the Kremlin to impose some measure of conformity on Eastern Europe in defense of its own interests. The Brezhnev Doctrine of November 1968 carried Soviet pretensions in Eastern Europe beyond any previous declaration. Said the Soviet leader: "When the internal and external forces hostile to Socialism seek to turn back the development of any Socialist country toward the restoration of the Capitalist order . . . this is no longer only a problem of the people of that country, but also a common problem of concern for all Socialist countries." The doctrine warned the westerly Communist states against edging too far either toward political and economic liberalization, as had Alexander Dubcek's Czechoslovakia, or toward excessive commercial and political relations with the West.

If Slavic Europe remained the Kremlin's private preserve, it was not monolithic. Rumania, Hungary, and Poland, careful not to threaten Soviet security with anti-Soviet policies and ideologies, had long enjoyed some degree of independence. For Russia the experience of maintaining its hegemony over reluctant and highly nationalistic states was both costly and unpromising. Outside its direct sphere of influence the Soviet Union dominated a number of Communist parties, but always in adverse proportion to the importance of those parties and their leaders. In China the Soviets never exercised control and, after the mid-1950s, very little influence. The Peking regime was fiercely independent in its ideological assertions, its policies, and its behavior. The open Sino-Soviet split after 1960 over matters of ideology and interest did not necessarily weaken either Russia or China militarily, but it re-established for each a powerful, historic antagonist and thereby reduced the ambitions of both toward the non-Communist world.

This burgeoning danger of confrontation with China exposed Russia's western flank where the Soviet hegemony contributed little security. China, with five embassies in Eastern Europe, made every effort to undermine Soviet influence in that region. At best the Russian position in Eastern Europe was unstable; after a quarter century it still rested on the might of Soviet arms. To the west of Poland lay West Germany, a country that could become difficult in the event of a Sino-Soviet war. In 1969, when the Soviets still accused the Germans of revanchism, one young Russian complained: "In two world wars, they nearly defeated us even while fighting on two fronts. But now, it is we who have arranged to have enemies on two fronts—7000 miles apart—and to have antagonized nearly all the nations in the world capable of helping our sick economy." It was not strange that Moscow's failures in Eastern Europe and its preoccupation with Peking encouraged a search for better relations with the United States and Western Europe.

In the United States as well, the costs of the Cold War spiraled beyond what most Americans regarded as an adequate or needed return for their vast expenditure of money and effort. The consumption of some $1.5 trillion over a quarter century had purchased neither peace nor security—at least not on American terms. Nor was the end of the expenditure in sight. What to American critics had sustained the arms race had been the search for absolute security in a world perceived to be profoundly dangerous. This search for security produced defense systems of astonishing destructiveness and sophistication which could never be adequate. Those who had placed American policy on the altar of American power could measure the success of that policy only by the diminution of the danger which encouraged the creation of the power. But twenty years of American Cold War effort had eliminated neither Soviet power nor the Soviet hegemony from Eastern Europe. Nor had the West eliminated the Soviet adherence to Communist dogma.

Long before 1970 the decades of Cold War without victory over either Soviet power or Soviet ideology demonstrated that American security and wellbeing, as well as that of most countries of the world, did not require the restoration of the Versailles order after all. In Europe containment had won. As an end it has stabilized the division of Europe with a vengeance. As a means to an end—the negotiation of a new order in Europe—it had failed simply because no Western military structure could undo the Soviet political and territorial gains which flowed from Hitler's collapse. That the United States had coexisted with a world that did not measure up to its precepts of self-determination with such perennial success and no little security created doubts regarding the wisdom of the search for some more ideological perfect order.

THE REQUIREMENTS OF LEGITIMACY

Such doubts lay at the heart of the Nixon-Kissinger approach to Russia. Nixon accepted advisor Henry A. Kissinger's concept that the foundation of stability was not peace but a generally accepted legitimacy. As Kissinger expressed it in his study of Metternich, *A World Restored:* " 'Legitimacy' . . . should not be confused with justice. It means no more than an international agreement about the nature of workable arrangements and about the permissible aims and methods of foreign policy. It implies the acceptance of the framework of the international order by all major powers. . . ." A legitimate order did not eliminate conflict, but only its scope. Conflicts would be fought, if at all, in the name of the existing order. Agreements could have significance only when they contributed to a "stable structure of peace" which all nations shared and therefore wished to preserve. No international arrangement could succeed unless it harmonized the interests and values of each. In his relations with the Kremlin Nixon hoped essentially to move from the mere assertion to the harmonization of national interests. Still the achievement of a peaceful harmonization necessitated the acceptance by all nations of existing conditions as the basis of international life.

What had made possible the legitimacy of post-Napoleonic Europe was the French renunciation of its previous revolutionary policies and Europe's general retreat from the internationalist ideals of Czar Alexander's Holy Alliance. Nixon accepted the proposition, long seen by others, that the United States had neither the power nor the interest to push back the frontiers of the Communist world. He expressed this sense of limits in his address at the United States Naval Academy in June 1974. "America was no longer a giant," he said, "towering over the rest of the world with seemingly inexhaustible resources and a nuclear monopoly." If the United States could not have its way, it had no choice, believed Nixon, but to act pragmatically, eschewing results that were perfect in pursuit of those that were merely good. At the same time Nixon assumed that the divisions within the Communist world, dominated by the Sino-Soviet conflict, created the possibility that such countries would prefer international stability to revolution. If the U.S.S.R. wanted better relations with the United States, it must recognize the necessity of accepting the existing equilibrium, for as Nixon warned, "if either side sought to gain significant advantage over the other, it would inevitably lead to counter-activities aimed at redressing the balance. That in turn would jeopardize any progress that had already been achieved.'' Behind the Nixon-Kissinger approach to Russia was the fundamental belief that the U.S.S.R. had become or could be enticed to become a non-revolutionary, status quo power.

THE SUMMITS

Behind the summit meetings of the 1970s was a half decade of accumulating conviction that the Cold War drift in an increasingly fluid and restrictive world had ceased to serve the interests of either the United States or the U.S.S.R. The overriding concern of the two superpowers was the avoidance of war. Beyond that was the mutual desire to curb the ruinous arms race. For the Kremlin, questions of economics included as well greater access to Western technology and special trade agreements, supported by ample American credits and most-favored-nation status. Agreements on such questions would ease Russia's grain shortages and narrow that country's overall scientific-technological gap with the United States, Western Europe, and Japan.

On his road to the White House Nixon promised the American people a new age of negotiation. Still his early presidential observations on peace seemed to assure Americans and Europeans alike that any future negotiations with the Kremlin would demand general agreement on the old axiom that change to be legitimate had also to be peaceful. Throughout the Cold War that principle had demanded no less of the Soviets than their acceptance of a reconstituted Versailles order. For a full generation it had ruled out any basic Cold War settlements. Nixon's ultimate decision to discard both traditional Western revisionism toward the U.S.S.R. and the American mission to rid the world of Communist influence was the key to the new era of summitry.

Actually Western revisionism received its first inescapable challenge in West German Chancellor Willy Brandt's *Ostpolitik*. During 1970, after months of negotiation, Brandt signed treaties with both Moscow and Warsaw which recognized the postwar frontiers of Central Europe, acknowledging thereby that Russia, not Germany, had won World War II. By Autumn of that year the corresponding Soviet aim of increased cooperation with the West became apparent to Washington. Meanwhile a sharp crisis in the Middle East, with Syrian forces invading Jordan with Soviet tanks, almost destroyed the fragile Middle East ceasefire of August 1970. Almost simultaneously the Soviets moved submarines into Cuban waters. Such behavior, warned James Reston of *The New York Times*, would drive the President back to his old anti-Communist prejudices. Privately Kissinger reminded the Soviet ambassador that the Kremlin was violating the Khrushchev-Kennedy understanding of 1962 regarding Soviet bases in Cuba. Quickly the Soviets withdrew the submarines to end the crisis. During October 1970, Nixon invited Soviet Foreign Minister Andrei Gromyko to Washington to discuss the prospects for better United States-Soviet relations. That month the President addressed the United Nations and there stressed the need for concrete progress toward a more stable peace.

These limited initiatives produced the critical gains of 1971. In March Brezhnev outlined the new direction of Soviet policy before the Communist Party Congress. Nixon responded cautiously, determined to seek agreement on the broadest possible range of issues to relax tensions on all fronts. In May the President announced an important breakthrough in the ongoing Strategic Arms Limitation Talks (SALT). Then in September the Big Four, after long and tedious negotiations, reached an agreement on West Berlin. That month negotiations produced a draft treaty prohibiting the production or possession of biological weapons. Finally on October 12, 1971, the President announced: "In light of the recent advances in bilateral and multilateral negotiations involving the two countries, it has been agreed that a meeting [between the leaders of the United States and the Soviet Union] will take place in Moscow in the latter part of May, 1972." In November the American Secretary of Commerce began conversations in Moscow on the normalization of economic relations. In his February 1972, foreign policy report to Congress, Nixon explained that he had long believed that he could win the strugggle between the impulses toward hostility and relaxation within the Kremlin. At the same time Nixon reminded the nation that the issues that divided the United States and the U.S.S.R. were both genuine and serious.

During the spring of 1972 Kissinger flew to Moscow to work out guidelines for the summit conference with Chairman Brezhnev. Much of the presummit negotiation remained highly confidential. Following four days of secret talks in Moscow late in April, Kissinger, even as he refused to reveal their content, termed the talks "useful, frank, and satisfactory." Such careful preparations were indispensable to the smoothness and efficiency of the Moscow meeting. That the two powers shared a mutuality of interest in going to the summit received affirmation, at least in part, in the cordiality that characterized both the private and the formal exchanges between Nixon and Brezhnev.

Statesmen and journalists alike heralded the Nixon-Brezhnev meeting a milestone in the history of postwar American-Soviet relations. The actual agreements signed were impressive enough. The Soviet and American leaders sought to bind their two countries together so tightly with joint committees and projects that only with difficulty could remote conflicts of interest produce a direct confrontation. Eventually they arrived at a series of agreements carefully detailed in advance. One included an admission that "in the nuclear age there is no alternative to . . . peaceful coexistence." Others obligated the two nations to continue their quest for arms limitations and closer commercial, economic, scientific, technological, and cultural ties.

To achieve a more stable balance of terror at existing nuclear levels the negotiators at Moscow signed two nuclear arms pacts, one to assure the destruction of populations (as a deterrent) by limiting defensive missiles to two locations. Secondly, they froze offensive weapons to current levels for five years. In large measure this nuclear formula had been reached at the SALT talks during previous months. The Moscow agreements imposed no restraints on the qualitative improvement of existing weapons; thus Secretary of Defense Melvin R. Laird made it clear that expenditures for missile development would not be curtailed. The accords recognized formally the principle of nuclear parity. Henry Brandon of *The Sunday Times* in London noted the significance which Nixon attached to the Moscow agreements: "[W]hat was most reassuring to the President was that the Soviet leadership had finally come to understand the full implications of nuclear war, the need for imposing controls on the arms race, for redoubling the efforts to widen those controls and to grapple with the conceptual problem . . . of how to live with the most powerful enemy in a way that will not jeopardize each other's and everybody else's survival; in short, how to maintain order in the world."

Nixon and Brezhnev opened their Washington summit of June 1973, with mutual pledges to build world peace. During two days in Washington they signed four agreements for cooperation in oceanography, transportation, cultural exchange, and agriculture. The two men then retired to Camp David, Maryland, to focus on nuclear disarmament and troop reductions in Central Europe. Back in Washington they signed additional pacts; one required the two countries to work together when any third country endangered the peace. Their pact to avoid nuclear war they regarded the key to their achievements. Later the two leaders flew to the Nixon home at San Clemente. They terminated their working sessions by completing a 20-page communiqué calling for further détente between the two countries.

Kissinger's well-publicized, but largely futile, trip to Moscow in March 1974, presaged limited success for that year's summit, scheduled for Moscow in June. Disagreements within his own administration on nuclear policy limited Nixon's freedom to offer any formula on nuclear restrictions which the Soviets would accept. Eventually Washington proposed limits on multiple, independently-targetable re-entry vehicles (MIRVs), but the Kremlin failed to respond. The Nixon-Brezhnev agreements at Moscow were modest and failed to include any new arrangement on offensive nuclear weapons. Ultimately the two leaders signed accords to limit underground testing and to restrict to one the number of each country's anti-ballistic missile sites. The 1974 summit was a standoff; still it managed to keep the new relationship on track.

Meanwhile the Conference on Security and Cooperation in Europe (CSCE), meeting periodically, and often ineffectually, since mid-1973, had addressed two questions: a joint NATO-Warsaw Pact declaration against the use of force, and mutual and balanced force reductions (MBFR) across the heart of Europe. The U.S.S.R. joined by its Warsaw Pact allies, had pushed for the all-European conference as early as 1954, seeking through general agreement to legitimize Russia's special interests in Eastern Europe. Not until 1971 did the Communist bloc nations agree to United States and Canadian participation. For two years Washington resisted CSCE, still unprepared to recognize the Soviet hegemony formally. The Helsinki summit meeting of late July 1975, called to ratify the agreements reached by the CSCE, became a major landmark in the history of changing Soviet-American relations.

President Gerald Ford joined 34 other heads of state at Helsinki, Finland, to sign the lengthy document produced over the two previous years. The document itself was a statement of intent; it was not a treaty or a binding agreement under United States constitutional usage. It included ten principles on European security, among them the non-use of force, the inviolability of frontiers, territorial integrity, nonintervention in the internal affairs of other nations, respect for human rights, and the fulfillment of international obligations. The document provided for economic, scientific, technical, and environmental cooperation; for the freer movement of people and ideas; and for a future review conference in Belgrade in 1977. In recognizing officially the Soviet status in postwar Europe, the United States accepted the principle that détente, to endure, had to serve the interests of all.

TOWARD RAPPROCHEMENT WITH CHINA

Throughout the Kennedy-Johnson years, United States relations with China remained tense, at times belligerent. With Khrushchev's success in establishing a more reassuring relationship with the United States China emerged as a separate, but dominant, threat to Asian stability. Long before 1960 the evidence pouring out of Moscow and Peking dramatized the growing tensions between the two countries over a wide range of historic and ideological issues. Symbolically the break came in 1956 with Khrushchev's tirade again Stalin and his plea for a more realistic and less ideological competition between the Soviet and the non-Soviet worlds. China's denunciation of Soviet ideological moderation embraced claims to ideological purity, but it revealed as well vast differences in timing and character between the Russian and Chinese revolutions and the resulting disagreement over national purpose. The Quemoy crisis of August 1958, when Peking coordinated its attack on the Nationalist-held Chinese offshore islands with an effort to invoke its treaty arrangements with the U.S.S.R., clarified the growing divergence in Sino-Soviet perceptions of danger. Soviet abstinence, accompanied by clear warnings that Peking's troubles with the Republic of China were and would remain China's own, demonstrated the limited efficacy of the Chinese-Soviet alliance.

Despite the universal evidence of the Sino-Soviet rift after 1960, the Kennedy administration accepted the previous assumptions and postures regarding China with little attempt at re-examination. To official Washington the Moscow-Peking axis remained united on essentials and therefore dangerous. Secretary of State Dean Rusk denied in July 1961, that the prospects of a Sino-Soviet break could serve as the basis of sound policy. "I think," he declared, "there is solid evidence of some tensions between Moscow and Peiping, but I would use a little caution in trying to estimate the width of such gap as might be developing between them. . . . [H]ere are two great systems of power which are united in general in certain doctrinal framework and which together have certain common interests vis-à-vis the rest of the world." Whatever differences separated Peking from Moscow, the disagreements, ran Washington official view, were over means, not ends. As one administration spokesman remarked in February 1963, "A dispute over how to bury the West is no grounds for Western rejoicing."

Confronted with an escalating war in Vietnam, the Johnson administration became even more determined in its opposition to mainland China. In November 1965, Arthur Goldberg, in customary phraseology, defended the perennial American position before the UN. He denounced Peking for laying down its own conditions for membership. "The oldest of Peiping's conditions," he reminded the Assembly, "is the expulsion of the Republic of China. How can this Assembly even consider meeting that condition?" What mattered even more was China's alleged aggressiveness and its continued defiance of the principles of the United Nations Charter. "The admission of Peiping," warned Goldberg, "would bring into our midst a force determined to destroy the orderly and progressive world which the United Nations has been helping to build over the past 20 years." With arguments unchanged from the days of John Foster Dulles, Goldberg declared that recognition would only encourage Peking in its career of violence. Such assumptions of an aggressive China, responsible for Vietnam and a peril to the rest of Asia, faced no official challenge throughout the Johnson years.

It was Nixon who adopted the argument of the critics that the faltering American effort to isolate 700 million people diplomatically and economically served no useful purpose. Nixon wrote in the October 1967, issue of Foreign Affairs that "any American policy toward Asia must come urgently to grips with the reality of China." As President in 1969 Nixon recognized the need for a better relationship with the mainland as one essential component of a new American foreign policy. "I was fully aware," Nixon recalled, "of the profound ideological and political differences between our countries, . . . But I believed also that in this era we could not afford to be cut off from a quarter of the world's population. We had an obligation to try to establish contact . . . and perhaps move on to greater understanding." Nixon understood that the United States and China shared many historic interests and that the two decades of animosity had been a tragic, perhaps avoidable, aberration. To Nixon China posed a lesser danger than two decades of apocalyptic rhetoric had suggested.

As early as 1969 the Nixon administration, working cautiously through third countries, moved to establish better communication between Washington and Peking. Its efforts were largely unilateral— the granting of Americans the right to purchase Chinese goods without special permission; the validating of passports after March 1970, for travel in China; and the licensing after April 1970, of certain non-strategic American goods for export to China. During his stop in Rumania during October 1970, Nixon for the first time deliberately used Peking's official title, the Peoples Republic of China. Still if the normalization of United States-Chinese relations demanded new attitudes and perceptions in Washington, it required as well conditions elsewhere which would encourage China to identify its deepest interests with that normalization. No American initiatives toward China would have succeeded without the knowledge that they would be received with some graciousness.

Peking responded effectively to Nixon's overtures. During April 1971, in Nagoya, Japan, the Chinese pingpong team invited the American team, competing for the world championships, to visit the Chinese mainland. Prime Minister Chou En-lai addressed the visiting American team: "[W]ith your acceptance of our invitation, you have opened a new page in the relations of the Chinese and American people." Then on July 15 Nixon announced to the press that several days earlier Kissinger and Chou had held private talks in Peking. The premier had invited the President to visit China at some appropriate time before May 1972; Nixon had accepted that invitation. What lay behind the pingpong diplomacy of 1971 was Peking's admission that past antagonisms would prevent any beneficial response to the new, more promising international environment. Among those factors that encouraged the new Chinese pragmatism were the pervading nature of the Sino-Soviet rift, which official American rhetoric had persistently denied; the reemergence of Japan as a major factor in the life of Asia; and the expectation of peace in Vietnam.

Nixon's new approach to China culminated in his trip to Peking in February 1972, and the establishment of a permanent American liaison office in Peking during 1973. By acknowledging the legitimacy of the Chinese government—which four previous administrations had refused to do—Nixon expected Peking to accept the legitimacy of the existing diplomatic order and the limits of proper political conduct. Late in 1971 the Peking government replaced the Republic of China in the United Nations without producing distress among the American people or bringing disaster to either the UN or the free nations of Asia. Fortunately the earlier tensions never disintegrated into open conflict. Yet the perennial posture of nonrecognition and the language which underwrote it were not without their costs. For as Walter Lippman observed, they made China the enemy and propelled the country into a wide variety of treaties and guarantees around the eastern fringes of the Pacific with consequences which could require a generation to correct.

That the President's new diplomacy enjoyed the almost universal approval of the American people was not strange. For many the older attitudes and intentions toward mainland China, defended with such flamboyant phraseology, never made much sense. Indeed, that language belonged largely to a minority which had a direct political and emotional stake in this country's special attachment to the Republic of China. Long before the seventies the charges of Chinese aggression ceased to carry much conviction. William Pfaff argued in *The New Yorker* of June 3, 1972, that Nixon's initiatives merely capitalized on a suppressed popular impulse for change. "It reversed," wrote Pfaff, "an American China policy that under a succession of previous Administrations had delivered blows, bluster, and grand denunciations in the name of democracy and liberty. That way of conducting ourselves before the world . . . had become so corrupt in recent years, so sterile and thick with hypocrisy, that the country was ready for some Metternichian realism. . . ."

Clearly the Asia of the seventies scarcely resembled the former vision of a continent engulfed by a dangerous and revolutionary bipolar conflict. The developments of the early seventies suggested that the lines of major tension in Asia were receding before a realignment of world power. Washington's initiatives toward Moscow and Peking in 1972 encouraged Japan to establish closer relationships with both China and Russia. Japan's influence in Asia expanded with that country's trade and investment around the continent's eastern and southern rim. For hard economic reasons the powerful bonds between the United States and Japan showed signs of strain. China and the U.S.S.R. were in direct confrontation everywhere across Asia. As early as 1969 Moscow offered defense pacts to the countries of Southeast Asia against an allegedly aggressive China. Peking retaliated in 1972 by inviting the United States to maintain its bases in Southeast Asia as a guarantee against Soviet encroachment.

Much of the President's new pentagonal world embraced Asia where four powers competed in a fluid relationship. Nothing dramatized more clearly the revolution in the American perception of Asia and the world than the President's assumption of a new balance of power. "We must remember," he declared in January 1972, "the only time in the history of the world that we have had any extended period of peace is when there has been a balance of power. . . . I think it will be a safer world and a better world if we have a strong, healthy United States, Europe, Soviet Union, China, Japan—each balancing the other. . . ." Thereafter the new American outlook toward Asia set the stage for a limited, ordered relationship with China. What continued to marr that relationship as late as 1975 was the issue of Taiwan where the United States perpetuated its special arrangements with the Republic of China, and the continuing American pursuit of détente with the U.S.S.R., a country which the Chinese viewed as a special danger to their interests and security in Asia.

NIXON'S PROGRAM FOR VIETNAM

In Vietnam Nixon inherited a disastrous policy without a guiding strategy for victory or withdrawal. But the new President was determined to succeed where previous administrations had failed. Kissinger had outlined a plan for disengagement without defeat in the January 1969, issue of *Foreign Affairs*. For the next four years every Nixon proposal began with Kissinger's two-track formula, one seeking a military settlement, the other a political solution for South Vietnam. The former required a stronger South Vietnamese army to permit the gradual withdrawal of United States forces; the second, Saigon's willingness to broaden its base so that it might meet the Communist challenge more effectively. For Kissinger the dual approach presaged a rapid and honorable disengagement. "Give us six months," he told a group of Quaker critics, "and if we haven't ended the war by then, you can come back and tear down the White House fence." Kissinger no less than others regarded the American escalation of the Johnson years a tragic blunder. Still he believed that a great nation had no choice but to maintain even a mistaken commitment. "However we got into Vietnam, whatever the judgment of our actions," he warned, "ending the war honorably is essential for the peace of the world. Any other solution may unloose forces that would complicate prospects for international order."

Why Kissinger's approach to Vietnam would fail was clear as early as January 1969, when Nixon dispatched Henry Cabot Lodge to Paris and instructed him to call for a military withdrawal of all American and North Vietnamese forces from South Vietnam. Washington and Saigon hoped thereby to end the fighting with minimum changes in the political structure of South Vietnam. Indeed, the South Vietnamese negotiators in Paris denied that the peace conference had any right to decide the political future of South Vietnam at all. But Hanoi and the NLF, having pursued nothing other than the destruction of the Saigon regime, insisted that a political settlement must precede any withdrawal of military forces. The power of the insurgency to influence the political future of South Vietnam lay in its military effectiveness, not in its capacity to win an election. As long as Saigon would concede its enemies no chance to gain power by political means, Hanoi and its allies had no choice but to accept a settlement dictated by Saigon or continue to struggle. Hanoi warned the Nixon administration that it would fight rather than recognize the Saigon regime or American military superiority on the battlefield.

During February Kissinger received a massive bureaucratic report on Vietnam which revealed almost total disagreement and confusion within the government on every aspect of the American involvement. The war was a sinking tragedy, but United States officials were still determined to find some escape without capitulating. What changed under Nixon were the means whereby the United States would achieve the success it required. Upon his return from Saigon in March, Defense Secretary Laird informed Congress that the United States would soon increase the fighting capacity of the South Vietnamese army beyond the levels contemplated by the previous administration. Johnson had sought only sufficient combat capacity to permit Saigon to cope with internal insurgency after the achievement of peace. But Laird ordered the creation of South Vietnamese combat forces capable of replacing Americans in the continuing war itself. When the South Vietnamese army had achieved self-sufficiency, there would be a reduction of American forces. By promising both victory and the eventual de-Americanization of the war, Laird had created the foundations of an acceptable Vietnam policy.

To reassure South Vietnamese President Thieu that the United States would never negotiate away his country's right to self-determination, Nixon conferred with him on Guam in June 1969. There Nixon announced his decision to withdraw an initial 25,000 men from Vietnam by August 1969. In September the President announced a second troop withdrawal. Still it was not apparent that the South Vietnamese army had achieved any greater capacity to handle the military burden. Critics argued that Vietnamization would never succeed militarily and that no amount of military pressure would modify Hanoi's demands. Six Rand Corporation analysts warned in early October: "Even if a new strategy should produce military successes in Vietnam, substantially reduce U.S. costs and dampen domestic opposition, Hanoi could not be induced to make any concessions—so long as they implied recognition of the authority of the Saigon government.'' Throughout the autumn of 1969 the antiwar movement centered on the campuses where student activists organized the nationwide moratorium on October 15 and the giant mobilization on Washington a month later.

Nixon met the student challenge head-on with a nationally televised speech on November 3. In this massive effort to win popular support, the President argued effectively that the nation had two choices if it would end the war, either ''a precipitate withdrawal of all Americans from Vietnam without regard to the effects of that action'' or a ''search for a just peace through a negotiated settlement if possible, or through continued implementation of our plan for Vietnamization if necessary. . . .'' The President quickly disposed of the first alternative, for certainly the American people would never accept disaster for South Vietnam and the cause of peace. The American stakes in Vietnam still demanded victory. But Vietnamization combined with the gradual withdrawal of American forces, the President promised, would bring the war to a successful conclusion whether the peace negotiations in Paris succeeded or not. By posing two alternatives, one promising victory and peace, the other presaging humiliation and disaster, the President aroused the overwhelming support of the silent majority. Again he managed to skirt the alternatives posed by the war's critics—a modification of the Saigon regime or a war without foreseeable end. Not without reason South Vietnam's president declared the speech ''the greatest and most brilliant I have known a United States President to make.''

CAMBODIA AND AFTER

Nixon had neutralized the antiwar appeal to the nation's silent majority and guaranteed himself the support of Congress. But seven months later, with his Cambodian venture of May 1970, he ran the risk of losing that support. His rationalization of Cambodia did not convince his critics, but it kept the nation in line. The movement of North Vietnamese men and supplies into Cambodia, he said, gave the United States no choice but ''to go to the heart of the trouble. That means cleaning out major North Vietnamese and Vietcong occupied sanctuaries which serve as bases for attacks on both Cambodia and American and South Vietnamese forces in South Vietnam.'' The action, he warned, was indispensable for the success of Vietnamization and the achievement of a just peace. The President had moved, finally, to protect American prestige. "It is not," he said, "our power but our will and character that is being tested tonight. . . . If we fail to meet this challenge all other nations will be on notice that despite its overwhelming power the United States, when a real crisis comes, will be found wanting."

Beyond the destruction of food and munitions the gains from the Cambodian operation were not clear. The enemy's main line units had moved into the heart of Cambodia, taking most essential material with them. Despite their estimated losses, the North Vietnamese had far greater numbers in Cambodia at the end of June than earlier, and had expanded their control over a much larger area of Cambodia and Laos. During July they returned to their sanctuaries along the South Vietnamese border. That summer American planes flew a hundred sorties a day into Cambodia. Costs remained limited, but the Cambodian venture had transformed that country into a battleground and increased the scope of America's involvement in Southeast Asia.

During July 1970, the President opened his new peace offensive by naming former ambassador to England, David K. E. Bruce, as chief negotiator in Paris. Unfortunately successful negotiations required a new formula far more than a new negotiator. To break the deadlock Nixon offered a cease-fire in place but insisted that control of the political negotiations be left with Saigon. Predictably the Communist negotiators in Paris rejected the proposal outright. They insisted that Saigon accept them politically in the south before they would agree to a cease-fire and a mutual troop withdrawal. The basic conflict had not changed. Nor would it in the future. As late as June 3, 1971, Bruce complained in Paris: "We seek an end to the killing now, even before the other military and political issues are resolved. You insist that the fighting and killing go on unless and until the political and military issues are resolved entirely in your favor."

Faced with resistance that would never end, Washington had no choice but to compromise or to claim ever greater success for Vietnamization. Not even the disastrous South Vietnamese retreat from Laos early in 1971, following a dismal effort to close the Ho Chi Minh Trail, placed any curbs on official American rhetoric. Ambassador Ellsworth Bunker assured the American Chamber of Commerce at Saigon in February: "The Vietnamese armed forces have grown in strength and effectiveness. . . . In pacification, the emphasis has shifted from expansion to consolidation. Constitutional government has been strengthened." On April 7, 1971, President Nixon informed the nation via television that the South Vietnamese incursion into Laos had been more damaging to the North Vietnamese than the 1970 operations in Cambodia. "Consequently," he concluded, "tonight I can report that Vietnamization has succeeded." A month later Assistant Secretary Marshall Green told a House committee: "Security in Viet-Nam has greatly improved. Pacification continues to move steadily forward. . . . Vietnamization is succeeding." In his annual foreign policy report of February 1972, the President again boasted, "As our role has diminished, South Vietnam has been able increasingly to meet its own defense needs and provide growing security to its people."

Long before his reelection campaign in 1972 Nixon had eliminated Vietnam as a troublesome political issue. If the war raged on, the President's Vietnamization program had successfully shifted the burden of American involvement from the ground to the air. Indeed, beginning in early 1971 the administration had unleashed on Vietnam the heaviest air war in history. This permitted extensive troop withdrawals and a precipitous reduction in American casualties. By early 1972, the United States had less than 200,000 troops in Vietnam—a decrease of almost 400,000 from the Johnson years. The President promised to continue troop withdrawals until he reached the goal of a residual force of some 30,000. Having proclaimed Vietnamization a success, Nixon offered to terminate all United States war activity in Vietnam and withdraw all American troops in four months if Hanoi agreed to an internationably supervised cease-fire and the release of all American prisoners.

Nixon's Vietnam strategy rendered the Democratic leadership vulnerable on the war issue. In 1972, Americans rejected any policy that threatened the existence of the Saigon government. Stewart Alsop attacked the bipartisan maneuver in Congress to cut aid to South Vietnam. "To force those who have fought on our side to surrender," he wrote, "would be a terrible betrayal, an act of gross immorality." Democratic Presidential candidate George McGovern's long-standing opposition to the war comprised no threat. But when frontrunning Edmund Muskie, in February, unveiled his peace plan for Vietnam, the administration responded fiercely with the charge that he was undermining the government's peace strategy in Paris. Muskie's warning to Saigon that the United States would not support the war indefinitely exposed him to accusations that he was prepared to accept defeat in Southeast Asia. Clearly the President had full command of the Vietnam issue.

FAILURE IN SOUTH VIETNAM

Twice during Nixon's first term the Senate passed amendments that would have eliminated funds for the Vietnam war and compelled the president to withdraw American forces. The House refused to agree on the ground that such restrictions were an improper abridgement of the President's authority to conduct foreign policy. During January 1973, House Democrats, by a vote of 154 to 75, and Senate Democrats, by a vote of 36 to 12, resolved to pass legislation that would end the Indochinese involvement. Still the Democrats in Congress faced the widespread notion, encouraged by the President, that such action would destroy the peace efforts in Paris. Nixon's advantage was still profound. If the cease-fire negotiations failed, the administration's critics would carry the responsibility. If the negotiations succeeded, their warnings that the cease-fire would not produce a genuine settlement mattered little, for any agreement that achieved a return of all United States prisoners and extricated the United States from the war would be overwhelmingly acceptable to the American people. On January 27, 1973, the four Vietnam belligerents signed the cease-fire agreement for Indochina that provided for the return of all American prisoners and the withdrawal of all United States military personnel in 60 days. Nixon could scarcely conceal his resentment toward those editors and congressmen who refused to praise his "peace with honor." But the critics could see little honor in the 10-year American involvement. Nor would they agree with the President that American withdrawal from the war was synonymous with peace. The war, they predicted, would continue.

This cease-fire, in large measure, left the struggle for Vietnam where Americans had found it twelve years earlier. In those years the United States had sent two million men to Vietnam; in its long pursuit of victory it had spent some $150 billion. Now it had retreated from the war with no more than its returned prisoners. Again North and South Vietnam faced each other in a conflict that knew no political or territorial bounds. There had been change; the Vietnam of 1973 was not that of 1961. Combatants could not fight a war of that magnitude, tearing apart so much of the countryside and creating over two million refugees, without effecting some transfer of power. But whether the effort had given Saigon the political and military energy to survive was doubtful. Nothing which the United States had done diminished the goals of either Saigon or Hanoi. Saigon still avoided the reality that Ho Chi Minh had freed all Indochina from French rule and that after 1954 the South Vietnamese regime had attempted to snatch victory from defeat—an objective sustained only by the burgeoning commitment of the United States. For a dozen years the United States had fought in Vietnam without coming to grips with the Vietnamese challenge at all.

After January 1973, Nixon's purpose in Cambodia was the negotiation of a cease-fire between the Lon Nol government in Phnom Penh and its enemies. By April the cease-fire was still nonexistent and the level of fighting around the capital had increased. The president responded to the continued insurgency with another massive air offensive, although administration spokesmen admitted that bombing targets were scarce. What disturbed some members of Congress was Secretary of Defense Elliot Richardson's assertion that the administration would continue the bombing whether Congress authorized the expenditure or not. The president, he said, would reduce troop levels in Europe, if necessary, to cover the cost of the Cambodian operation. Convinced that the administration's war in Cambodia had no constitutional support, Senate leaders, Republicans and Democrats alike, introduced measures to cut off funds for any military action in Cambodia that was not specifically approved by Congress. During May a Gallup Poll revealed that almost 60 percent of the American people disapproved of the Cambodian bombing and that over 75 percent believed that the president should seek congressional approval before carrying out any additional military action in Southeast Asia. Clearly the president's policy in Cambodia was doomed.

Republican leaders in the House hoped to head off a vote that would curtail the president's authority, but in mid-May the House voted 219 to 188 to prevent the Pentagon from using appropriated funds to carry on the bombing. Then by a vote of 224 to 172, it forbade the use of money in a $2.9 billion supplemental appropriation bill anywhere in the vicinity of Cambodia. Early in June the Senate attached a restrictive rider to a $3.4 billion supplemental appropriation bill that, its backers believed, the president dared not veto. The House passed the measure and then attached it to the even more vital appropriation bill for funding the operations of government. The president vetoed the first bill, declaring that it would undo his work in obtaining an honorable peace in Indochina. "We are now involved," he warned, "in concluding the last element of that settlement. It would be nothing short of tragic if this great accomplishment, bought with the blood of so many Asians and Americans, were to be undone by Congressional action." It was this argument that had sustained his control of Congress and the public through four years. This time it failed. Congress moved rapidly toward a showdown with the president. It began to attach riders restricting the use of federal funds in Cambodia to increasingly

essential financial legislation until the administration had either to ca-
pitulate or see the whole government grind to a halt. Finally the House
and Senate agreed to the president's proposal of a cutoff on August 15.
That day the long American war in Southeast Asia came to an end.

Thereafter Nixon preserved the United States commitment to
Saigon with secret promises of aid, under the continuing assumption
that the perpetuation of that regime would guarantee the peace of Asia.
Publicly Kissinger, Secretary of State since September 1973, insisted
that the United States had no formal commitment to South Vietnam,
but he informed Congress that the long involvement in Vietnam bound
the country, politically and morally. For that reason, he said, the
United States must continue its support of Saigon as long as it was
needed. During May 1974, the Senate reduced the Vietnam appropriation from $2.4 billion to $1.1 billion. The administration reacted bitterly. Said one official: "We believe that whether or not we adequately
support South Vietnam . . . will be an index of our reliability to our
allies. And should that reliability be called into question, the global effects could be most dangerous to our national security."

Throughout the spring of 1975 the inexorable disasters in South
Vietnam created a profound moral and intellectual crisis in Washington. A decade of official United States policy was approaching the
end long predicted. Still Kissinger and the administration battled
Congress into March and April for military aid appropriations to save
the South Vietnamese and Cambodian regimes. Vice President Nelson
A. Rockefeller predicted the extermination of a million Vietnamese in a
Communist takeover. If that were true, only a genuine, permanent victory for Saigon would prevent it, something which no one contemplated any longer. Kissinger led the attack on Congress for its refusal
to appropriate the requested $722 million in military aid for Cambodia
and South Vietnam. What kind of people, he asked, would deliberately
destroy an ally? Arguing against the principle of "selective reliability,"
he warned that any break in the American effort would cause the whole
international order to collapse.

Even as the Secretary described the fall of Saigon an event of
potentially cataclysmic significance, he refused to recommend the
commitment of a single American soldier to save it. Never had the gap
between words and policy been greater. Throughout the crisis the
administration hoped less to save Saigon than to effect a graceful escape from its self-imposed dilemma. The overriding task of 1975 was
that of assuring the world that whatever the outcome of the Indochina
struggle, it would not be the fault of the United States. As one United
States official in Cambodia explained, "Sometimes you have to go

through the motions. Sometimes the motions are more important than the substance.'' To the end every move to save Vietnam was designed to avoid a decision. But if United States interests demanded a graceful withdrawal from Southeast Asia under conditions of political stability, why did Washington fail to encourage the Saigon and Phnom Penh regimes to seek a political settlement with their insurgent enemies while they still possessed some bargaining power? And if the military and political resiliency of these two pro-American governments was essential to the satisfactory solution of the Southeast Asian problem, why did the United States not insist on a higher level of honesty and efficiency in those governments? To attach this nation's global standing to regimes at once weak and inflexible could lead only to disaster.

As Ambassador Graham Martin, in a final demonstration of the American failure, left the embassy roof in Saigon aboard a helicopter, analysts and writers who had predicted such an ending for a full decade reminded the American people that the evidence of continuing disaster had been available no less to those in Washington who had carried the nation into Vietnam. Still the administration assumed no responsibility for what it and previous administrations had done. In late April 1975, Kissinger explained why the long Vietnam experience would sink into history without compensation even in some form of public enlightenment. ''I think this is not the occasion, when the last American has barely left Saigon,'' he told newsmen, ''to make an assessment of a decade and a half of American foreign policy, because it could equally well be argued that if five Administrations that were staffed, after all, by serious people, dedicated to the welfare of their country, came to certain conclusions, that maybe there was something in their assessment, even if for a variety of reasons the effort did not succeed. . . . [S]pecial factors have operated in recent years. But I would think that what we need now in this country . . . is to heal the wounds and to put Viet-Nam behind us and to concentrate on the problems of the future. . . .'' If the American people would demand no explanation of a disastrous policy at the moment of its collapse, they would not do so thereafter. For them no less than for official Washington Vietnam no longer mattered.

THE LIMITS OF DÉTENTE

Whatever the damaging impact of Vietnam on Kissinger's reputation, his successes in dealing with Russia and China perpetuated through 1975 his reputation as Washington's dominant personality and, for some, the country's most successful Secretary of State in the twentieth century. Kissinger sought essentially to negotiate a formal diplomatic settlement of the Cold War. More than his predecessors he was willing to accept changes wrought by the Russian victories of 1944 and 1945. He refused to criticize the Kremlin for its repression of Eastern Europe and its failure to liberalize the Soviet political system. Much of his success, therefore, hinged on his lack of public concern for human rights inside the Soviet bloc, although he insisted that he could serve those rights more effectively with policies aimed at relaxation rather than tension. Countless Americans, tired of Washington's perennial Cold War posture which seemed to achieve little beyond a stabilized Europe, agreed. For them Kissinger's diplomacy was credible, even praiseworthy.

But Kissinger's pursuit of détente with the U.S.S.R. troubled a wide spectrum of analysts and observers. Some denied that the Soviet Union had become a fundamentally status quo power. Harvard Historian Richard Pipes spoke for many when he observed, "The Soviet aim is world hegemony at nothing less than the level that Britain occupied in the nineteenth century." Those who shared that perception of the Soviet threat could discover no gains from détente. If the United States lost little in legitimizing the Soviet hegemony, it received little in exchange. Indeed, for some critics détente was synonymous with sellout. Every agreement, they charged, enhanced Russia's global position. Thus the pact to eliminate nuclear war merely encouraged new Soviet expansionist ventures in Asia, Africa, and Latin America.

Equally disturbing for some Americans was Soviet naval expansion which managed to transform Russia for the first time into a genuine global power. Whereas the United States appeared to reduce its world commitments and slow its arms program, the Soviet Union seemed determined to extend its leadership in certain categories of military power and to enlarge the area of its activities. Former Secretary of Defense James Schlesinger warned the country in March 1976, that it had not faced a threat of such magnitude since the 1930's. Former State Department officials Paul H. Nitze and Charles Burton Marshall observed in the February 8, 1976, issue of *The New York Times* that the profound disagreements on the meaning of peace which had underwritten the Cold War would demand a strategic approach to peace as long as they continued. "Détente has brought changes," they wrote, "but their sum amounts to modification and not mutation of relationships. The main change involves tone of discourse. In the United States version, détente dwells upon concord, however slight, and soft-pedals differences, however basic. . . . By blunting people's sense of distinction between favorable and adverse trends, the general effect is to produce dull indifference." Détente, even its adherents admitted, was an ill-chosen word, creating expectations beyond those justified by past agreements. In practice détente proved to be another name for peaceful coexistence, with all the limited expectations which that term implied.

Defined as competitive coexistence détente suffered little loss of support. It was not clear how the country would pursue anything less. "Foreign policy," Kissinger declared in November 1975, "must be based on reality, not rhetoric, and today's reality is that we live in a world of nuclear equality. . . . It could not have been prevented; it cannot be ignored or reversed by unilateral decision. It means that we must manage a fundamental conflict of values in the shadow of nuclear holocaust. We are striving to preserve peace while defending our essential principles and interest." Defending his policies against Republican and Democratic challengers alike, Kissinger reminded the nation again at Boston during March 1976, that the capacity of both superpowers to devastate the world in a few hours compelled the administration to guard its relations with the Kremlin. None of the critics, the Secretary complained, were very specific in enumerating Soviet gains and American losses. Nor did any of them suggest a precise alternative to administration policy.

For Washington the central challenge to foreign policy remained that of determining what changes on the world scene threatened the international order and thus the security of the United States. In its initial approaches to Russia and China the Nixon administration had assumed that both Communist powers had accepted the legitimacy of the existing order. On that assumption the United States sold millions of tons of grain to the U.S.S.R. and negotiated numerous agreements designed to avoid direct confrontation with that country. At the same time the United States battled the recipients of Soviet aid in Asia and Africa as if they were indeed a threat to the international order. It did so again during 1975 when the Soviets, using Cuban mercenaries, backed the victorious faction struggling for control of Angola. Congress quickly terminated the administration's burgeoning effort in what it regarded as an unpromising and unnecessary cause. The repeated American reverses in the Afro-Asian world, noted Georgi Arbatov, director of the Soviet Academy of Sciences Institute of United States and Canadian Studies, "are connected with the invariable U.S.

stand in defense of obviously doomed undertakings and regimes, be it South Vietnam or the groupings in Angola operating in alliance with the South African racists and colonialist mercenaries. It is not the Soviet Union that is responsible for this, but the traditions and survivals of the Cold War and blind anti-Communism inherent in it." Nationalism, not communism, remained the dominant force in determining the purposes and behavior of peoples.

Still Washington continued to oppose change that appeared to favor any Communist cause. Kissinger warned the Italian and French governments that NATO could not tolerate the participation of the burgeoning Communist parties of their countries in member governments. Enrico Berlinguer, head of the Italian Communist Party, accused Washington of interfering in Italy's internal affairs. "We favor membership in NATO and friendship with the U.S.A.," he said. ". . . What does Washington want for Europe and Italy?" In March 1976, Kissinger warned the Kremlin that the United States would oppose any further Angola-style Soviet interventions. "We can never tolerate a shift in the strategic balance against us," he said, "either in unsatisfactory agreements, violations of agreements, or by neglect of our own defense requirements. . . . [W]e are determined to defend peace by systematic resistance to pressures and irresponsible actions." The Secretary informed Congress that any further Cuban action in Africa would endanger the security of the United States. In its concern for global defense against communism in all its forms, the United States, with few exceptions, exerted no pressure toward freedom and humaneness in those governments that it supported.

Through the long Cold War the Soviet-American competition in Asia and Africa had proved costly and unsatisfactory for both countries. The Soviets gained little from their perennial efforts to influence China and the Middle East; it was not clear that they would achieve more in Africa. To oppose communism in Asia the United States inflicted grievous injury on itself without reaping any commensurate rewards. Amid the burgeoning changes of the sixties and seventies the two superpowers controlled less and less as major and minor states asserted interests of their own. The nations of the world, for better or worse, had long been moving in directions that had no relationship to world communism, liberation, or containment. Only those Slavic countries under direct Soviet control had not stepped fully out of the roles to which the great powers had assigned them at the dawn of the Cold War. But the new independence and diversity of international life did not serve the United States badly. For this country's essential concern for world stability received reinforcement wherever sovereign nations pursued their own interests and displayed some willingness to defend their borders. If the resulting restraints on national power and influence were severe, they did not eliminate the possibilities for effective action where it mattered.

PART TWO

Documents

1

Cordell Hull's Radio Address, April 9, 1944[1]

Perhaps no speech of the war years illustrates bettter the purposes and hopes of American leadership in fighting the war than Hull's speech over the Columbia Broadcasting System on April 9, 1944. To Hull the United States, with its Allies, was seeking victory to establish a world based on the principles of the Atlantic Charter. Only the necessity of defeating Germany and Japan permitted the Secretary of State to obscure the incompatibility between the purpose of achieving Soviet compliance with this peacetime goal and the demonstrated Russian desire to maintain some tangible evidence of victory.

. . . In talking about foreign policy it is well to remember, as Justice Holmes said, that a page of history is worth a volume of logic. There are three outstanding lessons in our recent history to which I particularly wish to draw your attention. In the first place, since the outbreak of the present war in Europe, we and those nations who are now our allies have moved from relative weakness to strength. In the second place, during that same period we in this country have moved from a deep-seated tendency toward separate action to the knowledge

1. Leland M. Goodrich and Marie J. Carroll (eds.), *Documents on American Foreign Relations, July 1943–June 1944* (Vol. VI, Boston, 1945), pp. 25–35.

and conviction that only through unity of action can there be achieved in this world the results which are essential for the continuance of free peoples. And, thirdly, we have moved from a careless tolerance of evil institutions to the conviction that free governments and Nazi and Fascist governments cannot exist together in this world because the very nature of the latter requires them to be aggressors and the very nature of free governments too often lays them open to treacherous and well-laid plans of attack. . . .

The allied strength has now grown to the point where we are on the verge of great events. Of military events I cannot speak. It is enough that they are in the hands of men who have the complete trust of the American people. We await their development with absolute confidence. But I can and should discuss with you what may happen close upon the heels of military action.

As I look at the map of Europe, certain things seem clear to me. As the Nazis go down to defeat they will inevitably leave behind them in Germany and the satellite states of southeastern Europe a legacy of confusion. It is essential that we and our Allies establish the controls necessary to bring order out of this chaos as rapidly as possible and do everything possible to prevent its spread to the German-occupied countries of eastern and western Europe while they are in the throes of reestablishing government and repairing the most brutal ravages of the war. If confusion should spread throughout Europe it is difficult to overemphasize the seriousness of the disaster that may follow. Therefore, for us, for the world, and for the countries concerned, a stable Europe should be an immediate objective of allied policy.

Stability and order do not and cannot mean reaction. Order there must be to avoid chaos. But it must be achieved in a manner which will give full scope to men and women who look forward, men and women who will end Fascism and all its works and create the institutions of a free and democratic way of life.

We look with hope and with deep faith to a period of great democratic accomplishment in Europe. Liberation from the German yoke will give the peoples of Europe a new and magnificent opportunity to fulfill their democratic aspirations, both in building democratic political institutions of their own choice and in achieving the social and economic democracy on which political democracy must rest. It is important to our national interest to encourage the establishment in Europe of strong and progressive popular governments, dedicated like our own to improving the social welfare of the people as a whole—governments which will join the common efforts of nations in creating the conditions of lasting peace and in promoting the expansion of production, employment, and the exchange and consumption of goods, which are the material foundations of the liberty and welfare of all peoples. . . .

However difficult the road may be, there is no hope of turning victory into enduring peace unless the real interests of this country, the British Commonwealth, the Soviet Union, and China are harmonized and unless they agree and act together. This is the solid framework upon which all future policy and international organization must be built. It offers the fullest opportunity for the development of institutions in which all free nations may participate democratically, through which a reign of law and morality may arise, and through which the material interests of all may be advanced. But without an enduring understanding between these four nations upon their fundamental purposes, interests, and obligations to one another, all organizations to preserve peace are creations on paper and the path is wide open again for the rise of a new aggressor. . . .

The road to agreement is a difficult one, as any man knows who has ever tried to get two other men, or a city council, or a trade gathering, or a legislative body, to agree upon anything. Agreement can be achieved only by trying to understand the other fellow's point of view and by going as far as possible to meet it.

Although the road to unity of purpose and action is long and difficult we have taken long strides upon our way. The Atlantic Charter was proclaimed by the President and the Prime Minister of Great Britain in August 1941. Then, by the Declaration of the United Nations of January 1, 1942, these nations adopted the principles of the Atlantic Charter, agreed to devote all their resources to the winning of the war, and pledged themselves not to conclude a separate armistice or peace with their common enemies.

After that came the declaration signed at Moscow on October 30, 1943. Here the four nations who are carrying and must carry the chief burden of defeating their enemies renewed their determination by joint action to achieve this end. But they went farther than this and pledged cooperation with one another to establish at the earliest practicable date, with other peace-loving states, an effective international organization to maintain peace and security, which in principle met with overwhelming nonpartisan approval by the Congress in the Connally and Fulbright resolutions.

Further steps along the road of united allied action were taken at the conference at Cairo, where the President and Mr. Churchill met with Generalissimo Chiang Kai-shek, and at the conference at Tehran, where they met with Marshal Stalin. At Tehran the three Allies fighting in Europe reached complete agreement on military plans for winning the war and made plain their determination to achieve harmonious action in the period of peace. That concert among the Allies rests on broad foundations of common interests and common aspirations, and it will endure. The Tehran declaration made it clear also that in the tasks of peace we shall welcome the cooperation and active participation of all nations, large and small, which wish to enter into the world family of democratic nations.

The Cairo declaration as to the Pacific assured the liquidation of Japan's occupations and thefts of territory to deprive her of the power to attack her neighbors again, to restore Chinese territories to China, and freedom to the people of Korea. . . .

There has been discussion recently of the Atlantic Charter and of its application to various situations. The Charter is an expression of fundamental objectives toward which we and our Allies are directing our policies. It states that the nations accepting it are not fighting for the sake of aggrandizement, territorial or otherwise. It lays down the common principles upon which rest the hope of liberty, economic opportunity, peace, and security through international cooperation. It is not a code of law from which detailed answers to every question can be distilled by painstaking analysis of its words and phrases. It points the direction in which solutions are to be sought; it does not give solutions. It charts the course upon which we are embarked and shall continue. That course includes the prevention of aggression and the establishment of world security. The Charter certainly does not prevent any steps, including those relating to enemy states, necessary to achieve these objectives. What is fundamental are the objectives of the Charter and the determination to achieve them. . . .

We have found no difference of opinion among our Allies that the organization and purposes of the Nazi state and its Japanese counterpart, and the military system in all of its ramifications upon which they rest, are, and by their very nature must be, directed toward conquest. There was no disagreement that even after the defeat of the enemy there will be no security unless and until our victory is used to destroy these systems to their very foundation. The action which must be taken to achieve these ends must be, as I have said, agreed action. We are working with our Allies now upon these courses.

The conference at Moscow . . . established the European Advisory Commission, which is now at work in London upon the treatment of Germany. Out of these discussions will come back to the governments for their consideration proposals for concrete action.

Along with arrangements by which nations may be secure and free must go arrangements by which men and women who compose those nations may live and have the opportunity through their efforts to improve their material condition. As I said earlier, we will fail indeed if we win a victory only to let the free peoples of the world, through any absence of action on our part, sink into weakness and despair. The heart of the matter lies in action which will stimulate and expand production in industry and agriculture and free international commerce from excessive and unreasonable restrictions. . . .

I shall not on this occasion be able to explain the work which has been done—and it is extensive—in these fields. In many of them proposals are far advanced toward the stage of discussion with members of the Congress prior to formulation for public discussion.

I hope, however, that I have been able in some measure to bring before you the immensity of the task which lies before us all, the nature of the difficulties which are involved, and the conviction and purpose with which we are attacking them. Our foreign policy is comprehensive, is stable, and is known of all men. As the President has said, neither he nor I have made or will make any secret agreement or commitment, political or financial. The officials of the Government have not been unmindful of the responsibility resting upon them, nor have they spared either energy or such abilities as they possess in discharging that responsibility. . . .

2

Speech of Captain Thorneycroft in the British House of Commons, February 28, 1945[2]

Captain Thorneycroft, addressing the House of Commons on the subject of the Yalta Agreement, recognized what many American leaders refused to do—that the control of Eastern Europe had passed to the Soviets and that the Yalta Agreement was the best settlement possible. For him the maintenance of the alliance was more important than a struggle over Poland.

I believe that the decisions which were arrived at at the Crimea Conference and, in particular, the decision relating to Poland, were wise decisions which were taken in circumstances of very considerable difficulty. . . . As I have said, each of these heads of States was laying down the future path we were likely to follow in our foreign affairs, and on the choice of that road hangs the issue as to whether, in another 30 years, we shall have another war or peace. We have had to face issues of this kind before. They are horribly familiar.

Twenty-five years ago, towards the end of another war, we were also discussing the rights of small Powers, and the future organisation of peace, and I have no doubt that on that occasion we made many mistakes. At any rate, it is certain that in the unhappy years which

2. *Parliamentary Debates, House of Commons, Fifth Series*, Vol. 408, pp. 1454–61.

followed we made mistakes, and none of us wants to reiterate the sad story of the path which led a Germany not totally disarmed to the reoccupation of the Rhineland, through Munich and Berchtesgaden, and eventually to war. It seems to me, looking at that past history, that the mistakes we made were not so much on detailed decisions of British statesmen trying to stave off disaster, as in the failure to face the real issues in foreign policy at an early enough date. . . . If we are to enter in another period in which the facts of a certain situation in foreign affairs are to be tortured to fit into some international document to which we have affixed our signature we shall enter upon a course which must eventually lead us to another war, a war in which we shall have very few friends, and a process which will be detrimental to British honour. . . .

I do not believe that this Crimea Conference is the first milestone in the downward path. I do not believe that this Polish settlement is a betrayal of Poland or of British honour. Polish and British interests are to a large extent the same. We each have an interest to see that no one Power should dominate the whole of Europe. But the first British interest that we have is to finish this war at the earliest possible date. It is common ground that the German people have, or had, until recently, only one hope, and that was that the Allies would fall out among themselves. If the decisions taken at the Crimea Conference are supported by this House then that hope will be finally dispelled. . . .

I do not want to elaborate on the international organisation, because I think that that would be out of order now, but I think that when it is said that Poland can rely upon an international organisation to see that this settlement is kept she is entitled to ask what that international organisation will amount to. If there is one lesson we have learned from the history of the last quarter of a century it is that an international organisation, unless backed up by military power, is both valueless and dangerous. Under the Yalta Agreement, we are committed to the provision of an occupation Army on German soil. We are committed to a number of agreements which, if not world wide, will be very wide indeed. I presume that the Government have gone into the logistics of this matter. I presume that they have estimated what Forces will be required in order to carry out these commitments. The next step which is required is not so much a decision on voting rights at San Francisco as a forthright statement from this Government, the National Government, to the British people as to what sacrifices will be involved. What is required is a statement as to the Forces we shall have to raise in order to carry out what we shall have to do, and a clear statement as to whether compulsory military service will be necessary, as I think it will be. . . .

I believe the settlement we have reached with regard to Poland is the best settlement we could have got. It is worth while remembering that in statesmanship and politics what counts is not the art of getting what is best, but the art of getting what is possible. I concede at once—and this may be embarrassing for the Government—that I do not regard the Polish settlement as an act of justice. It may be right or wrong, it may be wise of foolish, but at any rate it is not justice as I understand the term. It is not the sort of situation in which you get two parties to a dispute putting their case forward in front of a disinterested body and in which the strength and power of one of the parties is never allowed to weigh in the balance. The sooner we recognize that we are a long way from that sort of thing happening the better.

The Government had two choices only. They could have postponed the issue. . . . They could have said, "No, we want this submitted to arbitration. We cannot do anything without the consent of the London Polish Government." No one knows what would happen in those circumstances, but one can safely say that it is unlikely that there would in any circumstance be a free, independent and democratic Poland. The Red Army is in occupation of that country and the Lublin Committee is in control. . . . The second course that they could adopt was to make the best settlement they could and impose it deliberately on the Poles. They have done that. They have bargained the Eastern frontier for the chance of a free Government of Poland within the new frontier. . . . We have encouraged the London Polish Government to negotiate, and have criticised them because they did not negotiate very well. We have told them they must make concessions, and then we have blamed them because they did not make concessions. I do not regard that as a sensible or an honourable course. I do not believe you can ask a Pole to decide to hand over a half of his country. I do not think it is a fair thing to ask any Pole to do. If they agreed to do that, they would divide Poland for a generation, perhaps for all time, into those who thought they were patriots and those who thought they were traitors. This is to perpetuate civil war. Nor could you ask the Poles as an act of policy to take a large slice of their powerful neighbouring State. It is a big decision to take from Germany the whole of East Prussia or the land up to the Oder. It is like taking Wales from England. That is a decision which must be taken by more powerful States. I do not believe that you save your honour in this matter by imposing on others the obligation of making a decision which you ought to make yourself.

I believe the real difficulty in which my hon. Friends find themselves is not so much Poland at all. I believe it is in the apparent conflict between documents like the Atlantic Charter, and the facts of the European situation. We talk to two different people in two different languages. In the East we are talking to the Russians. The Russians are nothing if not realists. I believe Marshal Stalin's motives are entirely honourable. I believe that the Russian Foreign Office is perhaps more in tune with the advice which would be given to the Tsars than to the potentates of the twentieth century. In such circumstances we talk in language not far removed from power politics. In the West we are faced by the Americans. They are nothing if not idealists. To them we talk in the polite language of the Atlantic Charter. Somehow or other we have to marry those two schools of thought. If I could persuade the Americans, particularly in the Middle West, to have something of the Russian realism in international relations, and persuade the Russians to have the idealism that exists on the East coast of America, we might get somewhere, but let us face the fact that the process will be a long and painful one. You do not move suddenly from a world in which there are international rivalries, into a world where there is international co-operation. It is the world that we are in that the Prime Minister has to deal with. We could not come back from Yalta with a Blue-print for a new Utopia. The fundamental error into which my hon. Friends have fallen is this. The rights of small nations are not safeguarded by signing documents like the Atlantic Charter, and quarrelling with anyone who does not agree with your interpretation of them. The rights of small nations are safeguarded by a mixture of diplomacy and military power and, in using those things, you are liable to come into conflict with your friends. . . . The Government are trying to obtain a free, independent and democratic Poland, when the country is occupied by a foreign, though a friendly, Army belonging to a country which has not quite the same interpretation of what is free, independent and democratic as ourselves. . . . But throughout this process the Government have pursued a consistent course. They have sought by every means in their power to obtain from the wreck of Europe two independent and free States. To the Poles I would say that I believe this settlement gives them an opportunity of playing a part in the future of their country which they can never do from London. They should take that opportunity. To the Russians I would say that this is regarded as a test case. The proof of this pudding is in the eating. Russia has many friends in this country. On the decision and action that she takes in the coming weeks with regard to Poland will depend not only whether she keeps those friends but the whole future of co-operation between our two countries. As regards ourselves, I would say that this document provides what may be the basis of future peace. It will only be that, if we are prepared to face up to the sacrifices and the efforts which it involves and to recognize that those sacrifices and efforts are, indeed, worth while.

3

Churchill's Speech at Fulton, Missouri, March 5, 1946[3]

Winston Churchill was one of the first Western leaders to view Russia as a military threat. In his famous "Iron Curtain" speech at Fulton he suggested a military response comprising the creation of a joint United States-British military establishment. Churchill made no effort to analyze Soviet intentions, but he knew from experience that the possession of superior military power by one nation leads to aggression unless countered by opposing military power.

. . . The United States stands at this time at the pinnacle of world power. It is a solemn moment for the American democracy. With primacy in power is also joined an awe-inspiring accountability to the future. As you look around you, you must feel not only the sense of duty done but also feel anxiety lest you fall below the level of achievement. Opportunity is here now, clear and shining, for both our countries. To reject it or ignore it or fritter it away will bring upon us all the long reproaches of the aftertime. It is necessary that constancy of mind, persistency of purpose and the grand simplicity of decision shall guide

3. *Vital Speeches of the Day,* XII (March 15, 1946), pp. 329–32.

and rule the conduct of the Englishspeaking peoples in peace as they did in war. We must and I believe we shall prove ourselves equal to this severe requirement.

When American military men approach some serious situation they are wont to write at the head of their directive the words, "over-all strategic concept." There is wisdom in this as it leads to clarity of thought. What, then, is the over-all strategic concept which we should inscribe today? It is nothing less than the safety and welfare, the freedom and progress of all the homes and families of all the men and women in all the lands. . . .

To give security to these countless homes they must be shielded from the two gaunt marauders—war and tyranny. We all know the frightful disturbance in which the ordinary family is plunged when the curse of war swoops down upon the bread winner and those for whom he works and contrives. The awful ruin of Europe, with all its vanished glories, and of large parts of Asia, glares in our eyes. When the designs of wicked men or the aggressive urge of mighty states dissolve, over large areas, the frame of civilized society, humble folk are confronted with difficulties with which they cannot cope. For them all is distorted, broken or even ground to pulp. . . . Our supreme task and duty is to guard the homes of the common people from the horrors and miseries of another war. . . .

I now come to the second danger which threatens the cottage home and ordinary people, namely tyranny. . . . It is not our duty at this time, when difficulties are so numerous, to interfere forcibly in the internal affairs of countries whom we have not conquered in war, but we must never cease to proclaim in fearless tones the great principles of freedom and the rights of man, which are the joint inheritance of the English-speaking world and which, through Magna Carta, the Bill of Rights, the habeas corpus, trial by jury and the English common law, find their most famous expression in the Declaration of Independence.

All this means that the people of any country have the right and should have the power by constitutional action, by free, unfettered elections, with secret ballot, to choose or change the character or form of government under which they dwell, that freedom of speech and thought should reign, that courts of justice independent of the executive, unbiased by any party, should administer laws which have received the broad assent of large majorities or are consecrated by time and custom. Here are the title deeds of freedom, which should lie in every cottage home. Here is the message of the British and American peoples to mankind. Let us preach what we practice and practice what we preach. . . .

Neither the sure prevention of war, nor the continuous rise of world organization will be gained without what I have called the fraternal association of the English-speaking peoples. This means a special relationship between the British Commonwealth and Empire and the United States. This is no time for generalities. I will venture to be precise. Fraternal association requires not only the growing friendship and mutual understanding between our two vast but kindred systems of society but the continuance of the intimate relationships between our military advisers, leading to common study of potential dangers, similarity of weapons and manuals of instruction and interchange of officers and cadets at colleges. It should carry with it the continuance of the present facilities for mutual security by the joint use of all naval and air-force bases in the possession of either country all over the world. This would perhaps double the mobility of the American Navy and Air Force. . . .

A shadow has fallen upon the scenes so lately lighted by the Allied victory. Nobody knows what Soviet Russia and its Communist international organization intends to do in the immediate future, or what are the limits, if any, to their expansive and proselytizing tendencies. I have a strong admiration and regard for the valiant Russian people and for my war-time comrade, Marshal Stalin. . . . We understand the Russians need to be secure on her western frontiers from all renewal of German aggression. We welcome her to her rightful place among the leading nations of the world. Above all we welcome constant, frequent and growing contacts between the Russian people and our own people on both sides of the Atlantic. . . .

From Stettin in the Baltic to Trieste in the Adriatic, an iron curtain has descended across the Continent. Behind that line lie all the capitals of the ancient states of central and eastern Europe. Warsaw, Berlin, Prague, Vienna, Budapest, Belgrade, Bucharest, and Sofia, all these famous cities and the populations around them lie in the Soviet sphere and all are subject in one form or another, not only to Soviet influence but to a very high and increasing measure of control from Moscow. . . .

In front of the iron curtain which lies across Europe are other causes for anxiety. In Italy the Communist party is seriously hampered by having to support the Communist trained Marshal Tito's claims to former Italian territory at the head of the Adriatic. Nevertheless the future of Italy hangs in the balance. Again one cannot imagine a regenerated Europe without a strong France. All my public life I have worked for a strong France and I never lost faith in her destiny, even in the darkest hours. I will not lose faith now. However, in a great number of countries, far from the Russian frontiers and throughout the world, Communist fifth columns are established and work in complete unity and absolute obedience to the directions they receive from the Communist center. Exception in the British Commonwealth and in this United States, where Communism is in its infancy, the Communist parties or fifth columns constitute a growing challenge and peril to Christian civilization. . . .

The outlook is also anxious in the Far East and especially in Manchuria. The agreement which was made at Yalta, to which I was a party, was extremely favorable to Soviet Russia, but it was made at a time when no one could say that the German war might not extend all through the summer and autumn of 1945 and when the Japanese war was expected to last for a further eighteen months from the end of the German war. . . .

On the other hand I repulse the idea that a new war is inevitable; still more that it is imminent. It is because I am so sure that our fortunes are in our own hands and that we hold the power to save the future, that I feel the duty to speak out now that I have an occasion to do so. I do not believe that Soviet Russia desires war. What they desire is the fruits of war and the indefinite expansion of their power and doctrines. But what we have to consider here today while time remains, is the permanent prevention of war and the establishment of conditions of freedom and democracy as rapidly as possible in all countries. Our difficulties and dangers will not be removed by closing our eyes to them. They will not be removed by mere waiting to see what happens; nor will they be relieved by a policy of appeasement. What is needed is a settlement and the longer this is delayed the more difficult it will be and the greater our dangers will become. From what I have seen of our Russian friends and allies during the war, I am convinced that there is nothing they admire so much as strength, and there is nothing for which they have less respect than for military weakness. For that reason the old doctrine of a balance of power is unsound. We cannot afford, if we can help it, to work on narrow margins, offering temptations to a trial of strength. If the western democracies stand together in strict adherence to the principles of the United Nations Charter, their influence for furthering these principles will be immense and no one is likely to molest them. If, however, they become divided or falter in their duty, and if these all-important years are allowed to slip away, then indeed catastrophe may overwhelm us all. . . .

If the population of the English-speaking commonwealth be added to that of the United States, with all that such co-operation implies in the air, on the sea and in science and industry, there will be no quivering, precarious balance of power to offer its temptation to ambition or adventure. On the contrary, there will be an overwhelming assurance of security. . . .

4

Truman's Speech to Congress, March 12, 1947[4]

In this noted speech, President Harry S. Truman publicized the concept of a global, ideological struggle between the United States and the U.S.S.R. In his request for economic and military aid for Greece and Turkey, he divided the world into free nations and oppressed nations and committed the United States to support all free governments struggling to maintain themselves against their own minorities or external pressures.

. . . The United States has received from the Greek Government an urgent appeal for financial and economic assistance. Preliminary reports from the American Economic Mission now in Greece and reports from the American Ambassador in Greece corroborate the statement of the Greek Government that assistance is imperative if Greece is to survive as a free nation. I do not believe that the American people and the Congress wish to turn a deaf ear to the appeal of the Greek Government.

Greece is not a rich country. Lack of sufficient natural resources has always forced the Greek people to work hard to make both ends

4. *The New York Times,* March 13, 1947.

meet. Since 1940, this industrious, peace loving country has suffered invasion, four years of cruel enemy occupation, and bitter internal strife. . . .

The Greek Government has also asked for the assistance of experienced American administrators, economists and technicians to insure that the financial and other aid given to Greece shall be used effectively in creating a stable and self-sustaining economy and in improving its public administration.

The very existence of the Greek state is today threatened by the terrorist activities of several thousand armed men, led by Communists, who defy the Government's authority at a number of points, particularly along the northern boundaries. A commission appointed by the United Nations Security Council is at present investigating disturbed conditions in Northern Greece and alleged border violations along the frontiers between Greece on the one hand and Albania, Bulgaria, and Yugoslavia on the other.

Meanwhile, the Greek Government is unable to cope with the situation. The Greek Army is small and poorly equipped. It needs supplies and equipment if it is to restore the authority of the Government throughout Greek territory.

Greece must have assistance if it is to become a self-supporting and self-respecting democracy. The United States must supply that assistance. We have already extended to Greece certain types of relief and economic aid but these are inadequate. There is no other country to which democratic Greece can turn. No other nation is willing and able to provide the necessary support for a democratic Greek Government. . . .

Greece's neighbor, Turkey, also deserves our attention. The future of Turkey as an independent and economically sound state is clearly no less important to the freedom-loving peoples of the world than the future of Greece. The circumstances in which Turkey finds itself today are considerably different from those of Greece. Turkey has been spared the disasters that have beset Greece. And during the war, the United States and Great Britain furnished Turkey with material aid. Nevertheless, Turkey now needs our support. . . . I am fully aware of the broad implications involved if the United States extends assistance to Greece and Turkey, and I shall discuss these implications with you at this time.

One of the primary objectives of the foreign policy of the United States is the creation of conditions in which we and other nations will be able to work out a way of life free from coercion. This was a fundamental issue in the war with Germany and Japan. Our victory was won over countries which sought to impose their will, and their way of life upon other nations.

To ensure the peaceful development of nations, free from coercion, the United States has taken a leading part in establishing the United Nations. The United Nations is designed to make possible lasting freedom and independence for all its members. We shall not realize our objectives, however, unless we are willing to help free people to maintain their free institutions and their national integrity against aggressive movements that seek to impose upon them totalitarian regimes. This is no more than a frank recognition that totalitarian regimes imposed on free peoples, by direct or indirect aggression, undermine the foundations of international peace and hence the security of the United States.

The peoples of a number of countries of the world have recently had totalitarian regimes forced upon them against their will. The Government of the United States has made frequent protests against coercion and intimidation, in violation of the Yalta Agreement, in Poland, Rumania and Bulgaria. I must also state that in a number of other countries there have been similar developments. At the present moment in world history nearly every nation must choose between alternative ways of life. The choice is too often not a free one.

One way of life is based upon the will of the majority, and is distinguished by free institutions, representative government, free elections, guarantees of individual liberty, freedom of speech and religion, and freedom from political oppression.

The second way of life is based upon the will of a minority forcibly imposed upon the majority. It relies upon terror and oppression, a controlled press and radio, fixed elections, and the suppression of personal freedoms.

I believe that it must be the policy of the United States to support free peoples who are resisting attempted subjugation by armed minorities or by outside pressures.

I believe that we must assist free peoples to work out their own destinies in their own way.

I believe that our help should be primarily through economic and financial aid which is essential to economic stability and orderly political processes.

The world is not static, and the status quo is not sacred. But we cannot allow changes in the status quo in violation of the Charter of the

United Nations by such methods as coercion, or by such subterfuges as political infiltration. In helping free and independent nations to maintain their freedom, the United States will be giving effect to the principles of the Charter of the United Nations. . . .

Should we fail to aid Greece and Turkey in this fateful hour, the effect will be far reaching to the West as well as to the East. We must take immediate and resolute action. . . .

5

Marshall's Speech at Harvard University, June 5, 1947[5]

In this speech Secretary of State George C. Marshall not only argued for an expanded economic aid program for Europe but also, with the advice of the Policy Planning Staff of the State Department, attempted to extricate American foreign policy from the ideological context to which the Truman Doctrine had consigned it. Marshall made it clear that United States economic aid, under the new program, would be aimed at poverty and economic dislocation, not at any ideology or nation.

I need not tell you gentlemen that the world situation is very serious. That must be apparent to all intelligent people. I think one difficulty is that the problem is one of such enormous complexity that the very mass of the facts presented to the public by press and radio make it exceedingly difficult for the man in the street to reach a clear appraisement of the situation. Furthermore, the people of this country are distant from the troubled areas of the earth and it is hard for them to comprehend the plight and consequent reactions of the long-suffering

5. Raymond Dennett and Robert K. Turner (eds.), *Documents on American Foreign Relations, January 1–December 31, 1947* (Vol. IX, Princeton, 1949), pp. 1–11.

peoples, and the effect of those reactions on their governments in connection with our efforts to promote peace in the world.

In considering the requirements for the rehabilitation of Europe, the physical loss of life, the visible destruction of cities, factories, mines and railroads was correctly estimated, but it has become obvious during recent months that this visible destruction was probably less serious than the dislocation of the entire fabric of European economy. For the past ten years conditions have been highly abnormal. . . . The breakdown of the business structure of Europe during the war was complete. Recovery has been seriously retarded by the fact that two years after the close of hostilities a peace settlement with Germany and Austria has not been agreed upon. But even given a more prompt solution of these difficult problems, the rehabilitation of the economic structure of Europe quite evidently will require a much longer time and greater effort than had been foreseen. . . .

The division of labor is the basis of modern civilization. At the present time it is threatened with breakdown. The town and city industries are not producing adequate goods to exchange with the food-producing farmer. Raw materials and fuel are in short supply. Machinery is lacking or worn out. The farmer or the peasant cannot find the goods for sale which he desires to purchase. So the sale of his farm produce for money which he cannot use seems to him an unprofitable transaction. . . . Meanwhile people in the cities are short of food and fuel. So the governments are forced to use their foreign money and credits to procure these necessities abroad. This process exhausts funds which are urgently needed for reconstruction. . . .

The truth of the matter is that Europe's requirements for the next three or four years of foreign food and other essential products—principally from America—are so much greater than her present ability to pay that she must have substantial additional help, or face economic, social and political deterioration of a very grave character. . . .

It is logical that the United States should do whatever it is able to do to assist in the return of normal economic health in the world, without which there can be no political stability and no assured peace. Our policy is directed not against any country or doctrine but against hunger, poverty, desperation and chaos. Its purpose should be the revival of a working economy in the world so as to permit the emergence of political and social conditions in which free institutions can exist. Such assistence, I am convinced, must not be on a piecemeal basis as various crises develop. Any assistance that this Government may render in the future should provide a cure rather than a mere palliative. Any government that is willing to assist in the task of recovery will find full cooperation, I am sure, on the part of the United States Government. Any government which maneuvers to block the recovery of other countries cannot expect help from us. Furthermore, governments, political parties or groups which seek to perpetuate human misery in order to profit therefrom politically or otherwise will encounter the opposition of the United States.

It is already evident that, before the United States Government can proceed much further in its efforts to alleviate the situation and help start the European world on its way to recovery, there must be some agreement among the countries of Europe as to the requirements of the situation and the part those countries themselves will take in order to give proper effect to whatever action might be undertaken by this Government. It would be neither fitting or efficacious for this Government to undertake to draw up unilaterally a program designed to place Europe on its feet economically. This is the business of the Europeans. The initiative, I think, must come from Europe. . . . The program should be a joint one, agreed to by a number, if not all, European nations.

An essential part of any successful action on the part of the United States is an understanding on the part of the people of America of the character of the problem and the remedies to be applied. Political passion and prejudice should have no part. With foresight, and a willingness on the part of our people to face up to the vast responsibility which history has clearly placed upon our country, the difficulties I have outlined can and will be overcome.

6

Acheson's Speech in Washington, April 22, 1950[6]

This speech of Secretary of State Dean G. Acheson before the American Society of Newspaper Editors comprised a good summary of his concept of containment of the Soviet Union. He made it clear that he sought a settlement with Russia, not that country's destruction. He did not here or elsewhere enumerate any achievable conditions for such a settlement.

I would like to discuss with you the thing that is most important to all of us: the well-being and happiness and security of the United States. I ask you to put aside, for the moment, all considerations that are less important, to forget all differences of opinion that are less than vital. . . .

We are faced with a threat—in all sober truth I say this—we are faced with a threat not only to our country but to the civilization in which we live and to the whole physical environment in which that civilization can exist. This threat is the principal problem that confronts the whole United States in the world today. . . .

There is no miracle that will make it disappear from the earth.

6. The Department of State, *Strengthening the Forces of Freedom: Selected Speeches and Statements of Secretary State Acheson, February 1949–April 1950* (Washington, 1950), pp. 1–9.

Having recognized this truth, we need not for a moment be discouraged or downhearted. We have open to us, and we are now pursuing, many lines of action that will meet the challenge confronting us. May I mention six lines of action.

Our first line of action—and this seems to me the basis of all the others I shall discuss—is to demonstrate that our own faith in freedom is a burning and a fighting faith. We are children of freedom. We cannot be safe except in an environment of freedom. We believe in freedom as fundamentally as we believe anything in this world. We believe in it for everyone in our country. And we don't restrict this belief to freedom for ourselves. We believe that all people in the world are entitled to as much freedom, to develop in their own way, as we want ourselves. . . .

We must use every means we know to communicate the value of freedom to the four corners of the earth. Our message must go out through leaflets, through our free press, radio programs and films, through exchange of students and teachers with other countries, and through a hundred other ways. . . .

Thirdly, it is not enough that one should have a faith and should make that faith articulate. It is also essential that we, and those who think like us, should have the power to make safe the area in which we carry that faith into action. This means that we must look to our defenses. It means that we must organize our defenses wisely and prudently, with all the ingenuity and all the methods in which we are best versed to make ourselves strong.

Every element of promise is present in our situation. We have the ingenuity, we have the productive power, we have the determination, we have the resources. But this is not a subject on which I am competent to dwell at length. The President's chief advisers in this field are our Secretary of Defense and our service secretaries, in whom we can have complete faith and confidence.

Fourthly, beyond faith and preachment and defense there lies the necessity of translating all of these into terms of the daily lives of hundreds of millions of peoples who live in this free world of ours. I am talking about the effort we are now making to help create a better material life for ourselves and for other people in many parts of the world.

One part of this effort has to do with setting in operation again the great workshops of the free world. Since the end of the war we have worked steadily at this problem and we have had a vast measure of success. The chimneys of these factories are smoking again, raw materials are moving into them, finished goods are moving out. Hundreds of millions of people see the spector of insecurity in their daily lives being pushed further back. . . .

Now while we are helping to get workshops going—old and new— and to get people producing in Europe and other parts of the world, we have to do still another thing. And that is to develop a sensible system of trade to exchange the goods which are being and will be produced. . . .

We are going to have to make a great national effort, also, to get our own trade with the rest of the world into balance, to get out of the situation where we are selling abroad much more than we are buying and making up the difference out of the pockets of American taxpayers. Nobody here or abroad wants that situation to continue indefinitely. As part of the remedy we shall have to buy more from abroad, and that will demand a concerted national effort.

The fifth line of action is in the political field. In this political field we have so far only scratched the surface of what can be done to bring the free world closer together, to make it stronger and more secure and more effective.

There are many ways of organizing the free world for common action and many different opinions on how it should be done. But I think it is important in this hour of danger to concentrate our minds and our energies on using the machinery we have at hand, on expanding it and making it work. When you look over the field, you will see that we now have created a great deal of good machinery.

There is the whole machinery of the United Nations which we are continually learning to use more effectively. Within the framework of the United Nations we have other machinery, like the North Atlantic Treaty and the Organization of American States.

The free nations of Europe have banded together in the Council of Europe, in the Marshall Plan organization, and in a smaller group known as the Western Union. We can work with all of these organizations. We can use whichever is best suited to accomplish a particular purpose. What we need to do is to expand the machinery we have, to improve it, to use it with boldness and imagination, and, when necessary, to supplement it with new machinery.

Now our program of action would not be complete if I did not go on to a sixth field, and that is the area of our relations with the Soviet Union and the countries that have fallen under Communist control. In this field, as in our relations with the free nations, we have the machinery of negotiation at hand. In the United Nations we have a dozen or more conference tables at which our differences could be thrashed out, where unfortunately the Soviet chair stands empty at the present time. We shall go on trying to find a common ground for agreement, not perfect or eternal agreement, but at least a better arrangement for living together in greater safety. . . .

We do not propose to subvert the Soviet Union. We shall not attempt to undermine Soviet independence. And we are just as determined that Communism shall not by hook or crook or trickery undermine our country or any other free country that desires to maintain its freedom. That real and present threat of aggression stands in the way of every attempt at understanding with the Soviet Union. For it has been wisely said that there can be no greater disagreement than when someone wants to eliminate your existence altogether.

If, as, and when that idea of aggression, by one means or another, can be ruled out of our relations with the Soviet Union, then the greatest single obstacle to agreement will be out of the way. As the results of our actions become clear and the free world becomes stronger, it will, I believe, become progressively easier to get agreements with the Soviet Union. . . .

7

Acheson's Speech in Washington, January 12, 1950[7]

Acheson's speech before the National Press Club comprised a complete statement of American Far Eastern policy at mid-century. This policy, the Secretary pointed out, was anchored to the assumption of a vast revolutionary upheaval blanketing the Orient. He defined the nation's defense commitment in the Far East, including specifically Japan, the Ryukyus, and the Philippines. Recognizing the force of the Asiatic upheaval, he warned that henceforth the fundamental decisions in Asia would lie in Asian hands.

. . . I am frequently asked: Has the State Department got an Asian policy? And it seems to me that that discloses such a depth of ignorance that it is very hard to begin to deal with it. The peoples of Asia are so incredibly diverse and their problems are so incredibly diverse that how could anyone, even the most utter charlatan, believe that he had a uniform policy which would deal with all of them. On the other hand, there are very important similarities in ideas and in problems among the peoples of Asia and so what we come to, after we understand these diversities and these common attitudes of mind, is the fact that there must be certain similarities of approach, and there must be very great dissimilarities in action. . . .

7. *The Department of State Bulletin*, XXII (January 23, 1950), pp. 111–119.

There is in this vast area what we might call a developing Asian consciousness, and a developing pattern, and this, I think, is based upon two factors. . . .

One of these factors is a revulsion against the acceptance of misery and poverty as the normal condition of life. Throughout all of this vast area, you have that fundamental revolutionary aspect in mind and belief. The other common aspect that they have is the revulsion against foreign domination. Whether that foreign domination takes the form of colonialism or whether it takes the form of imperialism, they are through with it. They have had enough of it, and they want no more. . . .

Now, may I suggest to you that much of the bewilderment which has seized the minds of many of us about recent developments in China comes from a failure to understand this basic revolutionary force which is loose in Asia. The reasons for the fall of the Nationalist Government in China are preoccupying many people. All sorts of reasons have been attributed to it. Most commonly, it is said in various speeches and publications that it is the result of American bungling, that we are incompetent, that we did not understand, that American aid was too little, that we did the wrong things at the wrong time. . . . Now, what I ask you to do is to stop looking for a moment under the bed and under the chair and under the rug to find out these reasons, but rather to look at the broad picture and see whether something doesn't suggest itself. . . .

What has happened in my judgment is that the almost inexhaustible patience of the Chinese people in their misery ended. They did not bother to overthrow this government. There was really nothing to overthrow. They simply ignored it. . . . They completely withdrew their support from this government, and when that support was withdrawn, the whole military establishment disintegrated. Added to the grossest incompetence ever experienced by any military command was this total lack of support both in the armies and in the country, and so the whole matter just simply disintegrated.

The Communists did not create this. The Communists did not create this condition. They did not create this revolutionary spirit. They did not create a great force which moved out from under Chiang Kai-shek. But they were shrewd and cunning to mount it, to ride this thing into victory and into power. . . .

Now, let me come to another underlying and important factor which determines our relations and, in turn, our policy with the peoples of Asia. That is the attitude of the Soviet Union toward Asia, and particularly towards those parts of Asia which are contiguous to the

Soviet Union, and with great particularity this afternoon, to north China.

The attitude and interest of the Russians in north China, and in these other areas as well, long antedates communism. This is not something that has come out of communism at all. It long antedates it. But the Communist regime has added new methods, new skills, and new concepts to the thrust of Russian imperialism. This Communistic concept and techniques have armed Russian imperialism with a new and most insidious weapon of penetration. Armed with these new powers, what is happening in China is that the Soviet Union is detaching the northern provinces [areas] of China from China and is attaching them to the Soviet Union. This process is complete in outer Mongolia. It is nearly complete in Manchuria, and I am sure that in inner Mongolia and in Sinkiang there are very happy reports coming from Soviet agents to Moscow. This is what is going on. It is the detachment of these whole areas, vast areas—populated by Chinese—the detachment of these areas from China and their attachment to the Soviet Union.

I wish to state this and perhaps sin against my doctrine of nondogmatism, but I should like to suggest at any rate that this fact that the Soviet Union is taking the four northern provinces of China is the single most significant, most important fact, in the relation of any foreign power with Asia.

What does that mean for us? It means something very, very significant. It means that nothing that we do and nothing that we say must be allowed to obscure the reality of this fact. All the efforts of propaganda will not be able to obscure it. The only thing that can obscure it is the folly of ill-conceived adventures on our part which easily could do so, and I urge all who are thinking about these foolish adventures to remember that we must not seize the unenviable position which the Russians have carved out for themselves. We must not undertake to deflect from the Russians to ourselves the righteous anger, and the wrath, and the hatred of the Chinese people which must develop. It would be folly to deflect it to ourselves. We must take the position we have always taken—that anyone who violates the integrity of China is the enemy of China and is acting contrary to our own interest. That, I suggest to you this afternoon, is the first and the greatest rule in regard to the formulation of American policy toward Asia.

I suggest that the second rule is very like the first. That is to keep our own purposes perfectly straight, perfectly pure, and perfectly aboveboard and do not get them mixed-up with legal quibbles or the attempt to do one thing and really achieve another. . . .

What is the situation in regard to the military security of the Pacific area, and what is our policy in regard to it?

In the first place, the defeat and the disarmament of Japan has placed upon the United States the necessity of assuming the military defense of Japan so long as that is required, both in the interest of our security and in the interests of the security of the entire Pacific area and, in all honor, in the interest of Japanese security. We have American—and there are Australian—troops in Japan. I am not in a position to speak for the Australians, but I can assure you that there is no intention of any sort of abandoning or weakening the defenses of Japan and that whatever arrangements are to be made either through permanent settlement or otherwise, that defense must and shall be maintained.

This defensive perimeter runs along the Aleutians to Japan and then goes to the Ryukyus. We hold important defense positions in the Ryukyu Islands, and those we will continue to hold. In the interest of the population of the Ryukyu Islands, we will at an appropriate time offer to hold these islands under trusteeship of the United Nations. But they are essential parts of the defensive perimeter of the Pacific, and they must and will be held.

The defensive perimeter runs from the Ryukyus to the Philippine Islands. Our relations, our defensive relations with the Philippines are contained in agreements between us. Those agreements are being loyally carried out and will be loyally carried out. Both peoples have learned by bitter experience the vital connections between our mutual defense requirements. We are in no doubt about that, and it is hardly necessary for me to say an attack on the Philippines could not and would not be tolerated by the United States. But I hasten to add that no one perceives the imminence of any such attack.

So far as the military security of other areas in the Pacific is concerned, it must be clear that no person can guarantee these areas against military attack. But it must also be clear that such a guarantee is hardly sensible or necessary within the realm of practical relationship.

Should such an attack occur—one hesitates to say where such an armed attack could come from—the initial reliance must be on the people attacked to resist it and then upon the commitments of the entire civilized world under the Charter of the United Nations which so far has not proved a weak reed to lean on by any people who are determined to protect their independence against outside aggression. But it is a mistake, I think, in considering Pacific and Far Eastern problems to become obsessed with military considerations. Important as they are, there are other problems that press, and these other problems are not capable of solution through military means. These other problems arise out of the susceptibility of many areas, and many countries in the Pacific area, to subversion and penetration. That cannot be stopped by military means.

The susceptibility to penetration arises because in many areas there are new governments which have little experience in governmental administration and have not become firmly established or perhaps firmly accepted in their countries. They grow, in part, from very serious economic problems. . . . In part this susceptibility to penetration comes from the great social upheaval about which I have been speaking. . . .

So after this survey, what we conclude, I believe, is that there is a new day which has dawned in Asia. It is a day in which the Asian peoples are on their own, and know it, and intend to continue on their own. It is a day in which the old relationships between east and west are gone, relationships which at their worst were exploitations, and which at their best were paternalism. That relationship is over, and the relationship of east and west must now be in the Far East one of mutual respect and mutual helpfulness. We are their friends. Others are their friends. We and those others are willing to help, but we can help only where we are wanted and only where the conditions of help are really sensible and possible. So what we can see is that this new day in Asia, this new day which is dawning, may go on to a glorious noon or it may darken and it may drizzle out. But that decision lies within the countries of Asia and within the power of the Asian people. It is not a decision which a friend or even an enemy from the oustide can decide for them.

8

Dulles' Statement on Liberation, January 15, 1953[8]

John Foster Dulles first publicized his concept of liberation in his article, "A Policy of Boldness," Life, May 19, 1952. This concept he then wrote into the Republican platform of 1952. When he appeared before the Senate Foreign Relations Committee the following January, prior to becoming Secretary of State, he insisted that the liberation of China and the Soviet satellites could be achieved without war or even revolution. Precisely how he hoped to achieve this he never stated, either here or elsewhere.

. . . The CHAIRMAN. I am particularly interested in something I read recently, to the effect that you stated you were not in favor of the policy of containment. I think you advocated a more dynamic or positive policy.

Can you tell us more specifically what you have in mind? . . . .

Mr. DULLES. There are a number of policy matters which I would prefer to discuss with the committee in executive session, but I have no objection to saying in open session what I have said before: namely, that we shall never have a secure peace or a happy world so

8. *Hearing before the Committee on Foreign Relations, United States Senate, Eighty-Third Congress, First Session, on the Nomination of John Foster Dulles, Secretary of State-Designate, January 15, 1953* (Washington, 1953), pp. 5–6.

long as Soviet communism dominates one-third of all the peoples that there are, and is in the process of trying at least to extend its rule to many others.

These people who are enslaved are people who deserve to be free, and who, from our own selfish standpoint, ought to be free because if they are the servile instruments of aggressive despotism, they will eventually be welded into a force which will be highly dangerous to ourselves and to all of the free world.

Therefore, we must always have in mind the liberation of these captive peoples. Now, liberation does not mean a war of liberation. Liberation can be accomplished by processes short of war. We have, as one example, not an ideal example, but it illustrates my point, the defection of Yugoslavia, under Tito from the domination of Soviet communism. Well, that rule of Tito is not one which we admire, and it has many aspects of despotism, itself; but at least it illustrates that it is possible to disintegrate this present monolithic structure which, as I say, represents approximately one-third of all the people that there are in the world.

The present tie between China and Moscow is an unholy arrangement which is contrary to the traditions, the hopes, the aspirations of the Chinese people. Certainly we cannot tolerate a continuance of that, or a welding of the 450 million people of China into the servile instruments of Soviet aggression.

Therefore, a policy which only aims at containing Russia where it now is, is, in itself, an unsound policy; but it is a policy which is bound to fail because a purely defensive policy never wins against an aggressive policy. If our only policy is to stay where we are, we will be driven back. It is only by keeping alive the hope of liberation, by taking advantage of that wherever opportunity arises, that we will end this terrible peril which dominates the world, which imposes upon us such terrible sacrifices and so great fears for the future. But all of this can be done and must be done in ways which will not provoke a general war, or in ways which will not provoke an insurrection which would be crushed with bloody violence, such as was the case, for example, when the Russians instigated the Polish revolt, under General Bor, and merely sat by and watched them when the Germans exterminated those who were revolting.

It must be and can be a peaceful process, but those who do not believe that results can be accomplished by moral pressures, by the weight of propaganda, just do not know what they are talking about.

I ask you to recall the fact that Soviet communism, itself, has spread from controlling 200 million people some 7 years ago to controlling 800 million people today, and it has done that by methods of political warfare, psychological warfare and propaganda, and it has not actually used the Red Army as an open aggressive force in accomplishing that.

Surely what they can accomplish, we can accomplish. Surely if they can use moral and psychological force, we can use it; and, to take a negative defeatest attitude is not an approach which is conducive to our own welfare, or in conformity with our own historical ideas. . . .

9

Dulles' Speech in New York, January 12, 1954[9]

This dramatic statement of Dulles' total concept of foreign affairs was critical of the Truman policies because they had been piecemeal and had always left the initiative to the Kremlin. It was necessary, he said, for the United States to develop long-range policies which would protect the nation's security at reduced cost. He found the answer in "massive retaliation." But he went far beyond the assurance that the United States could prevent aggression simply by threatening to employ its weapons of mass destruction, for he promised that the time gained by preventing aggression would produce erosion within the enemy states and thus eventually give this nation a victory in the cold war. This speech thus tied the concept of massive retaliation to the concept of peaceful liberation. It not only promised ultimate victory but also promised it at little risk and at reduced expenditures.

. . . We live in a world where emergencies are always possible, and our survival may depend upon our capacity to meet emergencies. Let us pray that we shall always have that capacity. But, having said that, it is necessary also to say that emergency measures—however

9. *The Department of State Bulletin*, XXX (January 25, 1954), pp. 107–10.

good for the emergency—do not necessarily make good permanent policies. Emergency measures are costly; they are superficial; and they imply that the enemy has the initiative. They cannot be depended on to serve our long-time interests.

"The long time" factor is of critical importance. The Soviet Communists are planning for what they call "an entire historical era," and we should do the same. . . .

In the face of this strategy, measures cannot be judged adequate merely because they ward off an immediate danger. It is essential to do this, but it is also essential to do so without exhausting ourselves.

When the Eisenhower administration applied this test, we felt that some transformations were needed. It is not sound military strategy permanently to commit U.S. land forces to Asia to a degree that leaves us no strategic reserves. It is not sound economics, or good foreign policy, to support permanently other countries; for in the long run, that creates as much ill will as good will. Also, it is not sound to become permanently committed to military expenditures so vast that they lead to "practical bankruptcy." . . . We need allies and collective security. Our purpose is to make these relations more effective, less costly. This can be done by placing more reliance on deterrent power and less dependence on local defensive power.

This is accepted practice so far as local communities are concerned. We keep locks on our doors, but we do not have an armed guard in every home. We rely principally on a community security system so well equipped to punish any who break in and steal that, in fact, would-be aggressors are generally deterred. That is the modern way of getting maximum protection at a bearable cost.

What the Eisenhower administration seeks is a similar international security system. We want, for ourselves and the other free nations, a maximum deterrent at a bearable cost.

Local defense will always be important. But there is no local defense which alone will contain the mighty landpower of the Communist world. Local defenses must be reinforced by the further deterrent of massive retaliatory power. A potential aggressor must know that he cannot always prescribe battle conditions that suit him. Otherwise, for example, a potential aggressor, who is glutted with manpower, might be tempted to attack in confidence that resistance would be confined to manpower. He might be tempted to attack in places where is superiority was decisive. . . .

But before military planning could be changed, the President and his advisers, as represented by the National Security Council, had to

take some basic policy decisions. This has been done. The basic decision was to depend primarily upon a great capacity retaliate, instantly,
by means and at places of our choosing. Now the Department of
Defense and the Joint Chiefs of Staff can shape our military establishment to fit what is *our* policy, instead of having to try to be ready to
meet the enemy's many choices. . . . As a result, it is now possible to
get, and share, more basic security at less cost.

Let us now see how this concept has been applied to foreign
policy, taking first the Far East. In Korea this administration effected a
major transformation. The fighting has been stopped on honorable
terms. That was possible because the aggressor, already thrown back
to and behind his place of beginning, was faced with the possibility that
the fighting might, to his own great peril, soon spread beyond the limits
and methods which he had selected. . . .

I have said in relation to Indochina that, if there were open Red
Chinese armed aggression there, that would have "grave consequences which might not be confined to Indochina." I expressed last
month the intention of the United States to maintain its position on
Okinawa. This is needed to insure adequate striking power to imple-
ment the collective concept which I describe.

All of this is summed up in President Eisenhower's important
statement of December 26. He announced the progressive reduction of
the U.S. ground forces in Korea. He pointed out that U.S. military
forces in the Far East will now feature "highly mobile naval, air and
amphibious units"; and he said in this way, despite some withdrawal of
land forces, the United States will have a capacity to oppose aggression "with even greater effect that heretofore." . . .

At the April meeting of the NATO Council, the United States put
forward a new concept, now known as that of the "long haul." That
meant a steady development of defensive strength at a rate which will
preserve and not exhaust the economic strength of our allies and
ourselves. This would be reinforced by the striking power of a strategic
air force based on internationally agreed positions. . . .

There are still some strategic spots where the local governments
cannot maintain adequate armed forces without some financial support
from us. In these cases, we take the judgment of our military advisers
as to how to proceed in the common interest. For example, we have
contributed largely, ungrudgingly, and I hope constructively, to end
aggression and advance freedom in Indochina. The technical
assistance program is being continued, and we stand ready to meet
nonrecurrent needs due to crop failures or like disasters. But, broadly

speaking, foreign budgetary aid is being limited to situations where it clearly contributes to military strength. . . .

If we can deter such aggression as would mean general war, and that is our confident resolve, then we can let time and fundamentals work for us. We do not need self-imposed policies which sap our strength. . . . We intend that our conduct and example shall continue, as in the past, to show all men how good can be the fruits of freedom.

If we rely on freedom, then it follows that we must abstain from diplomatic moves which would seem to endorse captivity. That would, in effect, be a conspiracy against freedom. I can assure you that we shall never seek illusory security for ourselves by such a "deal." We do negotiate about specific matters, but only to advance the cause of human welfare. . . .

If we persist in the courses I outline we shall confront dictatorship with a task that is, in the long run, beyond its strength. For unless it changes, it must suppress the human desires that freedom satisfies—as we shall be demonstrating. If the dictators persist in their present course, then it is they who will be limited to superficial successes, while their foundation crumbles under the tread of their iron boots. . . .

We can be sure that there is going on, even within Russia, a silent test of strength between the powerful rulers and the multitudes of human beings. Each individual no doubt seems by himself to be help-less in this struggle. But their aspirations in the aggregate make up a mighty force. There are signs that the rulers are bending to some of the human desires of their people. There are promises of more food, more household goods, more economic freedom.

That does not prove that the Soviet rulers have themselves been converted. It is rather thay they may be dimly perceiving a basic fact, that is that there are limits to the power of any rulers indefinitely to suppress the human spirit. In that God-given fact lies our greatest hope. It is a hope that can sustain us. For even if the path ahead be long and hard, it need not be a warlike path; and we can know that at the end may be found the blessedness of peace.

10

Dulles' Defense of U.S. China Policy, June 28, 1957[10]

In this speech, delivered in San Francisco, Mr. Dulles repeated the rationale developed by American officials after 1952 to explain and defend American policy toward China. These arguments were molded into a pattern which never varied. For that reason one need read only one full defense of the policy of nonrecognition to grasp the full argumentation.

. . . On the China mainland 600 million people are ruled by the Chinese Communist Party. That party came to power by violence and, so far, has lived by violence. It retains power not by will of the Chinese people but by massive, forcible repression. It fought the United Nations in Korea; it supported the Communist war in Indochina; it took Tibet by force. It fomented the Communist Huk rebellion in the Philippines and the Communists' insurrection in Malaya. It does not disguise its expansionist ambitions. It is bitterly hateful of the United States, which it considers a principal obstacle in the way of its path of conquest.

In the face of this condition the United States has supported, morally and materially, the free nations of the Western Pacific and

10. *The Department of State Bulletin*, XXXVII (July 15, 1957), pp. 91–95.

Southeast Asia. Our security treaties make clear that the violation of these nations by international communism would be considered as endangering our own peace and safety and that we would act accordingly. Together we constitute a goodly company and a stout bulwark against aggression.

As regards China, we have abstained from any act to encourage the Communist regime—morally, politically, or materially. . . .

United States diplomatic recognition of Communist China would have the following consequences:

(1) The many mainland Chinese, who by Mao Tse-tung's own recent admission seek to change the nature of their government, would be immensely discouraged.

(2) The millions of overseas Chinese would feel that they had no Free China to which to look. Today increasing numbers of these overseas Chinese go to Free China to study. Six years ago there were less than 100 Chinese students from Southeast Asia and Hong Kong studying in Taiwan. Now there are nearly 5,000. . . .

If the United States recognized the Chinese Communist regime, many of the millions of overseas Chinese in free Asian countries would, reluctantly, turn to acceptance of the guiding direction of the Communist regime. This would be a tragedy for them; and it would imperil friendly governments already menaced by Chinese Communist subversion.

(3) The Republic of China, now on Taiwan, would feel betrayed by its friend. That Government was our ally in the Second World War and for long bore alone the main burden of the Far Eastern war. It had many tempting opportunities to compromise with the Japanese on terms which would have been gravely detrimental to the United States. It never did so. . . . We are honorbound to give our ally, to whom we are pledged by a mutual defense treaty, a full measure of loyalty.

(4) The free Asian governments of the Pacific and Southeast Asia would be gravely perplexed. They are not only close to the vast Chinese land mass, but geographically and, to some extent, politically, they are separated as among themselves. The unifying and fortifying influence is, above all, the spirit and resolution of the United States. If we seemed to waver and to compromise with communism in China, that would in turn weaken free Asia resistence to the Chinese Communist regime and assist international communism to score a great success in its program to encircle us.

United States recognition of Communist China would make it probable that the Communist regime would obtain the seat of China in the United Nations. That would not be in the interest either of the United States or of the United Nations. . . . Should a regime which in 7 years has promoted five foreign or civil wars—Korea, Indochina, Tibet, the Philippines, and Malaya . . . be given a permanent seat, with veto power, in the body which under the charter has "primary responsibility for the maintenance of international peace and security"?

Communist Russia, with its veto power, already seriously limits the ability of the United Nations to serve its intended purposes. Were Communist China also to become a permanent, veto-wielding member of the Security Council, that would, I fear, implant in the United Nations the seeds of its own destruction. . . .

Trade with Communist China is not a normal trade. It does not provide one country with what its people want but cannot well produce for themselves, in exchange for what other people want but cannot well produce themselves. Trade with Communist China is wholly controlled by an official apparatus, and its limited amounts of foreign exchange are used to develop as rapidly as possible a formidable military establishment and a heavy industry to support it. . . .

We also doubt the value of cultural exchanges, which the Chinese Communists are eager to develop. They want this relationship with the United States primarily because, once that example were given, it would be difficult for China's close neighbors not to follow it. These free nations, already exposed to intense Communist subversive activities, could not have the cultural exchanges that the Communists want without adding greatly to their danger.

These are the considerations which argue for a continuance of our present policies. What are the arguments on the other side?

There are some who say that we should accord diplomatic recognition to the Communist regime because it has now been in power so long that it has won the *right* to that. That is not sound international law. Diplomatic recognition is always a privilege, never a right.

Of course, the United States knows that the Chinese Communist regime exists. We know that very well, for it has fought us in Korea. . . . For nearly 2 years we have been, and still are, dealing with it in an effort to free our citizens and to obtain reciprocal renunciations of force.

But diplomatic recognition gives the recognized regime valuable rights and privileges, and, in the world of today, recognition by the United States gives the recipient much added prestige and influence at home and abroad. . . .

Another argument beginning to be heard is that diplomatic recognition is inevitable, so why not now?

First, let me say emphatically that the United States need never succumb to the argument of ''inevitability.'' We, with our friends, can fashion our own destiny. We do not accept the mastery of Communist forces. . . . The reality is that a governmental system which tolerates diversity has a long life expectancy, whereas a system which seeks to impose conformity is always in danger. That results from the basic nature of human beings. . . .

We always take into account the possibility of influencing the Communist regime to better ways if we had diplomatic relations with it, or if, without that, we had commercial and cultural contacts with it. But the experience of those who now recognize and deal with the Chinese Communist regime convinces us that, under present conditions, neither recognition, nor trade, nor cultural relations, nor all three, would favorably influence the evolution of affairs in China. The probable result, internally, would be the opposite of what we hope for. . . .

Do we see any chance that the potentially great Chinese nation, with its rich and ancient culture and wisdom, will again be able to play a constructive part in the councils of the nations? We confidently answer these questions in the affirmative. Our confidence is based on certain fundamental beliefs. One is a belief in the future of human freedom. . . .

We can confidently assume that international communism's rule of strict conformity is, in China, as elsewhere, a passing and not a perpetual phase. We owe it to ourselves, our allies, and the Chinese people to do all that we can to contribute to that passing.

If we believed that this passing would be promoted by trade and cultural relations, then we would have such relations. If we believed that this passing would be promoted by our having diplomatic relations with the present regime, then we would have such relations. If we believed that this passing would be promoted by some participation of the present regime in the activities of the United Nations, then we would not oppose that.

We should be, and we are, constantly testing our policies, to be as certain as we can be that, in the light of conditions as they from time to time are, our policies shall serve the great purposes to which our Nation has been dedicated since its foundation—the cause of peace, justice, and human liberty. . . .

Many free nations seek to coordinate their foreign policies with ours. Such coordination is indeed indispensable if the free world is to have the cohesion needed to make it safe. But United States policies will never serve as rallying points for free peoples if the impression is created that our policies are subject to change to meet Communist wishes for no reason other than that communism does not want to change. If communism is stubborn for the wrong, let us be steadfast for the right.

The capacity for change is an indispensable capacity. Equally indispensable is the capacity to hold fast that which is good. Given those qualities, we can hopefully look forward to the day when those in Asia who are yet free can confidently remain free and when the people of China and the people of America can resume their long history of cooperative friendship.

11

Dean Rusk's Statement Before the Senate Committee on Foreign Relations, February 18, 1966[11]

With time the United States government's defense of its policies in Vietnam assumed a standard formula. No American official expressed it more often and with more consistency than did Dean Rusk, Secretary of State through the Kennedy and Johnson administrations. The statement which follows, broadcast over nationwide television, explains why five successive administrations avoided a negotiated settlement in Vietnam and preferred to sustain the American commitment to victory. That struggle, Rusk warned, involved "our largest interests and deepest purposes." The perception of global danger in Vietnam rendered the argument for involvement predictable, the goal of victory beyond challenge. Still the Secretary, having defined the danger which allegedly confronted the country, presented no evidence for its existence.

Why are we in Viet-Nam? Certainly we are not there merely because we have power and like to use it. We do not regard ourselves as the policeman of the universe. We do not go around the world looking for quarrels in which we can intervene. Quite the contrary. We have recognized that, just as we are not gendarmes of the universe, neither

11. The Department of State *Bulletin*, LIV (March 7, 1966), pp. 346–356.

are we the magistrate of the universe. If other governments, other institutions, or other regional organizations can find solutions to the quarrels which disturb the present scene, we are anxious to have this occur. But we are in Viet-Nam because the issues posed there are deeply intertwined with our own security and because the outcome of the struggle can profoundly affect the nature of the world in which we and our children will live.

The situation we face in Southeast Asia is obviously complex but, in my view, the underlying issues are relatively simple and are utterly fundamental. I am confident that Americans, who have a deep and mature understanding of world responsibility, are fully capable of cutting through the underbrush of complexity and finding the simple issues which involve our largest interests and deepest purposes. I regard it, therefore, as a privilege to be able to discuss these problems with the committee this morning—to consult with you—and at the same time to try to clarify for the American people the issues we must squarely face.

I do not approach this task on the assumption that anyone, anywhere, has all the answers or that all wisdom belongs to the executive branch of the Government, or even to the Government itself. The questions at issue affect the well-being of all Americans, and I am confident that all Americans will make up their own minds in the tradition of a free and independent people. Yet those of us who have special responsibilities for the conduct of our foreign policy have had to think hard and deeply about these problems for a very long time. The President, his Cabinet colleagues, and the Congress, who share the weightiest responsibilities under our constitutional system, have come to certain conclusions that form the basis for the policies we are now pursuing.

Perhaps it is worth pointing out that those who are officially responsible for the conduct of our public affairs must make decisions— and must make decisions among existing alternatives. None of us in the executive or the legislative branch has fulfilled our responsibilities merely by formulating an opinion—we are required to decide what this nation shall do and shall not do and are required to accept the consequences of our determinations.

What are our world security interests involved in the struggle in Viet-Nam?

They cannot be seen clearly in terms of Southeast Asia only or merely in terms of the events of the past few months. We must view the problem in perspective. We must recognize that what we are seeking to achieve in South Viet-Nam is part of a process that has continued for a long time—a process of preventing the expansion and extension of Communist domination by the use of force against the weaker nations on the perimeter of Communist power.

This is the problem as it looks to us. Nor do the Communists themselves see the problem in isolation. They see the struggle in South Viet-Nam as part of a larger design for the steady extension of Communist power through force and threat.

I have observed that some objection has been raised to the use of the term "Communist aggression." It seems to me that we should not confuse ourselves or our people by turning our eyes away from what that phrase means. The underlying crisis of this postwar period turns about a major struggle over the very nature of the political structure of the world. Before the guns were silent in World War II, many governments sat down and thought long and hard about the structure of international life, the kind of world which we ought to try to build, and wrote those ideas into the United Nations Charter. That charter establishes an international society of independent states, large and small, entitled to their own national existence, entitled to be free from aggression, cooperating freely across national frontiers in their common interests, and resolving their disputes by peaceful means.

But the Communist world has returned to its demand for what it calls a "world revolution," a world of coercion in direct contradiction to the Charter of the United Nations. There may be differences within the Communist world about methods, and techniques, and leadership within the Communist world itself, but they share a common attachment to their "world revolution" and to its support through what they call "wars of liberation."

So what we face in Viet-Nam is what we have faced on many occasions before—the need to check the extension of Communist power in order to maintain a reasonable stability in a precarious world. That stability was achieved in the years after the war by the valor of free nations in defending the integrity of postwar territorial arrangements. And we have achieved a certain stability for the last decade and a half. It must not be overthrown now.

Like so many of our problems today, the struggle in South Viet-Nam stems from the disruption of two world wars. The Second World War completed a process begun by the first. It ripped apart a structure of power that had existed for 100 years. It set in train new forces and energies that have remade the map of the world. Not only did it weaken the nations actively engaged in the fighting, but it had far-reaching secondary effects. It undermined the foundations of the colonial structures through which a handful of powers controlled one-third of the world's population. And the winds of change and progress that have blown fiercely during the last 20 years have toppled those structures almost completely.

Meanwhile the Communist nations have exploited the turmoil of a time of transition in an effort to extend Communist control into other areas of the world. . . .

We fought the Korean war, which like the struggle in Viet-Nam occurred in a remote area thousands of miles away, to sustain a principle vital to the freedom and security of America—the principle that the Communist world should not be permitted to expand by overrunning one after another of the arrangements built during and since the war to mark the outer limits of Communist expansion by force.

Before the Korean war had ended, the United States, under President Truman, moved to settle and consolidate the situation in the Pacific through a peace treaty with Japan, and through bilateral security treaties with Japan and the Philippines, and through the ANZUS treaty with Australia and New Zealand.

Hardly had the Korean war been finished when France, which had been fighting a protracted struggle in Indochina, decided to relinquish its political presence in Southeast Asia. After a brief negotiation it came to terms with the Communist forces that had captured the nationalist movement. The result was the division of Indochina into four parts: a Kingdom of Cambodia, a Kingdom of Laos, and Viet-Nam divided at the 17th parallel between the Communist forces in the North and a non-Communist Vietnamese government in the South. . . .

In order to give support to the nations of Southeast Asia, the United States took the lead in the creation of an alliance embodied in a treaty and reinforced by a collective security system known as SEATO—the Southeast Asia Treaty Organization. In this alliance the United States joined with Great Britain, France, Australia, New Zealand, Thailand, Pakistan, and the Philippines to guarantee the security not only of the member nations but also to come to the aid of certain protocol states and territories if they so requested.

South Viet-Nam was included in this protocol. The United States had not been a party to the agreements made in Geneva in 1954, which France had concluded with the Communist Vietnamese forces known as the Viet Minh. But the Under Secretary of State, Walter Bedell Smith, stated under instruction that the United States would not disturb the agreements and "would view any renewal of the aggression in violation of the . . . agreements with grave concern and as seriously threatening international peace and security."

Under Secretary Smith's statement was only a unilateral declaration, but in joining SEATO the United States took a solemn treaty engagement of far-reaching effect. Article IV, paragraph 1, provides that "each Party recognizes that aggression by means of armed attack . . . would endanger its own peace and safety, and agrees that it will in that event act to meet the common danger in accordance with its constitutional processes."

It is this fundamental SEATO obligation that has from the outset guided our actions in South Viet-Nam.

The language of this treaty is worth careful attention. The obligation it imposes is not only joint but several. The finding that an armed attack has occurred does not have to be made by a collective determination before the obligation of each member becomes operative. Nor does the treaty require a collective decision on actions to be taken to meet the common danger. If the United States determines that an armed attack has occurred against any nation to whom the protection of the treaty applies, then it is obligated to "act to meet the common danger" without regard to the views or actions of any other treaty member.

The far-reaching implications of this commitment were well understood by this committee when it recommended, with only the late Senator [William] Langer dissenting, that the Senate consent to the ratification of the treaty. The committee's report states:

> The committee is not impervious to the risks which this treaty entails. It fully appreciates that acceptance of these additional obligations commits the United States to a course of action over a vast expanse of the Pacific. Yet these risks are consistent with our own highest interests. There are greater hazards in not advising a potential enemy of what he can expect of us, and in failing to disabuse him of assumptions which might lead to a miscalculation of our intentions.

Following this committee's recommendation, the Senate gave its advice and consent to the treaty by a vote of 82 to 1, the late Senator Langer dissenting. All members of this distinguished committee who were then Senators voted for that treaty.

Our multilateral engagement under the SEATO treaty has been reinforced and amplified by a series of bilateral commitments and assurances directly to the Government of South Viet-Nam. On October 1, 1954, President Eisenhower wrote to President Diem offering "to assist the Government of Viet-Nam in developing and maintaining a strong, viable state, capable of resisting attempted subversion or aggression through military means." In 1957 President Eisenhower and President Diem issued a joint statement which called attention to "the large build-up of Vietnamese Communist military forces in North Viet-Nam" and stated:

> Noting that the Republic of Viet-Nam is covered by Article IV of the Southeast Asia Collective Defense Treaty, President Eisenhower and President Ngo Dinh Diem agreed that aggression or subversion threatening the political independence of the Republic of Viet-Nam would be considered as endangering peace and stability.

On August 2, 1961, President Kennedy declared that "the United States is determined that the Republic of Viet-Nam shall not be lost to the Communists for lack of any support which the United States can render."

On December 14, 1961, President Kennedy wrote to President Diem, recalling the United States declaration made at the end of the Geneva conference in 1954. The President once again stated that the United States was "prepared to help the Republic of Viet-Nam to protect its people and to preserve its independence." This commitment has been reaffirmed many times since.

These, then, are the commitments we have taken to protect South Viet-Nam as a part of protecting our own "peace and security." We have sent American forces to fight in the jungles of that beleaguered country because South Viet-Nam has, under the language of the SEATO treaty, been the victim of "aggression by means of armed attack."

There can be no serious question as to the existence and nature of this aggression. The war is clearly an "armed attack," cynically and systematically mounted by the Hanoi regime against the people of South Viet-Nam. . . .

In September 1960, the Lao Dong Party—the Communist Party in North Viet-Nam—held its Third Party Congress in Hanoi. That Congress called for the creation of a front organization to undertake the subversion of South Viet-Nam. Three months thereafter, the National Liberation Front was established to provide a political facade for the conduct of an active guerrilla war. Beginning in 1960 the Hanoi regime began to infiltrate into South Viet-Nam disciplined adherents whom the party had ordered North at the time of the settlement. In the intervening period since 1954, these men had been trained in the arts of sabotage and subversion. Now they were ordered to conscript young men from the villages by force or persuasion and to form cadres around which guerrilla units could be built. . . .

In the 3-year period from 1959 to 1961, the North Viet-Nam regime

infiltrated 10,000 men into the South. In 1962, 13,000 additional personnel were infiltrated. And by the end of 1964, North Viet-Nam may well
have moved over 40,000 armed and unarmed guerrillas into South Viet-
Nam.

Beginning over a year ago, the Communists apparently exhausted
their reservoir of Southerners who had gone North. Since then, the
greater number of men infiltrated into the South have been native-born
North Vietnamese. Most recently, Hanoi has begun to infiltrate elements of the North Vietnamese army in increasingly larger numbers.
Today there is evidence that nine regiments of regular North
Vietnamese forces are fighting in organized units in the South.

I have reviewed these facts—which are familiar enough to most of
you—because, it seems to me, they demonstrate beyond question that
the war in Viet-Nam is as much an act of outside aggression as though
the Hanoi regime had sent an army across the 17th parallel rather than
infiltrating armed forces by stealth. This point is important since it goes
to the heart of our own involvement. Much of the confusion about the
struggle in South Viet-Nam has arisen over a failure to understand the
nature of the conflict.

For if the war in South Viet-Nam were—as the Communists try to
make it appear—merely an indigenous revolt, then the United States
would not have its own combat troops in South Viet-Nam. But the evidence is overwhelming that it is, in fact, something quite different—a
systematic aggression by Hanoi against the people of South Viet-Nam.
It is one further effort by a Communist regime in one-half of a divided
country to take over the people of the other half at the point of a gun
and against their will.

Up to this point I have tried to describe the nature of our commitments in South Viet-Nam and why we have made them. I have sought
to put those commitments within the framework of our larger effort to
prevent the Communists from upsetting the arrangements which have
been the basis for our security. These policies have sometimes been attacked as static and sterile. It has been argued that they do not take account of the vast changes which have occurred in the world and are still
in train.

These contentions seem to me to miss the point. The line of policy
we are following involves far more than a defense of the *status quo*. It
seeks rather to insure that degree of security which is necessary if
change and progress are to take place through consent and not through
coercion. Certainly, as has been frequently pointed out, the world of
the mid-20th century is not standing still. Movement is occurring on

both sides of the Iron Curtain. Communism today is no longer monolithic; it no longer wears one face but many, and the deep schism
between the two great power centers of the Communist world—
Moscow and Peking—is clearly one of the major political facts of our
time.

There has been substantial change and movement within the Soviet Union as well—and perhaps even more among the countries of
Eastern Europe. These changes have not been inhibited because of our
efforts to maintain our postwar arrangements by organizing the
Western alliance. They have taken place because of internal developments as well as because the Communist regime in Moscow has
recognized that the Western alliance cannot permit it to extend its do-
minion by force.

Over time the same processes hopefully will work in the Far East.
Peking—and the Communist states living under its shadow—must
learn that they cannot redraw the boundaries of the world by force.

What we are pursuing, therefore, is not a static concept. For, unlike the Communists, we really believe in social revolution and not
merely in power cloaked as revolution. We believe in constructive
change and encourage it. That was the meaning of President Johnson's
initiatives at the Honolulu conference—to encourage the efforts of the
South Vietnamese Government to transform the country in a way that
will correct ancient injustices and bring about a better life for all the
people.

In meeting our commitments in South Viet-Nam we are using
substantial military forces. At the same time, we are making it quite
clear to North Viet-Nam and to the world that our forces are being employed for a limited and well-defined objective.

What we seek in South Viet-Nam is to bring about a restoration of
the conditions contemplated by the accords of 1954. We seek, in other
words, to restore the integrity of the settlement made between the
French Government and the Communist forces under Ho Chi Minh—a
settlement which was joined in by the United Kingdom, Communist
China, and Soviet Union, Laos, and Cambodia. This settlement forms
a part of the structure of arrangements that are the key to stability in
the present-day world.

Unfortunately, the limited nature of our purpose is foreign to the
philosophy of the Communist world. It may be hard, therefore, for
them to realize that the United States seeks no territorial aggrandizement in South Viet-Nam or anywhere in Southeast Asia. We do not
wish to maintain our troops in that area any longer than is necessary

to secure the freedom of the South Vietnamese people. We want no permanent military bases, no trade advantages. We are not asking that the Government of South Viet-Nam ally itself with us or be in any way beholden to us. We wish only that the people of South Viet-Nam should have the right and the opportunity to determine their future in freedom without coercion or threat.

For months now we have done everything possible to make clear to the regime in Hanoi that a political solution is the proper course. If that regime were prepared to call off the aggression in the South, peace would come in almost a matter of hours. When that occurred, the people of North Viet-Nam could safely go about their business. For we do not seek to destroy the Hanoi regime or to force the people of North Viet-Nam to accept any other form of government. And—under conditions of peace—we would be quite prepared for the North Vietnamese people to share with the other peoples of Southeast Asia in the economic and technical help that we and other nations are extending to that area.

This is the simple message that we have tried to convey to Hanoi through many channels. We have sought in every way to impress upon the Communist world the ease with which peace could be attained if only Hanoi were willing.

We have used every resource of diplomacy. I know of no occasion in history where so much effort has been devoted—not only on the part of the United States but of many other nations—in an effort to bring about a political solution to a costly and dangerous war. I know you are generally familiar with the record. . . .

Both Hanoi and Peking have repeatedly rejected our proposal for unconditional discussions. They have insisted instead that before any discussions can take place our side must agree in advance to the four points of Hanoi's program. The words that they have used have differed from formulation to formulation. Sometimes they have said their points are the "sole basis" for negotiations, sometimes the "most correct basis." But the effect is the same. What they are insisting upon is that we accept in advance their substantive position and then discuss only the ways in which it shall be given effect. The technique of demanding such substantive agreement in advance is a familiar Communist negotiating tactic. It does not mean that the basic points are open for discussion or that they can be loosely interpreted. It means just what it says.

We have subjected these four points to the most careful scrutiny. What do they reveal?

The first point calls for "recognition of the fundamental national rights of the Vietnamese people: sovereignty, independence, unity, and territorial integrity.'' This point also calls for the withdrawal of U.S. forces, dismantling of our military bases, and abolition of our military alliance with the Government of South Viet-Nam, "in strict conformity with the Geneva Agreements.''

The United States has made clear that we, too, are prepared to support a restoration of the provisions of the Geneva agreements and that we are prepared to withdraw our troops and dismantle military bases once there is compliance with the accords by all parties. We have said also that we would not expect or require a military alliance with a free South Viet-Nam.

The second point relates to the military clauses of the Geneva agreements, and these, too, we could agree to under the conditions I have indicated.

The fourth point provides that the issue of peaceful reunification should be settled by the Vietnamese people without foreign intervention. This also we could accept if it be clearly understood that conditions must first be created both in the North and South that will make it possible for truly free elections to be held.

It is in the third point that the core of the Communist position is disclosed. That point provides that "The internal affairs of South Viet-Nam must be settled by the South Vietnamese people themselves in accordance with the program of the National Liberation Front.''

To understand the significance of this point, it is necessary not only to examine what is meant by the "program of the National Liberation Front'' but to explore somewhat further the character of the Front itself and the purposes it serves in the tactics of the North Vietnamese regime.

Let us turn first to the Front itself. Both Hanoi and Peking have made clear again and again—and they have been joined in this by other Communist powers—that negotiations will be possible only when the United States recognizes the National Liberation Front as the "sole genuine representative of the entire South Vietnamese people.''

What are the implications of this proposal, and why are the Communists urging it so insistently?

The evidence is overwhelming that the National Liberation Front is exactly what its name implies—a Communist front organization intended to give support to the deliberate fiction that the war in Viet-Nam is an indigenous revolt. The Front is, as the facts make clear, an invention of the Communist Party of North Viet-Nam, to serve as a political cloak for its activities in the South. . . .

The People's Revolutionary Party has not concealed its role in the

Front. It has frankly stated that it is the dominant element. On February 15, 1961, the Viet Cong Committee for the South went even farther, stating that in time the Communist Party would "act overtly to lead the revolution in South Viet-Nam." In other words, the Communists have told their followers that, at the proper moment, they would emerge from cover and cast off the disguise of the National Liberation Front.

And so the Communists have a clear purpose in insisting that we recognize the National Liberation Front as the sole representative of the South Vietnamese people. For them this is not a procedural question but a major question of substance. They insist on our recognition of the Front as the sole spokesman for the people of South Viet-Nam since our acceptance of the Front in that capacity would in effect mean our acceptance of the Communist position as to the indigenous nature of the conflict and thus our acceptance of a settlement on Hanoi's terms—which would mean delivering South Viet-Nam into the control of the Communist North.

In spite of these clear realities, we have not asserted nor do we assert an unreasoning attitude with regard to the Front. The President said in his state of the Union message, "We will meet at any conference table, we will discuss any proposals—4 points or 14 or 40—and we will consider the views of any group"—and that, of course, includes the Front along with other groups.

To the extent then that the Front has any validity as a representative of a group, the views of that group can be heard and the issue of the Liberation Front should, as the President has said, not prove "an insurmountable problem."

It remains a problem only because Hanoi insists on using it to establish its own substantive position—that the Front represents the hopes and aspirations of the South Vietnamese people—and hence should control them.

The significance of this issue is clearly seen when one examines the so-called "Program of the National Liberation Front" as it was announced from Hanoi on January 29, 1961, and revised and amplified in a second publication on February 11 that same year. The first point of this program discloses the full Communist intention. It calls for the overthrow of the South Vietnamese Government in Saigon and the establishment of a coalition government from which the government in Saigon would be totally excluded. . . .

May I conclude, therefore, Mr. Chairman, with certain simple points which are at the heart of the problem and at the heart of United States policy in South Viet-Nam.

1. The elementary fact is that there is an aggression in the form of an armed attack by North Viet-Nam against South Viet-Nam.

2. The United States has commitments to assist South Viet-Nam to repel this aggression.

3. Our commitments to South Viet-Nam were not taken in isolation but are a part of a systematic effort in the postwar period to assure a stable peace.

4. The issue in Southeast Asia becomes worldwide because we must make clear that the United States keeps its word wherever it is pledged.

5. No nation is more interested in peace in Southeast Asia or elsewhere than is the United States. If the armed attack against South Viet-Nam is brought to an end, peace can come very quickly. Every channel or forum for contact, discussion, or negotiation will remain active in order that no possibility for peace will be overlooked.

12

Hans J. Morgenthau's Critique of American Involvement in Vietnam, January, 1968[12]

Hans J. Morgenthau, in 1968 the Albert A. Michelson Distinguished Service Professor of Political Science and Modern History at the University of Chicago, was one of the nation's leading critics of the American involvement in Vietnam. In the following essay Morgenthau asked the question: Why was the United States resolved to fight a war in Southeast Asia which, he argued, was "politically aimless, military unpromising, and morally dubious." He concluded that the issue was not American security but American prestige—not the prestige of the United States but the prestige of those responsible for the involvement. Such men, he concluded, "ought not to ask the nation to suffer for their false pride."

The policies the United States is pursuing in Vietnam are open to criticism on three grounds: they do not serve the interests of the United States; they run counter to American interests; and the United States objectives are not attainable, if they are attainable at all, without unreasonable moral liabilities and military risks.

In order to understand the rationale underlying our involvement in Southeast Asia one must go back to the spring of 1947 when the postwar policies of the United States were formulated and put into

12. "U.S. Misadventure in Vietnam," *Current History*, 54 (January, 1968), pp. 29–34.

practice—the policy of containment, the Truman doctrine and the Marshall Plan. These policies pursued one single aim by different means: the containment of communism. That aim derived from two assumptions: the unlimited expansionism of the Soviet Union as a revolutionary power, and the monolithic direction and control the Soviet Union exerted over the world Communist movement. . . .

It was against this essentially traditional military threat that the United States policy of containment was devised. Thus it partook of the rationale which since the beginning of the Republic has informed the policies of the United States with regard to Europe: the maintenance or, if need be, the restoration of the balance of power. It was for this reason that the United States intervened in two world wars on the seemingly weaker side, and it was for the same reason that it embarked on the policy of containing the Soviet Union. The Truman doctrine, itself originally applied to a specific, geographically limited emergency concerning Greece and Turkey, transformed this traditional and geographically limited commitment into a general principle of universal application by stipulating that the United States would come to the assistance of any nation threatened by Communist aggression or subversion.

The Marshall Plan served the purpose of the policy of containment in that it tried to make the nations of West Europe immune from Communist subversion and strong enough collectively to withstand Soviet aggression by restoring them to economic health. The spectacular success of the Marshall Plan had intellectual and political consequences similar to those of the policy of containment. The rationale underlying the Marshall Plan evolved into a general principle of American statecraft to be applied anywhere in the form of foreign aid.

It is against this background that one must consider the involvement of the United States in Southeast Asia. For the modes of thought and action growing from the specific European experiences of the postwar period still dominate today the foreign policies of the United States, paradoxically enough not so much in Europe as elsewhere throughout the world. The Administration consistently justifies its Asian policies by analogy with its European experiences. The United States thinks of Asia in 1968 as it thought of Europe in 1947, and the successes of its European policies have become the curse of the policies the United States is pursuing in Asia. For the problems Americans are facing in Asia are utterly different from those they successfully dealt with in Europe two decades ago, and the political world they were facing in Europe has been radically transformed.

The active involvement of the United States in Southeast Asia is a response to the Korean War. That war was interpreted by the United States government as the opening shot in a military campaign for world conquest under the auspices of the Soviet Union. In view of this interpretation, it was consistent for the United States to defend South Korea against the North Korean Communists, as it would have defended Western Europe against the Red Army had it stepped over the 1945 line of demarcation. Similarly, it was consistent for the United States to support with massive financial and material aid the French military effort to defeat the Vietnamese Communists. When France was threatened with defeat, in 1954, it was consistent for Secretary of State John Foster Dulles and Admiral Arthur Radford, then chairing the Joint Chiefs of Staff, to recommend that President Dwight Eisenhower intervene with American airpower on the side of France. Finally, it was a logical application of this policy of containing communism in Asia to establish and support an anti-Communist regime in South Vietnam, after the division of the country in 1954. However, when the disintegration of this regime became acute (roughly from 1960 onward), the United States continued this policy of containment as though the nature of world communism had not changed since 1950 and as though the political disintegration of South Vietnam posed for the United States an issue similar to the North Korean invasion of South Korea. It was at this point that our policy went astray.

While it was plausible—even though it has proven to be historically incorrect—to attribute the outbreak of the Korean War to a world-wide Communist conspiracy, there is no historical evidence whatsoever to interpret in that manner what has happened in Vietnam since 1960. The period of history since Nikita Khrushchev's denunciation of Joseph Stalin in 1956 has been characterized by the disintegration of the Communist bloc into its national components, each pursuing to a greater or lesser degree its own particular national policy within a common framework of Communist ideology and institutions. The influence that the Soviet Union and China are still able to exert over Communist governments and movements is not the automatic result of their common Communist character, but of the convergence of national interests and of particular power relations.

COMMUNISM IN VIETNAM

This has always been true of the Vietnamese Communists. Many of them were nationalists before they became Communists and it was only the indifference or hostility of the West that made them embrace communism. Even under the most unfavorable conditions of war with the United States, the government of North Vietnam has been able to retain a considerable measure of independence vis-à-vis both the Soviet Union and China by playing one off against the other. The Vietnamese Communists are not mere agents of either the Soviet Union or China. The sources of their strength and their aims are indigenous and must be judged on their own merits.

This being the case, the professed United States war aim, "to stop communism" in South Vietnam, reveals itself as an empty slogan. It must be made concrete by raising the questions: what kind of communism is the United States fighting in South Vietnam? and what is the relationship of that communism to the United States interest in containing the Soviet Union and China? The answers to these questions reveal the unsoundness of American policy. The fate of communism in South Vietnam is irrelevant to the containment of Soviet or Chinese communism since Vietnamese communism is not controlled by either of them. The United States fight against the South Vietnamese Communists is relevant only to its relations with South Vietnam, which, even if she were governed by Communists, could not affect the balance of power in Asia.

The instruments the United States is using to achieve its aim in Vietnam are three: "counter-insurgency" and "nation-building" in the South, and the bombing of the North. These instruments have failed as they were bound to fail.

COUNTER-INSURGENCY

It is to be held as an axiom, derived from the experience of many guerrilla wars, that a guerrilla war supported, or at least not actively opposed, by the indigenous population cannot be won, short of the physical destruction of that population. In the nature of things, the guerrilla is indistinguishable from the rest of the population, and in truth the very distinction is tenuous in a situation where the guerrilla is an organic element of the social and political structure. In such a situation, everyone is in a sense a potential guerrilla. The whole population is composed of full-time guerrillas, part-time guerrillas, auxiliaries who feed, clothe and hide the combatants, make arms, build hide-outs, and carry ammunition; only a minority is permanently passive or surreptitiously hostile to the guerrillas. What the United States is facing in South Vietnam is a primitive nation-in-arms, in a war which can be won only by incapacitating the total population.

It is for this reason that "pacification," repeated time and again for almost a decade under different names and auspices, has been a consistent failure. For it is based upon the misconception that the guerrillas are an 'alien element within the indigenous population, who therefore can be separated from that population by an appropriate technique. A Vietnamese village is pacified only when all the men capable of bearing arms are either dead or driven away and prevented from returning. The last condition is impossible to achieve. Thus many villages have been "pacified" time and again, only to fall back under guerrilla control when the military occupation was relaxed.

In Vietnam, what makes "counter-insurgency" so futile an undertaking is the difference between the motivation of the guerrillas and that of the professional army fighting them. No professional army could have withstood the punishment Americans have inflicted on the South Vietnamese guerrillas since the beginning of 1965. It is for this reason that United States military leaders have said repeatedly that the Viet Cong were on the verge of collapse, as they would have been were they professional soldiers. But, like the Spanish and Tyrolian guerrillas fighting the armies of Napoleon, they are fanatical protagonists of an ideal—social revolution or national survival or both—and they will die rather than admit defeat. Against them fights a professional army which does its duty efficiently as well as courageously and uses "counter-insurgency" as a mechanical contrivance, a particular kind of military tactic with which to fight "unorthodox" war. However, guerrilla war is not just "unorthodox" in the technical, tactical sense, but different in quality from traditional war; hence, it cannot be "won" in the traditional sense.

THE POLITICAL WAR

The United States government recognizes implicitly the truth of this analysis when it maintains that there are two wars in South Vietnam—a military war and a political war—and that victory in the latter will be decisive. In order to win that political war, the United States has embarked on a massive program of political, social and economic reconstruction in South Vietnam. It is the purpose of that program to establish the government of South Vietnam as a new focus that will attract the loyalties of the large mass of South Vietnamese who are indifferent to either side, as well as the disenchanted supporters of the Viet Cong. This program is up against three obstacles which, in the aggregate, appear insurmountable.

First, the government of South Vietnam is a military government and has remained so in spite of the democratic gloss which carefully circumscribed and managed elections have tried to put on it. The foundation of the government's power is the army, both in terms of the administrative structure and of what there is of loyal support. Yet the army is regarded by large masses of the population not as the expression of the popular will but as its enemy. This is so because of the oppressive behavior of the army toward the peasants and, more particularly, because there is reportedly no officer in the South Vietnamese army above the rank of lieutenant colonel who did not fight on the side of the French against his own people.

Second, this impression of an army fighting against its own people is reinforced by the massive presence of foreign armed forces without whom neither that army nor the government it supports could survive. Regardless of professed and actual American intention, the United States military presence, with its destructive economic, social and moral results for South Vietnam, appears to an ever-increasing number of South Vietnamese as an evil to be eliminated at any price. Thus our massive visible support for the government of South Vietnam, while indispensable and, in good measure, because it is indispensable, discredits that government in the eyes of the people of South Vietnam.

Finally, the hoped-for radical change in political loyalties requires radical social, economic and political reforms, especially with regard to the distribution of land. The achievement of such reforms has indeed earned the Viet Cong the allegiance of large masses of peasants. Both in its composition and policies, the government of South Vietnam represents the interests of a small group of absentee land owners and members of the urban upper middle class who would lose their economic, social and political privileges were that government really trying to counter the social revolution of the Viet Cong with radical social reforms of its own. The United States is facing here the same dilemma which has frustrated its foreign aid policies throughout the world, more particularly in the Alliance for Progress: it is trying to achieve radical social reforms through the instrumentality of governments which have a vital interest in the preservation of the status quo.

The universally recognized weaknesses of the government of South Vietnam—corruption, inefficiency, apathy, lack of public spirit, low military performance, a staggering desertion rate—result irremediably from the nature of that government. They are not to be remedied by American appeals to the South Vietnamese government to do more for the country or to let the South Vietnamese army take over a larger share of the fighting and pacification. A government imposed on an unwilling or at best indifferent people by a foreign power to defend the status quo against a national and social revolution is by dint of its very nature precluded from doing what Americans expect it to do. That nature dooms all efforts at politically effective reconstruction.

BOMBING OF THE NORTH

The third policy the United States is pursuing in Vietnam is the bombing of the North, to win the war in the South by interdicting the influx of men and material from the North, and to force the government of North Vietnam to the conference table by making it too costly for it to continue the war. Both purposes derive from a faulty perception of reality. The United States assumes that what it faces in South Vietnam is the result of foreign aggression and that there would be no unmanageable trouble in the South if only, in Secretary of State Dean Rusk's often repeated phrase, North Vietnam would leave her neighbor alone. It follows logically from this assumption that internal peace could be restored to South Vietnam if one could insulate South Vietnam from the North or compel the North to cease her assistance to the South. However, this assumption does not square with historic reality.

SOUTHERN ROOTS OF WAR

The roots of the trouble are in the South. They were deeply embedded in the nature of the Diem regime, which combined a fierce nationalism with a totalitarian defense of the economic and social status quo. Nobody doubts that the government of North Vietnam welcomed and aided and abetted the progressive disintegration of the Diem regime. But it did not cause it, nor was its support responsible for the Viet Cong's success. When, at the beginning of 1965, the government of South Vietnam was close to defeat at the hands of the Viet Cong, according to official estimates 90 per cent of the Viet Cong weapons were of American origin and the annual infiltration from the North amounted to no more than a few thousand men, mostly of Southern origin. Only a total of a few hundred were regulars of the North Vietnamese army.

Consequently, the war could not be won by bombing the North even if the bombing were more effective.

. . . [W]hat would happen [asks General Maxwell Taylor] if Hanoi were suddenly to disappear? Suppose everything of value in the North were destroyed; we would still have over 200,000 armed guerrillas in South Vietnam who would have to be accounted for in some way. For food they could live off the land without supplies from the North. If they avoided contact with large military forces, they could husband their weapons and ammunition stocks and maintain for a long time a low level of sustained depredations and terrorist activity. If they were determined to carry on the war, if their morale did not collapse at this disaster in the North, they could conceivably remain in action for the next ten years, or the next twenty years, and we might still be tied down by this vast guerrilla force.[13]

The situation would be no different if the government of North Vietnam were suddenly to collapse and to sign our peace terms on the dotted line. Who would impose these terms on the Viet Cong, who have not been defeated in the field and who continue to draw on the support or at least the indifference of large masses of the indigenous population?

It is precisely because we have been unable to win the war in the South that we continue to assume that the source of the war is in the North and that victory can be won by bombing the North. However, the day is close at hand when everything that appears to be worth bombing will have been bombed and the war in the South will still not be won. The next logical step will be the invasion of North Vietnam; for if North Vietnam is responsible for the war, then the conquest of North Vietnam will end the war. While it will not accomplish that end, it will conjure up the likelihood of a United States military confrontation with the Soviet Union or China or both. The Soviet Union has assured the United States that it will not stand idly by while the government of North Vietnam is destroyed, and China has made it clear that she will intervene, as she did in the Korean War, when a hostile army approaches her frontiers.

However, if the war in the South lasts long enough, the United States has a good chance of winning it. The United States is not likely to win the war in the traditional way by breaking the enemy's will to resist, but rather by killing so many enemies that there is no one left to resist. Killing in war has traditionally been a means to a psychological end. In this war, killing becomes an end in itself. The physical elimination of the enemy and victory become synonomous. Hence, the "body count," however fictitious in itself, is the sole measure of our success.

No civilized nation can wage such a war without suffering incal-

13. *Responsibility and Response* (New York: Harper and Row, 1967), p. 38.

culable moral damage. This damage is particularly grave since the nation can realize no plausible military or political benefit which could justify this killing for killing's sake. And it is particularly painful for a nation like the United States—founded as a novel experiment in government, morally superior to those that preceded it—which has throughout its history thought of itself as performing a uniquely beneficial mission not only for itself but for all mankind.

Why, then, is the United States evidently resolved to continue fighting a war which appears politically aimless, militarily unpromising and morally dubious? The answer is to be found in the concern for American prestige. If the United States should leave Vietnam without having won a victory, so it is argued, the credibility of its commitments throughout the world would suffer, Communist revolutions throughout the world would be encouraged, and the reputation of American invincibility would be impaired.

CONTAINING CHINA

Not only does the containment of Vietnamese communism not further the interests of the United States but, paradoxical as it may seem, it is even detrimental to those interests. The United States has a legitimate interest in the containment of China and its involvement in Vietnam is frequently explained in terms of this interest. But Vietnamese nationalism has been for a millenium a barrier to the expansion of Chinese power into Southeast Asia. There is no patriotic Vietnamese, North or South, Communist or non-Communist, Buddhist or Catholic, who does not regard China as the hereditary enemy of Vietnam. Yet to the degree that the United States weakens Vietnam as a national entity through the destruction of her human and material resources, it creates a political, military and social vacuum into which either the United States must move in virtual permanence or into which either the Soviet Union or China will move.

What about American prestige? Its decline because of the liquidation of United States involvement in Vietnam is a matter for speculation; its drastic decline by virtue of the involvement is a matter of fact. In the eyes of most of the world, the most powerful nation on earth is trying to force a nation of primitive peasants into submission by the massive use of all the modern means of mass destruction (with the exception of biological and nuclear weapons) and it is unable either to win or to liquidate that war. The champion of the "free world" is protecting the people of South Vietnam from communism by destroying them. And in the process, the world is moved closer and closer to an unwinnable war with China, if not to the cataclysm of nuclear war. This is the image which the United States presents today to most of the outside world; in consequence its prestige has never been so low.

If the United States were to liquidate the war, the damage to its prestige would at least in some measure be repaired. The United States would show that it is wise and strong enough to admit a mistake and correct it. The liquidation of the misadventure need not affect its future policies. Commitments are not entered into or honored by way of precedent, nor do precedents initiate revolutions. For better or for worse, history does not operate like the Supreme Court of the United States (and even the Supreme Court has been known to disregard precedent for reasons of principle and prudence).

What the argument about prestige really amounts to is a concern for the prestige not of the United States but of those who are responsible for its involvement in Vietnam. But those who are responsible for the straits in which the nation finds itself today should bear the consequences of their ideological blindness and political and military miscalculations. They ought not to ask the nation to suffer for their false pride.

Selected Bibliography

GENERAL HISTORIES OF THE COLD WAR

ACHESON, Dean G. *Present at the Creation.* New York, 1969.

AMBROSE, Stephen E. *Rise to Globalism: American Foreign Policy 1938–1970.* Baltimore, 1971.

BOHLEN, Charles E. *Witness to History, 1929–1969.* New York, 1973.

DEUTSCHER, Isaac. "Twenty Years of Cold War." *Ironies of History.* London, 1966.

DEUTCHER, Isaac. *The Great Contest: Russia and the West.* New York, 1960.

GATI, Charles, ed. *Caging the Bear: Containment and the Cold War.* Indianapolis, 1974.

HALLE, Louis B. *The Cold War as History.* New York, 1967.

HARRIMAN, W. Averell. *America and Russia in a Changing World: A Half Century of Personal Observation.* Garden City, N.Y., 1971.

HOROWITZ, David. *The Free World Colossus: A Critique of American Foreign Policy in the Cold War.* New York, 1965.

KENNAN, George F. *Russia and the West Under Lenin and Stalin.* Boston, 1961.

KNAPP, Wilfred. *A History of War and Peace, 1939–1965.* London, 1967.

238 SELECTED BIBLIOGRAPHY

LAFEBER, Walter. *America, Russia, and the Cold War, 1945–1966.* New York, 1971.

LAFEBER, Walter, ed. *America in the Cold War: Twenty Years of Revolutions and Response, 1947–1967.* New York, 1969.

LASCH, Christopher. "The Cold War, Revisited and Re-Visioned." *The New York Time Magazine,* January 14, 1968.

LERCHE, Charles O., Jr. *The Cold War and After.* Englewood Cliffs, N.J., 1965.

LUARD, Evan, ed. *The Cold War: A Reappraisal.* New York, 1964.

LUKACS, John. *A History of the Cold War.* Rev. ed. Garden City, N.Y., 1962.

MARSHALL, Charles Burton. *The Cold War: A Concise History.* New York, 1965.

MOSELY, Philip E. *The Kremlin and World Politics.* New York, 1960.

PATERSON, Thomas G., ed. *Containment and the Cold War: American Foreign Policy Since 1945.* Reading, Mass., 1973.

REES, David. *The Age of Containment: The Cold War, 1945–1965.* London, 1967.

ROBERTS, Henry L. *Russia and America: Dangers and Prospects.* New York, 1956.

SCHUMAN, Frederick L. *The Cold War: Retrospect and Prospect.* Baton Rouge, 1962.

SEABURY, Paul. *The Rise and Decline of the Cold War.* New York, 1967.

SHULMAN, Marshall D. *Beyond the Cold War.* New Haven, 1966.

SIRACUSA, Joseph M., ed. *The American Diplomatic Revolution: A Documentary History of the Cold War, 1941–1947.* Sydney, Australia, 1976.

SMITH, Gaddis. *Dean Acheson.* New York, 1972.

SPANIER, John W. *American Foreign Policy Since World War II.* New York, 1960.

WILLIAMS, William A. *The Tragedy of American Diplomacy.* Rev. ed. New York, 1962.

THE SECOND WORLD WAR

AMBROSE, Stephen E. *Eisenhower and Berlin, 1945: The Decision to Halt at the Elbe.* New York, 1967.

ARMSTRONG, Anne. *Unconditional Surrender: The Impact of the Casablanca Policy upon World War II.* New Brunswick, N.J., 1961.

BUCHANAN, A. Russell. *The United States and World War II.* 2 vols. New York, 1962.

BURNS, James MacGregor. *Roosevelt: The Soldier of Freedom, 1940–1945.* New York, 1970.

CHURCHILL, Winston. *The Second World War.* 6 vols. Boston, 1948–1953.

DAVIS, Lynn Etheridge. *The Cold War Begins: Soviet-American Conflict over Eastern Europe.* Princeton, N.J., 1974.

FEIS, Herbert. *Churchill, Roosevelt, Stalin: The War They Waged and the Peace They Sought.* Princeton, N.J., 1957.

FEIS, Herbert. *Between War and Peace: The Potsdam Conference.* Princeton, N.J., 1960.

FEIS, Herbert. *Japan Subdued.* Princeton, N.J., 1961.

HARRIMAN, W. Averell, and Elie ABEL. *Special Envoy to Churchill and Stalin, 1941–1946.* New York, 1975.

KOLKO, Gabriel. *The Politics of War: The World and United States Foreign Policy, 1943–1945.* New York, 1968.

LOEWENHEIM, Francis L., Harold D. LANGLEY, and Manfred JONAS, eds. *Roosevelt and Churchill: Their Secret Wartime Correspondence.* New York, 1975.

MCNEILL, William H. *America, Britain, and Russia: Their Cooperation and Conflict, 1941–1946.* London, 1953.

ROSE, Lisle A. *Dubious Victory: The United States and the End of World War II.* Kent, Ohio, 1973.

SMITH, Gaddis. *American Diplomacy During the Second World War, 1941–1945.* New York, 1965.

TUCHMAN, Barbara W. *Stilwell and the American Experience in China, 1911–1945.* New York, 1971.

ORIGINS OF THE COLD WAR

AGAR, Herbert. *The Price of Power.* Chicago, 1957.

ALPEROVITZ, Gar. *Atomic Diplomacy: Hiroshima and Potsdam.* New York, 1965.

ARKES, Hadley. *Bureaucracy, the Marshall Plan, and the National Interest.* Princeton, N.J., 1972.

CLEMENS, Diane. *Yalta.* New York, 1970.

DONNELLY, Desmond. *Struggle for the World: The Cold War and Its Causes.* London, 1965.

FENNO, Richard F., Jr., ed. *The Yalta Conference.* Boston, 1954.

FLEMING, D. F. *The Cold War and Its Origins, 1917–1950.* 2 vols. Garden City, N.Y., 1961.

GADDIS, John Lewis. *The United States and the Origins of the Cold War, 1941–1947.* New York, 1972.

GARDNER, Lloyd. *Architects of Illusion.* Chicago, 1970.

HAMBY, Alonzo L. *Beyond the New Deal: Harry S. Truman and American Liberalism.* New York, 1973.

HERZ, Martin F. *Beginnings of the Cold War.* Bloomington, Ind., 1966.

JONES, Joseph Marion. *The Fifteen Weeks.* New York, 1955.

KENNAN, George F. *Memoirs, 1925–1950.* Boston, 1967.

KUKLICK, Bruce. *American Policy and the Division of Germany: The Clash with Russia over Reparations.* Ithaca, N.Y., 1972.

LIPPMANN, Walter. *The Cold War.* New York, 1947.

MORGENTHAU, Hans J. *In Defense of the National Interest.* New York, 1951.

PATERSON, Thomas G. *Soviet-American Confrontation: Postwar Reconstruction and the Origins of the Cold War.* Baltimore, 1973.

PERKINS, Dexter. *The Diplomacy of a New Age.* Bloomington, Ind., 1967.

REITZEL, William et al. *United States Foreign Policy 1945–1955.* Washington, 1956.

SNELL, John L., ed. *The Meaning of Yalta.* Baton Rouge, La., 1956.

SNETSINGER, John. *Truman, the Jewish Vote, and the Creation of Israel.* Stanford, Cal., 1974.

WESTERFIELD, H. Bradford. *Foreign Policy and Party Politics, Pearl Harbor to Korea.* New Haven, 1955.

THE CONTINUING COLD WAR, 1950–1975

BEAL, John Robinson. *John Foster Dulles: A Biography.* New York, 1957.

CAMPBELL, John C. *Defense in the Middle East.* New York, 1960.

CHACE, James. *A World Elsewhere: The New American Foreign Policy.* New York, 1973.

DRAPER, Theodore. *Abuse of Power.* New York, 1966.

EPSTEIN, Leon D. *Britain—Uncertain Ally.* Chicago, 1954.

FINER, Herman. *Dulles over Suez.* New York, 1964.

FURNISS, Edgar S. *France, Troubled Ally.* New York, 1960.

GRAEBNER, Norman A. *The New Isolationism.* New York, 1956.

GRAUBARD, Stephen R. *Kissinger: Portrait of a Mind.* New York, 1973.

HOOPES, Townsend. *The Devil and John Foster Dulles.* New York, 1973.

HUGHES, Emmet John. *The Ordeal of Power.* New York, 1962.

KENNAN, George F. *Memoirs, 1950–1963.* Boston, 1972.

KENNAN, George F. *On Dealing with the Communist World.* New York, 1964.

KENNAN, George F. *Russia, the Atom, and the West.* New York, 1958.

KOLKO, Gabriel, and Joyce KOLKO. *The Limits of Power: The World and United States Foreign Policy, 1945–1954.* New York, 1972.

O'CONNOR, John F. *The Cold War and Liberation.* New York, 1961.

PATTERSON, Gardner, and Edgar S. FURNISS, Jr. *NATO: A Critical Appraisal.* Princeton, 1957.

STILLMAN, Edmund O., and William PFAFF. *The New Politics: America and the End of the Postwar World.* New York, 1961.

SULZBERGER, C. L. *What's Wrong with U.S. Foreign Policy.* New York, 1959.

THE COLD WAR IN ASIA

BARNET, Richard J. *Intervention and Revolution: America's Confrontation with Insurgent Movements Around the World.* New York, 1968.

BARNETT, A. Doak. *Communist China and Asia: A Challenge to American Policy.* New York, 1960.

FITZGERALD, Frances. *Fire in the Lake.* Boston, 1972.

HALBERSTAM, David. *The Best and the Brightest.* New York, 1972.

HALBERSTAM, David. *The Making of a Quagmire.* New York, 1965.

HIGGINS, Trumbull. *Korea and the Fall of MacArthur.* New York, 1960.

KAHIN, George M., and John W. LEWIS. *The United States and Vietnam.* New York, 1969.

MAY, Ernest R. *The Truman Administration and China, 1945–1949.* Philadelphia, 1975.

MCCARTHY, Mary. *Hanoi*. New York, 1968.

MEANY, Neville. "From the Pentagon Papers: Reflections on the Making of America's Vietnam Policy." *Australian Outlook, XXVI* (August 1972), 163–192.

PFEFFER, Richard M., ed. *No More Vietnams? The War and the Future of American Foreign Policy*. New York, 1968.

REISCHAUER, Edwin O. *Wanted: An Asian Policy*. New York, 1955.

ROSE, Lisle A. *Roots of Tragedy: The United States and the Struggle for Asia, 1945–1954*. Westport, Conn., 1975.

SHAPLEN, Robert. *The Lost Revolution: The U.S. in Vietnam, 1946–1966*. New York, 1966.

SIRACUSA, Joseph M. "The United States, Viet-Nam, and the Cold War: A Reappraisal." *Journal of Southeast Asia Studies, V* (March 1974), 82–101.

STEELE, Ronald. *Pax Americana*. New York, 1967.

TAYLOR, Telford. *Nuremburg and Vietnam*. New York, 1970.

TSOU, Tang. *America's Failure in China, 1941–1950*. Chicago, 1967.

ZAGORIA, Donald S. *The Sino-Soviet Conflict*. New York, 1962.

STUDIES OF POWER AND DIPLOMACY

ACHESON, Dean G. *Power and Diplomacy*. Cambridge, Mass., 1958.

BRODIE, Bernard. *Strategy in the Missile Age*. Princeton, 1959.

FINLETTER, Thomas K. *Power and Policy*. New York, 1954.

FINLETTER, Thomas K. *Foreign Policy: The Next Phase*. New York, 1958.

FULBRIGHT, J. William. *The Arrogance of Power*. New York, 1966.

FULBRIGHT, J. William. *The Crippled Giant: American Foreign Policy and Its Domestic Consequences*. New York, 1972.

KENNAN, George F. *American Diplomacy 1900–1950*. Chicago, 1951.

KENNAN, George F. *Realities of American Foreign Policy*. Princeton, 1954.

KISSINGER, Henry A. *Nuclear Weapons and Foreign Policy*. New York, 1957.

KOLKO, Gabriel. *The Roots of American Foreign Policy: An Analysis of Power and Purpose*. Boston, 1969.

KNORR, Klaus, ed. *NATO and American Security*. Princeton, 1959.

MARSHALL, Charles B. *Limits of Foreign Policy*. New York, 1954.

OSGOOD, Robert E. *Limited War*. Chicago, 1957.

PEARSON, Lester B. *Diplomacy in the Nuclear Age*. Cambridge, Mass., 1959.

STEVENSON, Adlai E. *Call to Greatness*. New York, 1954.

STILLMAN, Edmund O., and William PFAFF. *Power and Impotence*. New York, 1966.

THOMPSON, Kenneth W. *Political Realism and the Crisis of World Politics*. Princeton, 1960.

Index

244